The *Slumdog* Phenomenon

New Perspectives on World Cinema

The **New Perspectives on World Cinema** series publishes engagingly written, highly accessible, and extremely useful books for the educated reader and the student as well as the scholar. Volumes in this series will fall under one of the following categories: monographs on neglected films and filmmakers; classic as well as contemporary film scripts; collections of the best previously published criticism (including substantial reviews and interviews) on single films or filmmakers; translations into English of the best classic and contemporary film theory; reference works on relatively neglected areas in film studies, such as production design (including sets, costumes, and make-up), music, editing, and cinematography; and reference works on the relationship between film and the other performing arts (including theater, dance, opera, etc.). Many of our titles will be suitable for use as primary or supplementary course texts at undergraduate and graduate levels. The goal of the series is thus not only to address subject areas in which adequate classroom texts are lacking, but also to open up additional avenues for film research, theoretical speculation, and practical criticism.

Series Editors

Editorial Board

The *Slumdog* Phenomenon

A Critical Anthology

Edited by
Ajay Gehlawat

ANTHEM PRESS
LONDON · NEW YORK · DELHI

Anthem Press India
An imprint of Wimbledon Publishing Company India Private Limited (WPCIPL)
WPCIPL is a subsidiary of Wimbledon Publishing Company Limited (UK)

This edition first published in India 2014
by ANTHEM PRESS INDIA
www.anthempress.co.in

First published in UK and USA 2013
by ANTHEM PRESS
www.anthempress.com

ISBN-13: 978 93 80601 82 3 (Hbk)
ISBN-10: 93 80601 82 4 (Hbk)

TABLE OF CONTENTS

Notes on Contributors vii

List of Figures xi

Acknowledgments xiii

Introduction The *Slumdog* Phenomenon xv
Ajay Gehlawat

***SLUMDOG* AND THE NATION**

Chapter 1 National Allegory 3
Brian Larkin

Chapter 2 *Slumdog Millionaire* and the Emerging Centrality of India 9
Sharmila Mukherjee

Chapter 3 Slumlord Aesthetics and the Question of Indian Poverty 29
Nandini Chandra

Chapter 4 Watching Time: *Slumdog Millionaire* and National Ontology 39
Lakshmi Padmanabhan

***SLUMDOG* AND THE SLUM**

Chapter 5 *Slumdog Millionaire* and Epistemologies of the City 53
Ulka Anjaria and Jonathan Shapiro Anjaria

Chapter 6 A Million Dollar Exit from the Slum-World: *Slumdog Millionaire*'s Troubling Formula for Social Justice 69
Mitu Sengupta

Chapter 7 Slumdogs and Millionaires: Facts and Fictions of Indian (Under)development 91
Snehal Shingavi

SLUMDOG AND BOLLYWOOD

Chapter 8 Slumdogs, Coolies and Gangsters: Amitabh Bachchan and the Legacy of 1970s Bollywood in *Slumdog Millionaire* 109
Claus Tieber

Chapter 9 "It is Written" (in Invisible Ink): *Slumdog Millionaire*'s SFX and the Realist Overwriting of Bollywood Spectacle 121
Samhita Sunya

SLUMDOG'S RECEPTIONS

Chapter 10 Why the Sun Shines on *Slumdog* 143
Anandam Kavoori

Chapter 11 *Slumdog* Celebrities 149
Priya Jaikumar

Chapter 12 *Slumdog Millionaire* and the New Middlebrow 155
Robert Koehler

Chapter 13 Slumdog Comprador: Coming to Terms with the *Slumdog* Phenomenon 163
Ajay Gehlawat

Chapter 14 The Life-Cycle of *Slumdog Millionaire* on the Web 179
Thomas Elsaesser and Warren Buckland

Conclusion Jai *Who?* 201
Ajay Gehlawat

Select Bibliography 205

Films Cited 211

Index 213

NOTES ON CONTRIBUTORS

Ulka Anjaria is assistant professor of English at Brandeis University, with research interests in Indian literature and popular film, postcolonial studies and narrative theory. She is the author of *Realism in the Twentieth-Century Indian Novel: Colonial Difference and Literary Form*, published by Cambridge University Press in 2012. She is currently working on a second book on social realism in contemporary India.

Jonathan Shapiro Anjaria is assistant professor of anthropology at Brandeis University. He has published in *American Ethnologist, City and Community* and *Economic and Political Weekly*, among others. His co-edited volume (with Colin McFarlane), *Urban Navigations: Politics, Space and the City in South Asia*, was published by Routledge in 2011.

Warren Buckland is reader in film studies at Oxford Brookes University, UK. His research interests include film theory, narratology and contemporary American cinema. He has several books to his name, including: *Film Theory: Rational Reconstructions* (2012); *Film Theory and Contemporary Hollywood Movies* (ed., 2009); *Puzzle Films: Complex Storytelling in Contemporary Cinema* (ed., 2009); *Directed by Steven Spielberg: Poetics of the Contemporary Hollywood Blockbuster* (2006); *Studying Contemporary American Film: A Guide to Movie Analysis* (2002) (with Thomas Elsaesser); and *The Cognitive Semiotics of Film* (2000). He is also the editor of the quarterly journal *New Review of Film and Television Studies.*

Nandini Chandra teaches in the Department of English at the University of Delhi. Her book, *The Classic Popular: Amar Chitra Katha (1967–2007)*, was published by Yoda Press in 2008.

Thomas Elsaesser is professor emeritus of film and television studies at the University of Amsterdam, and, from 2006 to 2012, was visiting professor at Yale University. He has authored, edited and co-edited twenty volumes, many of which have been translated, notably into German, French, Italian, Korean and Chinese. Among his books are: *Studying Contemporary American Film* (2002, with Warren Buckland), *European Cinema: Face to Face with Hollywood* (2005); *Film Theory: An Introduction Through the Senses* (2010, with Malte Hagener) and *The Persistence of Hollywood* (2012).

Ajay Gehlawat is assistant professor of theatre and film in the Hutchins School of Liberal Studies at Sonoma State University. He is the author of *Reframing Bollywood: Theories of Popular Hindi Cinema* (Sage, 2010). His essays and articles have appeared in numerous journals and collections, including the *Journal of South Asian Popular Culture, TOPIA: Canadian Journal of Cultural Studies, Journal of African American Studies, CineAction, Quarterly Review of Film and Video,* and *South Asian Review.*

Priya Jaikumar is associate professor at the University of Southern California's School of Cinematic Arts, Department of Critical Studies. She studies the colonial pasts of European cinema, and transformations in Indian film policy and film form. Publications include the book *Cinema at the End of Empire* (Duke, 2006) and articles most recently featured in *Postcolonial Cinema Studies, Wasafari* and *Film and Empire.*

Anandam Kavoori is professor in the Grady College of Journalism and Mass Communication at the University of Georgia. He works in the areas of international communication, new media and media literacy. He is the author or editor of eight books including *Global Bollywood* (2008, with Aswin Punathambekar) and, most recently, *Digital Media Criticism* (2010).

Robert Koehler writes for *Variety, Cinema Scope, The Christian Science Monitor* and blogs on filmjourney.org.

Brian Larkin is the author of *Signal and Noise: Infrastructure, Media and Urban Culture in Nigeria*, and the co-editor of *Media Worlds: Anthropology on New Terrain.* He teaches anthropology at Barnard College, Columbia University.

Sharmila Mukherjee teaches English at the City University of New York's Bronx Community College and at New York University. She received her PhD in English from New York University. Her areas of scholarly interest include literature and globalization, and popular culture and globalization. Her debut novella will be published by Penguin India in the fall of 2012.

Lakshmi Padmanabhan is a PhD student and Chancellor Thomas Tisch Fellow in the Department of Modern Culture and Media at Brown University.

She has a BA in sociology from Stella Maris College, University of Madras and an MA in communication, culture and technology from Georgetown University. Her interests include contemporary South Asian film, new media philosophy, queer theory, race and globalization studies.

Mitu Sengupta is an associate professor in the Department of Politics at Ryerson University, Toronto, Canada. Mitu has published widely on Indian market liberalization and development, on labor and migration, and on the politics of sporting and cultural events. These writings are united by a concern for how knowledge about poverty, inequality, and "development" is produced, disseminated, interpreted and understood. Her new research builds on these critical inquiries to engage more directly with linking theory to practice, and is concerned with the creation of legal frameworks and policy interventions for poverty eradication in India and other developing countries, and for social and global justice.

Snehal Shingavi is an assistant professor in the Department of English at the University of Texas, Austin. He is the author of the forthcoming *The Mahatma Misunderstood: The Politics and Forms of Indian Literary Nationalism* (Anthem Press, 2013), has translated Munshi Premchand's *Sevasadan* (Oxford University Press, 2005) and has a forthcoming translation of Ajneya's *Shekhar: a Biography* (Oxford University Press, 2013).

Samhita Sunya is a PhD candidate at Rice University in Houston, Texas, and has also been a graduate research affiliate at the Centre for the Study of Culture and Society in Bangalore, Karnataka. Samhita is completing a pre-history of "viral" media and cinephilia in the digital era, through an account of Hindi film/songs. Her teaching and research interests include comparative media studies, sound and genre studies and adaptation studies.

Claus Tieber is research assistant at the University of Salzburg. He studied theatre, philosophy, political and communications studies at the University of Vienna. After years as a commissioning editor for the Austrian Broadcasting Corporation (ORF), he started an academic career in 2001, teaching film history and theory at the Universities of Vienna, Kiel and Salamanca. Recent publications include *Passages to Bollywood: Einführung in den Hindi-Film* (2006), *Schreiben für Hollywood: Das Drehbuch im Studiosystem* (2008), *Fokus Bollywood: Das indische Kino in wissenschaftlichen Diskursen* (2009) and *Stummfilmdramaturgie. Erzählweisen des amerikanischen Feature Films 1917–1927* (2011).

LIST OF FIGURES

4.1 Jamal and Salim stealing food from the train compartment. © 2008 Celador Films/Film4/Pathé Pictures International. All rights reserved. 43

5.1 Salim and Jamal looking out over the new urban landscape. © 2008 Celador Films/Film4/Pathé Pictures International. All rights reserved. 57

5.2 Images in Boyle's *Trainspotting* bend to reflect the distorted minds of its protagonists. © 1996 Channel Four Films/Figment Films/The Noel Gay Motion Picture Company. All rights reserved 59

5.3 A dystopic parody on urban transcendence – Renton descends into the toilet bowl. © 1996 Channel Four Films/Figment Films/The Noel Gay Motion Picture Company. All rights reserved 59

5.4 A feces-covered Jamal navigating through the crowd to reach the star. © 2008 Celador Films/Film4/Pathé Pictures International. All rights reserved. 61

9.1 Poster 1 for *Slumdog Millionaire*, ostensibly a love story. 127

9.2 Poster 2 for *Slumdog Millionaire* with the appearance of an indie documentary. 127

9.3 An online slideshow accompanies a 22 January 2009 column in the "Travel" section of the UK *Telegraph*. 128

9.4 The improbability of Jamal's success is implied in the film's opening moments (00:01:28). © 2008 Celador Films/Film4/Pathé Pictures International. All rights reserved. 133

9.5 Jamal's success is foreshadowed as fate (00:01:32).
© 2008 Celador Films/Film4/Pathé Pictures International.
All rights reserved. 133

11.1 The young stars of *Slumdog Millionaire* on Oscar night.
© 2009 Associated Press. All rights reserved. 150

12.1 Jamal, Latika and Salim as Mumbai street kids.
© 2008 Celador Films/Film4/Pathé Pictures International.
All rights reserved. 157

12.2 Jamal and *Millionaire* host Prem Kumar.
© 2008 Celador Films/Film4/Pathé Pictures International.
All rights reserved. 159

14.1 "Insights for Search" graph for "*Slumdog Millionaire*"
(May 2008–2009). 184

14.2 Regional interest and top ten search terms
for "*Slumdog Millionaire*." 184

14.3 "Insights for Search" graph for "*Slumdog Millionaire*"
(September 2008). 185

14.4 "Insights for Search" graph for "poverty porn"
(October 2008–2009). 188

ACKNOWLEDGMENTS

First and foremost I would like to thank all the contributors for their hard work and diligence. Thanks also to Tej Sood and Rob Reddick of Anthem, as well as to Janka Romero, for their sound editorial guidance, as well as to the external reviewers for their helpful comments and feedback. I would also like to thank Anuja Jain for her useful suggestion early on, Philippe Baudart for his technical assistance and, last but not least, Sylvie Baudart for all her invaluable advice throughout the various stages of this project.

Versions of the following chapters have been published previously. I am grateful for permission to reprint them in this volume.

"National Allegory," by Brian Larkin, first published in *Social Text* 27.3: 164–8. Copyright 2009, Duke University Press. All rights reserved. Reprinted by permission of the publisher.

"Slumlord Aesthetics and the Question of Indian Poverty," by Nandini Chandra, first published in *Monthly Review* (May 2009): 50–54.

"Slumdog Millionaire and Epistemologies of the City," by Jonathan Shapiro Anjaria and Ulka Anjaria, first published in *Economic and Political Weekly* 45.24 (2010): 41–6.

"A Million Dollar Exit from the Slum-world," by Mitu Sengupta, first published in *Third World Quarterly* 31.4 (2010): 599–616.

"Why the Sun Shines on *Slumdog*," by Anandam Kavoori, first published in *Global Media and Communication* 5.2: 259–62. Copyright 2009, SAGE Publications. Reprinted by permission of the publisher.

"Slumdog Celebrities," by Priya Jaikumar, first published in *Velvet Light Trap* 65: 22–4. Copyright 2010, the University of Texas Press. All rights reserved.

"*Slumdog Millionaire* and the New Middlebrow," by Robert Koehler, first published in *Cineaste* 34.2.

"Slumdog Comprador: Coming to Terms with the *Slumdog* Phenomenon," by Ajay Gehlawat, first published in *CineAction* 78 (2009): 2–9.

Introduction

THE *SLUMDOG* PHENOMENON

Ajay Gehlawat

It seems impossible to begin any discussion of *Slumdog Millionaire* (2008, hereafter *Slumdog*) without immediately mentioning how successful and controversial it has been – how many awards it has garnered,[1] how many cultural gurus have weighed in with damnation or praise (in some cases, damnation and then praise[2]) regarding its depictions of the slum, of India, its relationships with Bollywood, and its varying – in some cases, wildly divergent – receptions around the world. Yet the impossibility of avoiding such a discourse itself illuminates a salient point, namely, that the *Slumdog* phenomenon is precisely that – something viewed by so many people and resulting in so much passionate discussion that it has become more than just a film. *Slumdog* has become a cultural event, a phenomenon that speaks to many issues of our time, even as it illuminates several ongoing debates regarding the formation of cultural identities and relationships between global cultures (and culture industries) in the twenty-first century. Some of the issues *Slumdog* speaks to include: the rapidly transforming state of India; the increasing global dissemination of Indian culture (and the particular role Bollywood plays in this process); the exponential rise of Indian markets and, almost simultaneously, of Indian slums, especially those located in and around Bombay/Mumbai, where much of *Slumdog* takes place.[3]

This collection aims to address all of these issues and, in the process, provides a critical overview of the numerous debates surrounding the film, allowing readers to re-examine them in light of this anthology's multiple perspectives. Before providing an overview of this book's contents, I would briefly like to examine some of the key issues that *Slumdog* speaks to or, in some cases, elides. *Slumdog* comes at a time when India is seen as "rising," "shining" and otherwise answering all calls of the globe, part of a larger shift to the global South as the epicenter of the world. Rashmi Varma, for instance, describes a recent exhibition held at the Tate Modern in London, one year before the release of *Slumdog*, focusing on "global cities;" of the ten cities featured in the exhibition, only three

(London, Tokyo and Los Angeles) were from the so-called First World, while the remaining seven were from the postcolonial or so-called Third World.[4] This exhibit's make-up illuminates what Varma calls "a striking fact about the twenty-first century," namely, that the "key sites of rapid and mega-scale urbanization" are now located in the global South, in cities such as Bombay/Mumbai, whose population alone is expected to reach 50 million by 2050.[5]

Yet even as one can trace such a global shift, attendant issues immediately surface. Chief among these is the subsequent rise of slums. In these global cities, already roughly one billion people live in slums. More than half of Bombay's population live in slums or, indeed, are homeless; in Dharavi, the largest slum district of Bombay and quite possibly the largest slum concentration in Asia, over half a million people live in an area roughly one square mile.[6] At the same time, as Varma goes on to note, Bombay is seen as "the quintessential modern Indian, even Asian, city."[7] Such a juxtaposition – overwhelming slums and overwhelming modernity – indeed brings to mind Sunil Khilnani's characterization of Bombay as a city whose contrasts are "vividly adjacent."[8] Even as Varma notes that one of the key ideas informing the popular conception of Bombay is a "survival against all odds," she also notes the uneasy relationship – what she calls "one of the key contradictions at the heart of Bombay's popular and canonical representations" – between its urban reality (most vividly on display in the enormity of its slums) and its hyper-*un*-reality – "more like a movie set than the real thing."[9]

All of this is vividly on display in *Slumdog*. From the film's opening sequences, one is immediately thrust into the types of contradictions Varma points to and that give the film its name. Since its release, one of the bigger debates surrounding *Slumdog* has been whether it should be seen as a realistic work or art or as a fantasy – or, indeed, as both simultaneously. The film's director, Danny Boyle, himself commented on the contradictory juxtaposition comprising Bombay, describing it as a "maximum city," in which "everything's maximum. The horror that you see [...] but [also] the sense of joy."[10] In a similar vein, *Slumdog* has been characterized as "melodrama [...] fantas[y], and [...] real at the same time," by its director.[11] At the same time, as Pankaj Mishra notes in a review of Katherine Boo's recent book, *Behind the Beautiful Forevers: Life, Death, and Hope in a Mumbai Undercity* (2012), "the ostensible 'rise' of India has attracted its share of literary and journalistic buccaneers in recent years," many of which, Mishra argues, are "un-self-consciously suffused with the clichés of the age, speak[ing] of how free-market capitalism has ignited a general explosion of opportunity, fostering hope among the most destitute of Indians."[12] *Slumdog*, too, can be placed within such a trajectory, though the immediate question that comes to mind is: how does it function within such a movement?

Slumdog has invoked many literary and filmic parallels, including to the prose of Dickens and the films of Bollywood. However, relatively unmentioned in all of the parallels that have been made is one I would like to consider here, stemming from the term Mishra deploys in characterizing India's upward trajectory in the past years. Many commentators (beginning with the film's distributor, Fox Searchlight Pictures) have labeled *Slumdog* a "hopeful" film, directly referencing Barack Obama's narrative of hope in the process.[13] The parallel I would like to briefly take up is to the Gilded Age, an era of rapid economic and population growth in the United States during the late nineteenth century. During that period, as is the case with India today, the US economy rose at the fastest rate in its history, with several individuals becoming enormously (even obscenely) rich in a relatively short amount of time.[14] The noted American author, William Dean Howells, wrote about one such man in his novel, *The Rise of Silas Lapham* (1885). As is arguably the case with the exploding growth (of slums and fortunes) in India today, Howells depicted how his title character's "rise" (in affluence) coincided with a relative decline in morals. To follow Howells and look at what could arguably be called India's Gilded Age one can chart a similar rise and fall in what Mishra calls "India's desultory new culture of aspiration," which is nowhere more compellingly on display than in *Slumdog* – not just in the protagonist Jamal's quest to win millions on the Indian version of the television game show, *Who Wants to Be a Millionaire?* but, perhaps more fittingly, in his (bad) brother Salim's rise through the ranks of the local Mumbai mafia.[15]

In this way, one can also compare *Slumdog*'s protagonists (especially, perhaps, Salim) to the main character in Aravind Adiga's recent Booker Prize–winning novel, *The White Tiger*, released the same year as *Slumdog*. As is the case with Salim, Adiga's protagonist, Balram Halwai, faced with the declining morals of the new "culture of aspiration" in India, learns, in turn, to become a successful entrepreneur by adopting a Machiavellian mentality in his everyday life. As Adiga has noted, "there are a lot of self-made millionaires in India now," and, at the same time, "a lot of poorer Indians are left confused and perplexed by the new India that is being formed around them."[16] It is precisely in such a dog-eat-dog world that *Slumdog*'s young protagonists come of age and, in many ways, their upward struggle reflects the "rise" of India over the past two decades.

The first two sections of *The "Slumdog" Phenomenon* take this "rise" as their starting point. The first section, *Slumdog* and the Nation, begins with Brian Larkin's chapter "National Allegory," which updates the classic debate between Fredric Jameson and Aijaz Ahmad concerning how to interpret Third World texts via its application to Indian cinema, and to *Slumdog* in particular. In the process, even as the older paradigms of this famous exchange are reformulated through their application to *Slumdog*, Larkin examines how such a film becomes burdened with a sense of representation, is seen as speaking for the larger (Indian) nation and reflecting many of the popular (mis)conceptions surrounding this (national) construction. Larkin compares the debates surfacing today over *Slumdog* to the earlier controversies surrounding Satyajit Ray's film, *Pather Panchali* (1955), which was similarly (and simultaneously) seen as presenting both "the real India" and presenting India "improperly." As Larkin argues, Ray's film "brought tremendous prestige to India while, at the same time, destabilizing and threatening that prestige." Through these now canonical debates, Larkin commences his re-examination of *Slumdog*, asking in the process, what it means to be a cultural text, and indeed how such a text is created.

Building on Larkin's chapter, Sharmila Mukherjee, in her essay "*Slumdog* and the Emerging Centrality of India," considers the new global order in which India has emerged as a key player. Mukherjee examines how *Slumdog* reflects and celebrates this new status, even as it continues to be framed within an Other-izing discourse, which continues to invoke older, Orientalist motifs in describing the Indian nation. Employing and interrogating the analysis of Dipesh Chakrabarty, among others, Mukherjee argues that the formulation of the recent rising/ shining India is contingent upon a subsequent reformulation of its relationship with the West, which continues to serve as the silent referent in the construction of this new India. *Slumdog* (made at least in part by a British director[17]) thus functions as an apt reflection of India's new position in the world and as a Western articulation of such an emergence.

In keeping with this line of inquiry, the following chapter by Nandini Chandra explores the real-life fantasies set into motion through India's emerging new middle class, fueled by game shows such as *Millionaire*. Beginning her essay by looking at the case of an actual winner on this show – a "real-life Jamal," as it were – Chandra proceeds to contextualize what she calls the Cinderella effect of these game shows, wherein contestants are motivated to excel with promises of simultaneous escape (from poverty) and admission (into the new global economy) that can be read in tandem with both Jamal's and India's aspirations. Chandra invokes Partha Chatterjee's concept of a political society to (re)examine *Slumdog*'s characterization of the Indian underbelly, in which the slum, the brothel and child labor are all "stops on [the] guided tour,"[18] geared towards a neoliberal audience.

In the final essay in this section, "Watching Time: *Slumdog Millionaire* and National Ontology," Lakshmi Padmanabhan employs the concept of the media assemblage to examine the multiple emerging networks that *Slumdog Millionaire* encompasses. Drawing on the work of Gilles Deleuze and Amit Rai in particular, Padmanabhan examines not just the representations of India in *Slumdog* but what these representations *do*. As she notes, such an endeavor becomes particularly important given the numerous and conflicting invocations of differing nations – for example, India, Britain and the US – as ways of folding the film into (competing) national media assemblages. Such endeavors, Padmanabhan argues, paradoxically illuminate the transnational make up of *Slumdog* and (thus) the relative ease with which it can be appropriated by so many differing nationalist narratives. In the process, she pays particularly close attention to the differing senses of duration in the film, as well as what these, in turn, entail for the changing times of the nation.

Building on these introductory essays, the second section of the book examines *Slumdog*'s relationships with the slum. The first essay, "*Slumdog Millionaire* and Epistemologies of the City" by Ulka Anjaria and Jonathan Shapiro Anjaria, begins by addressing the underlying assumptions of much of the critical commentary surrounding the film, especially regarding what is considered to be a particular shortcoming – its melodramatic nature. Critiquing the implicit assumption that only a realist aesthetic could do justice to its subject matter, Anjaria and Anjaria reexamine how images of slums and poverty function within fantasy plots. In doing so the authors demonstrate how, despite eschewing realist conventions, *Slumdog* provides a mode of urban navigation (e.g., of the slum) that questions dominant narratives regarding the ubiquity of globalization. Key to such a rearticulation is an alternative realm of knowledge outside of the formal domains of the state, which "slumdogs" such as Jamal paradoxically have access to and utilize to their advantage.

The second essay in this section, Mitu Sengupta's "A Million Dollar Exit from the Slum-world," investigates the film's depictions of the slum and Indian poverty, arguing that these depictions do little to question the underlying structures of material inequality and, instead, reconceptualize slums as worthless, self-contained spaces. Simultaneously, Sengupta explains why a film like *Slumdog* was more successful with Indian audiences than previous films depicting similar settings, such as *City of Joy* (1992). This is partially due, Sengupta argues, to the absence of white bodies in *Slumdog* and its disregard for the labor struggles of the poor and simultaneous celebration of consumer capitalism. While noting that *Slumdog* is a film (and not a documentary), Sengupta illuminates how its narrative simultaneously presents the slum as devoid of internal resources and (thus) frames Jamal's "rescue" as one engineered by (magical) "destiny." Such an approach, she argues, reinforces earlier paradigms of the "culture of poverty," which paint unsympathetic portrayals of the urban poor and allow the state to remove slums (and their inhabitants) under the auspices of modernization.

In the final chapter of this section, "Slumdogs and Millionaires," Snehal Shingavi examines the facts and fictions underlying Indian (under)development, through a close examination of both *Slumdog* and the book it was loosely based on, Indian diplomat Vikas Swarup's *Q & A* (2005). Critiquing their respective approaches in depicting the slum, Shingavi claims that both film and novel paradoxically employ "facts" as a way of denying the realities of the poor. Both works are structured as exposés and fantasies, in which facts about poverty and urban life essentially become platitudes, providing little insight into how the poor actually live. Simultaneously, the mastery of such facts becomes a way for slumdogs such as Jamal (and the novel's Ram Mohammad Thomas) to escape from the slum. Such a fact-based ideology, Shingavi argues, aligns itself with a larger culture of English language education and the assimilation of Western trivia as modes of upward class mobility in India today.

Another key invocation that *Slumdog* makes is of Bollywood. Indeed, it should come as no surprise that the film arrives at precisely the moment when discussions over this latter industry – and the term itself – are burgeoning in the West where, prior to *Slumdog*, Bollywood was relatively unknown and, since its release (and overwhelming success), the two have largely become conflated (at least in the Western popular imaginary and press). The essays in the third section of this collection thus examine the various relationships between Bollywood (i.e., the popular Hindi film industry) and *Slumdog*, in order to develop a better understanding of both cinematic forms and the numerous ways in which *Slumdog* invokes, redefines and arguably replaces Bollywood.[19] Claus Tieber's essay, "Slumdogs, Coolies and Gangsters," examines *Slumdog*'s invocation of Bollywood's biggest star, Amitabh Bachchan, and how this larger-than-life figure is utilized by the film to conjure up multiple motifs stemming from 1970s Bollywood cinema. In the process, Tieber examines many of the traits *Slumdog*'s protagonists share with the angry young man persona that Bachchan made famous in the '70s, before moving on to consider Bachchan's subsequent "rehabilitation" as the original host of the Indian version of *Who Wants to Be a Millionaire?* which, in turn, becomes a key narrative device in *Slumdog*.

In the second essay of this section, "'It is Written' (in Invisible Ink)," Samhita Sunya argues that *Slumdog* invokes Bollywood as a way of reinforcing its credibility and authenticity. These invocations come equally through the visual components of the film and its aural components, Sunya argues, most notably via *Slumdog*'s award-winning soundtrack by veteran Bollywood composer A. R. Rahman. Invoking André Bazin's classical theories of filmic realism, Sunya examines how *Slumdog* develops a realist aesthetic through a process she labels overwriting, in which the film's aural and visual invocations of Bollywood paradoxically create an "effect of instant reality." Sunya develops this argument by carefully examining the invisible ways in which *Slumdog*'s scoring and song sequences lend credence to the film's realist portrayal of life in India and, in the process, function as a nod to classical Bollywood productions.

Finally, the essays in the last section of this collection examine the varying receptions of *Slumdog* around the globe. Beginning with Anandam Kavoori's useful overview, "Why the Sun Shines on *Slumdog*," in which the author sets forth some important contexts through which to gauge responses to the film, the pieces in this section examine why the film was so successful, particularly in the West, as well as what its resounding success implies for the future of such global, hybrid (co)productions. Priya Jaikumar's essay, "*Slumdog* Celebrities," examines the events of Oscar night 2009, when *Slumdog* swept to victory, paying particular attention to the reception the film's child stars received on Hollywood's red carpet, as well as what the film's success portends for the triumphant promise of transnational cinema. Robert Koehler's review, meanwhile, argues that *Slumdog* can most effectively be seen as a form of middlebrow cinema, in which it substitutes for an actual Bollywood film yet is successful in the West precisely because this sleight of hand goes unrecognized. In my essay, "Slumdog Comprador: Coming to Terms with the *Slumdog* Phenomenon," I examine the comprador phenomenon, in which critics who position themselves as speaking for India invoke a series of interrelated claims about *Slumdog* that simultaneously provide ideological cover for the film and its proponents. And in the final essay of this section, Thomas Elsaesser and Warren Buckland analyze the life cycle of *Slumdog* on the web, based on four layers of data which they use to assess the multiple meanings and intentions ascribed to the film by various communities, interest groups and experts.

Taken together, these essays comprise the first extended, in-depth study of a film that continues to generate controversy and conversation around the globe. The varying styles adopted by the pieces assembled here aptly reflect the multidisciplinary approach this collection takes as a whole, even as the book's four sections – moving from debates surrounding *Slumdog* and the Indian nation to the film's varying global receptions – build upon each other in a manner that allows for increasingly nuanced perspectives regarding the *Slumdog* phenomenon to emerge. In a late 2008 interview, Danny Boyle described his experience in India shooting *Slumdog* in the following manner:

> You do get shit all over you. There's nowhere to shit; people shit everywhere. Although you never see the women shitting. I was there a year, on and off, and for eight months full-time. You see men doing it all the time. But you never see women. There were all these rumors: "Oh, they get up in the night" – but I was up in the night, and I never saw them. There are these little plastic bags everywhere, tied up very neatly. It must be that; that's the only logical explanation.[20]

Reading Boyle's descriptions, and recalling one of the classic moments of the film, it could safely be said that shit becomes a key metaphor in *Slumdog*, frequently invoked not only by the film but, as is evident in the above passage, by its creator. From such a shitty metaphor emerges the following pearl: Boyle, knee-deep, as it were, searching for the (female) shit of India and awakening to find, like gifts from the Indian tooth fairy, neat little plastic bags of shit everywhere. These "brown paper packages tied up in string" become markers of *Slumdog*'s authenticity and ways of disposing of it (by consuming it). This collection, rather than flushing away the shit, plunges headfirst into it.

Notes

1 To provide what has now become the laundry list of accolades, *Slumdog* won eight Oscars, including for Best Picture, Best Director, Best Cinematography, Best Adapted Screenplay, Best Editing, Best Original Score and Best Original Song. In addition, the film won seven British Academy of Film and Television Arts (BAFTA) awards, including Best Film and Best Director, five Critics' Choice awards, four Golden Globes and numerous audience awards at multiple film festivals. Overall, the film won over fifty awards from organizations and film festivals around the world. For a full listing of the awards *Slumdog* either won or was nominated for, see http://www.imdb.com/title/tt1010048/awards (accessed 1 August 2012).

2 As in the case of Amitabh Bachchan, a central figure both in *Slumdog* and in its subsequent debates, as many of the essays in this collection go on to discuss.

3 I use Bombay and Mumbai interchangeably here (neither option seems particularly salutary, with one stemming from a colonial context and the other from a Hindu nationalist push to rename major Indian cities in the 1990s). At the same time, if one bears in mind Jamal's claim – made midway through *Slumdog* – that "Bombay had become Mumbai," then, within such a context, the difference (i.e., the name change) does become significant, with the latter term (Mumbai) correlating with the advent of globalization and the type of large-scale economic development that Jamal is referencing. Nevertheless, both terms continue to be used. For more regarding this name change, see Rashmi Varma, "Provincializing the Global City: from Bombay to Mumbai," *Social Text* 22.4 (2004): 65–89.

4 Rashmi Varma, *The Postcolonial City and its Subjects: London, Nairobi, Bombay* (New York: Routledge, 2012), xiii. The seven cities from the global South included in the 2007 Tate exhibit were Sao Paulo, Mexico City, Johannesburg, Cairo, Mumbai, Istanbul and Shanghai.

5 Ibid.

6 Ibid., 175n1, 202n49.

7 Ibid., 127.

8 Sunil Khilnani, *The Idea of India* (New York: Farrar Straus and Giroux, 1998), 138.

9 Varma, *The Postcolonial City*, 129. Bombay is also the center of Bollywood film production. For more regarding this industry, see, e.g., Manjunath Pendakur, *Indian Popular Cinema: Industry, Ideology, and Consciousness* (New York: Hampton Press, 2003); and Ranjani Mazumdar, *Bombay Cinema: An Archive of the City* (Minneapolis: University of Minnesota Press, 2007).

10 Ambrose Heron, "Interview: Danny Boyle on *Slumdog Millionaire*," in *Danny Boyle: Interviews*, edited by Brent Dunham (Jackson: University Press of Mississippi, 2011), 146. The phrase "maximum city" stems from Suketu Mehta's book about life in Bombay, *Maximum City: Bombay Lost and Found* (New York: Vintage, 2004).

11 Hank Sartin, "Boyle's Orders," in *Danny Boyle: Interviews*, 132.

12 Pankaj Mishra, "Fighting for Scraps," *New York Times Book Review*, 12 February 2012. Boo's book focuses on the Annawadi slum near Mumbai's airport.

13 Barack Obama was elected president of the United States at roughly the same time that *Slumdog* was making waves at various film festivals, en route to the Oscars, which took place approximately one month after Obama's inauguration. In many ways, one can chart similar trajectories between these two phenomena, as some of the essays in this collection go on to do. Fox Searchlight COO Nancy Utley described the film as "Obama-like" for its "message of hope in the face of difficulty," as well as its "underdog status." See Logan Hill, "Slumdog's Underdog," *New York*, 9 November 2008. Online: http://nymag.com/movies/features/52003/index1.html (accessed 1 August 2012).

14 Edward C. Kirkland, *Industry Comes of Age: Business, Labor, and Public Policy, 1860–1897* (New York: Quadrangle Books, 1961), 400–405.

15 Mishra, "Fighting for Scraps," 11. Indeed, the film juxtaposes these two "rises" (and at least one fall) from the very outset, juxtaposing shots of Jamal on the game show with the image of money falling into a bathtub in which Salim lies (and subsequently dies). As Varma notes in *The Postcolonial City*, "Ironically, the Mumbai mafia has produced its own forms of globalization by establishing transnational networks involving a variety of illegal enterprises through smuggling, piracy, narcotics, prostitution, construction, real estate, politics and Bollywood" (155).

16 Aravind Adiga, "A Conversation with Aravind Adiga," *The White Tiger* (New York: Free Press, 2008), 287–6. Adiga's latest novel, *Last Man in Tower* (2011), set in Bombay, also addresses the simultaneous "rise" (of monetary value) and "fall" (of morality) of the members of India's "new culture of aspiration."

17 The question of Loveleen Tandan's precise status also becomes a point of contention. While credited as the film's co-director, Boyle claims "she started out as casting director, but helped me in every way it's possible to imagine. [...] Culturally, she would tell me if I was wrong about things." In this way, Tandan might also be seen as playing the role of native informant. See Catherine Bray, "*Slumdog Millionaire*: Danny Boyle Interview," in *Danny Boyle: Interviews*, 140–41. Notably, despite Boyle's claims and her nominal listing as co-director, Tandan's name generally goes unmentioned in all of the award citations, which list Boyle as *Slumdog*'s sole *auteur*. For more regarding the concept of the native informant, see Gayatri Spivak, *A Critique of Postcolonial Reason: Toward a History of the Vanishing Present* (Cambridge: Harvard University Press, 1999); for additional discussion of Tandan's role in *Slumdog*, see Nandini Chandra's essay, "Slumlord Aesthetics and the Question of Indian Poverty," included in this collection.

18 Chandra, "Slumlord Aesthetics and the Question of Indian Poverty," 35 (included in this volume).

19 While some contemporary Hindi film theorists, for instance, Sangita Gopal and Priya Joshi, have invoked *Slumdog* in their efforts to delineate new forms of Bollywood cinema – what Gopal labels "New Bollywood" and Joshi, "Bollylite" – others, most recently Sangita Shresthova, have noted that, while it is "hardly a Bollywood film," *Slumdog*'s "runaway success" has "helped build Indian commercial cinema's presence in the popular imagination of the US public." See, respectively, Sangita Gopal, *Conjugations: Marriage and Form in New Bollywood Cinema* (Chicago: University of Chicago Press, 2011); Priya Joshi, "Bollylite in America," *South Asian Popular Culture* 8.3 (2010); and Sangita Shresthova, *Is It All About Hips? Around the World with Bollywood Dance* (New Delhi: Sage, 2011), 107.

20 Quoted in Bray, "*Slumdog Millionaire*," in *Danny Boyle: Interviews*, 139.

Part One

SLUMDOG AND THE NATION

Chapter 1
NATIONAL ALLEGORY

Brian Larkin

In January 2009, Amitabh Bachchan, the lion of Indian cinema, reacted on his blog to the increasing success of the film *Slumdog Millionaire* with a caution. Tapping into an anxiety about how India is represented abroad, he asserted: "If SM [*Slumdog Millionaire*] projects India as Third World dirty underbelly developing nation and causes pain and disgust among nationalists and patriots, let it be known that a murky under belly exists and thrives even in the most developed nations."[1] Bachchan intensified a furious controversy both inside India and abroad over whether the film was a form of "poverty porn,"[2] whether it was Indian or not and whether its representations showed real problems in India or a stereotype of poverty served up for foreign audiences.

Slumdog Millionaire is, perhaps, an ill fit for Fredric Jameson's argument in "Third World Literature in the Era of Multinational Capitalism" (*Social Text* 15 (1986)), that Third World texts operate as national allegories. Based on an Indian novel (*Q & A* by Vikas Swarup), adapted by a British screenwriter (Simon Beaufoy) and British director (Danny Boyle), co-directed by an Indian (Loveleen Tandan), financed from Europe, set in India and starring Indians – the film has origins complex enough for many Indians to claim it as *desi* while others disavow it as foreign. It is also not an allegory in Jameson's sense of private individual stories representing public political events. Yet the controversy itself is deeply Indian as it replays previous conflicts over the circulation of Indian cinema and what constitutes proper representations of India. What these controversies do is sharpen the focus on a dynamic central to the debate between Jameson and Aijaz Ahmad but relatively neglected in scholarly discussion.[3] Allegory is not always a feature immanent to a text but is something texts have placed upon them through the act of circulation across cultural difference. Bachchan's reaction to *Slumdog* as a story of a "dirty underbelly developing nation" rather than of the hard life of two children is an example of this. His reading of the film as a national allegory derives not from his experience of the film but from his reaction to its success in the West, and it is only after this movement that the film comes to stand for the nation (and thus become an object of critique). Allegory, in this mode, is not tied to the imagination of writer or director but is derived externally from the movement of the text in and out of different publics. This is particularly the case for successful films and novels such as *Slumdog* whose popularity heightens a dynamic inherent to the process of circulation itself.

In his article on Third World literature, Jameson attempts to lay out theoretical grounds for analyzing non-Western literature and through that to expand the literary canon. The publicity brought by the debate with Ahmad means this aim has been probably more successful than Jameson could have imagined (if not in the way he expected). His argument, famously, is that Third World intellectuals and the texts they produce exhibit an "obsessive return to the national situation" that comes from their position as structurally marginal to the centers of power in the contemporary world. He insists on a sharp cleavage between West and non-West. "Nothing is to be gained," he argues, "by passing over in silence the radical difference of non-canonical texts."[4] This difference emerges from the experience of imperial domination and living in the dark shadow of American hegemony that together lead to the formation of a different, more politicized non-Western intellectual. It is the experience of this marginality, Jameson argues, that accounts for the obsessive concern with allegory. Novels that purport to be about private, intimate stories "necessarily project a political dimension in the forms of national allegory: the story of the private individual destiny is always an allegory of the embattled situation of the public third world culture and society."[5]

Ahmad, of course, rejects the claim of difference and the argument that Third World texts are wholly concerned with national allegories (indeed he rejects the entire category of Third World literature as a theoretical unity). In most societies, he argues, there is a vast diversity of literature in which thematic concerns about the nation-state are either minor or wholly absent. Using the example of nineteenth-century Urdu literature, he argues this body of work betrays a preoccupation with the place of women and the rise of a petite bourgeoisie rather than any sustained discussion of the national question. It is only because Jameson has little access to vernacular literatures and relies on translated works, Ahmad argues, that he comes to conceive of Third World literature solely in terms of its marginality and opposition to "global American postmodernist culture."[6] While Ahmad makes some compelling points, he is curiously unconcerned with the basic question Jameson raises: what is the relation between cultural forms and nationalism? One can reject Jameson's totalizing summation ("all Third World texts") while still interrogating the close imbrication of nationalism, literature and film.

As the controversy over *Slumdog* reveals, the allegorical capacity of texts to stand for the nation stems not just from authorial intention but from the movement that looses them from original contexts of production and reception and opens them up to different publics that do not share the same contexts of understanding. While Jameson does not focus on this dynamic, it is central to his theoretical argument about the Western critical reception of non-Western texts. For Jameson, Third World texts come to the Western reader as estranged: "Western readers whose tastes [...] have been formed by our own modernisms"[7] cannot read in the same way as the public for which the text is originally intended. For readers like himself, Jameson argues, the text appears as "already-read."[8] The Westerner recognizes an "Other reader" standing between her and the text, at the same time realizing a "noncoincidence with that Other reader."[9] His argument here rests on a radical form of alterity that is reflexive in that the haunting presence of this second reader is ultimately the recognition of cultural, religious, political, and social difference. Jameson's analysis is grounded in the difficulty of translation across difference, and it is in that precise encounter that the force of national allegory is released.

To return to *Slumdog*, it is as these images circulate outside of India through film festivals and awards events, and as they assume popularity in these arenas, that they come to take on the increasing burden of representing the nation and so intensify the controversy that surrounds the film. In the case of India, this controversy replays earlier ones that frame how *Slumdog* is understood. The most important of these was the fierce reaction to the international success of Satyajit Ray's film *Pather Panchali* (1955). *Pather Panchali* was the first Indian film recognized within the realm of European art cinema and achieved the feat of making cinema acceptable to an Indian intelligentsia who were notoriously condescending toward Hindi film and of projecting India's artistic achievement to a worldwide critical audience. In her later years as a member of the Indian parliament, Nargis, one of the few Hindi film stars whose reputation matches that of Amitabh Bachchan, accused Ray of exporting Indian backwardness for foreign audiences. Her fear, and that of many nationalists, was that the film would merely confirm Western stereotypes of Indian poverty and deny the possibility of India representing herself as a modern nation, and she argued that Ray was only successful because he catered to the Western desire to see Indian poverty. Indian films should present images of a modern India that, for her, was defined by dams and development (itself a reference to the dam-building sequence in her most famous film, *Mother India* (1957).[10]

Accusations that *Pather Panchali* exported poverty had dogged the film from its release, long before Nargis's comments. Even though the film was selected to represent India at Cannes (where it won an award), attacks on the film led the Indian government to pass regulations directing that, in the future, "before any State Government sends films [...] abroad for exhibition, the State Government should ascertain the film's suitability from the point of view of external publicity."[11] The art historian Kajri Jain argues that these nationalist attempts to control representations of India are a secular equivalent to ideas of religious desecration. They exemplify "what film-makers in particular recognize as the 'proper light' syndrome referring to the way in which certain images [...] are rejected [...] by representatives of the state because they 'do not show India in a proper light.'"[12] In 1959 the Central Board of Film Censors reacted to the success of Ray's film abroad by extending its list of censorable images to include scenes representing "abject, disgusting poverty"[13] – a clear reference to *Pather Panchali* and one that confirms its peculiar status as a film that brought tremendous prestige to India while, at the same time, destabilizing and threatening that prestige. The assertion of government control over this process reveals an awareness that any film shown abroad might come to speak for the nation irrespective of its content or aesthetic form.

When Satyajit Ray made *Pather Panchali* according to the aesthetic norms of European art cinema at the time, it may be the case that he represented the sort of political intellectual Jameson wrote of, one for whom private stories were at the same time public narratives about the state of the nation. But the controversy that surrounded the film and more recently *Slumdog Millionaire* derives from Indian response to the critical success of these films as they traverse the festivals and cinemas of the West. Allegory, in these instances, is something external to the films. A cultural text is not a container of a meaning that lies inside of it waiting for the critic to release it but is already mediated by the process of circulation itself and accrues meaning by virtue of that traffic across difference. The Jameson–Ahmad debate has been mostly discussed in relation to its role in the analysis of postcolonial literature, but it has much to say about the difficulty in analyzing the traffic of cultural forms across national boundaries.[14] At stake is how we understand the specificity and forms of difference that gives rise to different intellectual publics for writers and critics and the dynamics of translation this involves.

Notes

1 Amitabh Bachchan, "Day 265," BigBlog, 13 January 2009. Online: http://blogs.siliconindia.com/Amitabhbachchan/DAY_265_Amitabh_Bachchan_Blog-bid-4w7V8hDF60689039.html (accessed 6 November 2012).

2 See, for instance, Alice Miles, "Shocked by Slumdog's Poverty Porn," *Times* (London), 14 January 2009. Online: www.timesonline.co.uk/tol/comment/columnists/alice_miles/article5511650.ece (accessed 14 January 2009).

3 See Aijaz Ahmad, "Jameson's Rhetoric of Otherness and the 'National Allegory,'" *Social Text* 17 (1987).

4 Fredric Jameson, "Third-World Literature in the Era of Multinational Capitalism," *Social Text* 15 (1986), 65.
5 Ibid., 69.
6 Ahmad, "Jameson's Rhetoric," 8.
7 Jameson, "Third-World Literature," 66.
8 Ibid.
9 Ibid.
10 D. A. Windsor, "Nargis, Rushdie, and the Real," *South Asia: Journal of South Asian Studies* 21 (1998): 229–42.
11 Cited in Erik Barnouw and S. Krishnaswamy, *Indian Film* (New York: Columbia University Press, 1963), 223.
12 Kajri Jain, *Gods in the Bazaar: The Commercial Sacred and Libidinal Economies of Indian Calendar Art* (Durham, NC: Duke University Press, 2007), 297.
13 Cited in Barnouw and Krishnaswamy, *Indian Film*, 224.
14 See special issues of *Social Text* 31/32 (1992), "Third World and Post-Colonial Issues," and *Social Text* 78 (2004), "Postcolonial Traces."

Chapter 2

SLUMDOG MILLIONAIRE AND THE EMERGING CENTRALITY OF INDIA

Sharmila Mukherjee

That used to be our slum. Can you believe that, huh? We used to live right there, man.
Now it's all business. India is at the center of the world now, *bhai*, and I,
I am at the center of the center.

You wanted to see a bit of real India? Here it is.
Well, here is a bit of the real America, son.

Halfway through Danny Boyle's 2008 magnum opus, *Slumdog Millionaire*, a remarkable imperial gloating comes from Salim Malik, the "slumdog" turned hip and rich factotum of billionaire gangster Javed Khan. In a scene of reunion between the film's two brothers as young adults, Salim, perched cockily atop the ramparts of an unfinished luxury condominium complex in the heart of metropolitan Mumbai, crows preeningly to his younger sibling Jamal about the emerging centrality of twenty-first century India in the global economy, and of his own omphalic position within this Indo-centric world. As he preens, his gaze sweeps across the blossoming Mumbai skyline which, framed by the force of the hyperbolic utterance, appears in excess of New York City's or Shanghai's. Salim's ethnocentric boast about his own arrival from abject marginality into the power and prestige of a Dolce & Gabbana–accessorized human/Indian subjectivity is aimed at converting his brother Jamal from idealist to pragmatist, such that he, too, can prioritize a dream of capital over a dream of love. It is also a brashly articulated affirmation of India's conversion from a "slumdog" nation to a "millionaire" capital of the world, from an aid recipient country to a major global player, a developer of the economies of other nations, even.[1]

In Salim's utterance we glimpse, among other things, the possibility of the formation of a new global order, coalescing around India as one of its powerful epicenters. Salim's affirmation of India's centrality is not a random, episodic instance of an eccentric, Bollywood-inspired hyperbole, though one could say that the tone in which it is delivered is indubitably Bollywoodian in its sweeping disavowal of the complex geographies of economic and geopolitical formations. The semiotics of exaltation foreground an emerging global discourse on India as the rising economic power of the twenty-first century alongside China and, by implication, on the country's thrilling ascent from being Third World to becoming a nation of emerging global modernity. Partaking in the discourse of an empowered India is Balram Halwai, the servant turned successful entrepreneur in Aravind Adiga's Booker Prize–winning novel, *The White Tiger* (2008), who reflects not only on his own unprecedented upward mobility within India, but also on that of India's in the world. As he says in a letter to the visiting dignitary, Chinese premier Wen Jiabao, the days of the "white man" are over, while the "brown" and "yellow" man are to be regarded as the emergent sovereignty of a globalizing world.[2] Both Salim's and Halwai's (fictional) reordering of the global power structure into an evolving Indian/brown center and a devolving American/white marginality, lack rigor and complexity. Yet they are indicative of a discernible shift in the way in which India's place in the current narrative of global power is being conceived of and discussed. The discursive formation of India as poised to emerge as an original knowledge-producing, rapidly modernizing entity, is taking place slowly but surely – not in a vacuum, but in the substantial context of a world that is increasingly becoming "post-American." This is because power, it is said, is moving seismically from the West to the "rest," the rest being a group of geographically diverse nations led by economic powerhouses such as India and China.[3]

Slumdog Millionaire (hereafter, *SDM*) captures India in its moment of triumphant ascension. In this chapter, I posit the film as a text that genuinely celebrates, or "Jai Hos," as it were, India's burgeoning globality and centrality. I predicate my reading of *SDM*'s celebratory stance, which I believe is expressed most piquantly in the Bollywood-style song and dance sequence at the end, on an implicit understanding that the film's ideology is in sync with the ideology of a new global paradigm of power, under whose aegis a twenty-first century India is produced discursively, as a subject rather than as an object of history. In other words, a history of the Indian present is produced not in a relationship of subordination but relative coevalness with Europe.[4] This is a refreshing departure from the usual mode of production of the East by the West. Western productions of non-Western histories, argues historian Dipesh Chakrabarty, have typically been "European" because, in the discourse of history, Europe remains the sovereign theoretical subject. He observes the peculiar way in which the writing of Indian, Chinese or Kenyan (among other) histories "tend to become variations on a master narrative that could be called the 'history of Europe.'"[5] What Chakrabarty avers is that, in cardinal ways, the discourse of history is always already mediated by Europe. Put otherwise, the discourse of history is predicated on Europe as the "silent," omniversal referent. In this chapter, I claim that in *SDM*'s construction of India, Europe as referent, though not entirely dissolved, is at least provincialized in so far as the film is infused with global content – screenwriter Simon Beaufoy claims to have been inspired by Bollywood films of the '70s in penning the story of *SDM* and the primary episteme employed by *SDM* is global, not Western.[6] This essay, however, does not attempt to arrive at or pitch a stable or unified category of a global episteme but instead contends that, produced through the grid of a global episteme, the India of *SDM*'s construing is fashioned not under the silent referent of Europe, but under the omniversal referent of Empire.[7] I wish to clarify that the India that is Jai Ho-ed, or catapulted by the film into discursive prominence (branded as being the center of the new world order) as a possible site of production of universal thought, is not composed in a referential vacuum (the "global" is not devoid of referentiality). On the contrary, I suggest that it is under the sign of a decentered and deterritorialized Empire that the formation of an India of hyper-real potential is administered.[8]

The predominant optic through which India is seen in *SDM* could, for argument's sake, be christened as the optic of globalization. In their book, *Empire*, theorists Antonio Negri and Michael Hardt attribute the emergence of this optic to the emergence of what they call the "postmodern Empire." Embedded in Empire or the new sovereignty, imply Negri and Hardt, is an optic of multipolarity through which the non-West is seen in its heterogeneity and difference, and not as an anachronistic variant of itself.[9] I take *SDM* to be a prime example of a paradigmatic visual text of the emergent imperial optic that represents contemporary India without Othering it into an abject form of subalternity but also confers on India a status of emergent centrality.[10] The cinematic assertion of India's rising centrality coincides with the real India's ascendancy in the global economic sphere, and the real and hyper-real converge to create conditions of possibility within the realms of textuality for the production of an India that can stake claims to universality.

In this chapter, I delight in *SDM*'s participation in a project of provincializing Europe and alternately, of conferring centrality on India. Yet I also deem such participation to be acutely problematic. Indeed, as I claim, the episteme on which *SDM*'s Western articulation of emergent Indian sovereignty is predicated is irresistibly inclusive. But in unpacking the film's representational strategies, I also raise the specter of latent structures of subjugation inhering in its and by default, in globalization's apparently liberatory gestures. I argue that the India that is poised to be modern globality's possible future in *SDM* is simultaneously a "translated" India, not an entirely unmediated enunciation of the real India. In the process of such a discovery, I find that in the global episteme, Europe's presence is not provincialized in totality; its presence has merely been diluted.

At a glance, it could be said that the Western ethnographic gaze, though born in a colonial era and constituting Western modernity, is adapting itself under the regnant power paradigm of the global present, to see the distinct practical conduct and value dynamics of Indian modernity on its own terms. Some broad conclusions can be drawn from the way in which Indian heterogeneity is being increasingly looked at through an optic of plurality: it can be said that Western consciousness is acclimatizing itself to an emerging global dispensation where power – economic, militaristic or cultural – is no longer the sole prerogative of the West to flex unilaterally. It has hybridized and detotalized itself such that it can be at home with the experience of postmodern globality and is, as a result, able to serve a new global logic of rule; one which has no center and observes no border dividing the multitude from the privileged, the central from the peripheral and the analytical from the pre-analytical. Yet if there has indeed been an attitudinal shift in the Western optic, from imperial to the convivial and the pluralistic in the way Western discourse is choosing to presence the "new" India, then it could also be argued that the shift is strategic, not disinterested or reflexive.[11] If the West's recent valorizing of India, both as a stunning economic "growth rate" performer and a nation where opposites co-exist in an unique form of modernity, is not spontaneous or gratuitous but politically motivated and conducted at the behest of a global sovereignty, then what, one might query, is the sovereignty that underwrites the onset of such a cultural mood vis-à-vis India, and what does it want? In other words, what authorizes the West's praise of India? Taking a cue from the Foucauldian premise that power, in one form or the other, is inextricably linked with systems of knowledge formation, it could be asked what new paradigm of power is normalizing the cheeky flamboyance of enunciations like that of Salim's in *SDM*?

It is not that Salim's kind of pulp-patriotic machismo, bent on legitimizing Indian centrality, has not been heard before; for where the business of discursively constituting India as an exemplary nation is concerned, Bollywood is no stranger to idioms of hyperbole and melodrama. Regardless of whether Bollywood (mass) cultural productions have troped India as the chaste body of the eternal mother, whose innate virtuosity stands resplendent in contradistinction to a morally decadent West, or as the glittering "dot" on the forehead of the global bride, beautifying the world by its presence or, more recently, as a "shining" and "rising" geopolitical and economic entity in the world, primed not only to exert hegemony over traditional regional rivals like Pakistan but also to aggressively outbid powerhouses like China and America as producers of global capital, they have routinely resorted to a rhetoric of bluster and sweeping sentimentality. But the sentimental Jai Ho-ing, or the foisting of India on a victory pedestal by a technically non-Bollywood/non-Indian artifact like *SDM*, is without precedence. Simply put, even if one were to discount Salim's patriotism as goofy rhetoric, one cannot help being seduced by the feeling that *SDM* casts a very twenty-first century gaze on a very twenty-first century India, by presencing its distinctive brand of disparate modernity through an unflinching and a seemingly unfiltered eye. The India of *SDM*, in other words, is not the Othered/Orientalized and dehistoricized India one typically encounters through the lens of Hollywood. The film, one can argue, is an instance of a Western cultural mediation where the East is apparently represented on its own terms, in the sense of being represented 'convivially', and is in the process transformed from being an object to a subject of history.

A modest qualifier is, however, in order here: to claim that the advent of a film like *SDM* has created the conditions of possibility for the arrival of what Anandam Kavoori describes as a very "specific kind of cultural hybridity" into the present of the global imaginary,[12] entails a certain division of critical labor between critiquing how the film produces India, and scrutinizing some of the voluminous discourse surrounding the film's reception in the US, the narratives about how the film was conceived and made, and about the film's putative social impact on the reality of children and slum poverty in India. Made primarily with a Western audience in mind, *SDM* is a relatively uncomplicated love story involving Jamal, a poor, semi-literate orphan, and Latika, a fellow orphan of an identical socio-economic ilk. Following the motif of traditional Bollywood films from the 1970s and 1980s, a flame of pure eternal desire burns in the breasts of both Jamal and Latika but they cannot be together because Jamal lacks capital. Not only does Jamal not possess the capital to make Latika his own and thereby rescue her from the corrupt, lustful and filthy rich godfather into whose clutches Latika has fallen, partly through her own complicity, but he also is not driven to acquire capital by sacrificing integrity. Jamal is shown to be an incorruptible *ingenue* whose sole objective in life is to find his lost-love Latika. In his quest, Jamal is fearless. Salim, who sees Jamal after many years of separation since childhood, is untutored in the art of Jamal's personal economy which is, in essence, a refusal of all real economies in favor of inhabiting the economy of unadulterated love. Salim wants to do his brotherly bit by initiating Jamal into the heart of twenty-first century India's burgeoning economy, and get him off the streets for good. Salim has become rich by participating fully in the economy and he is eager that Jamal enjoy similar fruits of success. However, the economy that Salim claims has put India at the center of the world turns out to be a sham economy of reckless fraudulence and gangsterism. Jamal is indifferent to Salim's economy. He is not even interested in the centrality of India. He is, as the film reveals in an interlude, content being a tea-server in a local call center in Mumbai. Not looking to move up the call center hierarchy, Jamal uses its available technology to find Latika's coordinates. At the television quiz show game, Jamal gives all the correct answers but he is not driven to win the million rupees prize money for the sake of personal enrichment; he sees the show as an opportunity to interface with Latika.

With such a protagonist at the core – staunchly adhering to the sentimental economy of love in an era marked by the reign of a neoliberal economy of capital – it is no surprise that *SDM* appealed to an international audience. However, while the film's global success could be attributed to the plot and the characters' legibility and universality, it could be said that *SDM* was a success in multiple registers beyond the merely commercial and the aesthetic. It not only had (American and British) audiences flocking to the theatres to watch the rags-to-riches odyssey of an Indian subaltern but also raised a discursive storm about the politics of globalization and its discontents and the ethicality of packaging "Eastern" poverty as visual cornucopia for Western consumption, among other related issues.[13] Most significantly, hailed as a cultural prodigy of globalization, *SDM* can be said to have spurred the creation of the conditions of possibility for producing India as a viable category of modernity in the global popular imaginary.

Yet should we be wary of making too much of this discursive arrival, as it were, of India in the global imaginary? It could be argued that the increasing normalization of the incorporation of an idea of India into the present of the global imaginary represents a cultural tipping point, rather than portending any major epistemological shift; or, as Dipesh Chakrabarty has forewarned in the context of what he describes as the project of "provincializing Europe," the fact of globalization notwithstanding, Western epistemology still prevails, albeit in a more hybrid and diffuse form, as the dominant determinant of all that is deemed modern, universal and historical.[14] Extending Chakrabarty's argument, one could say that the Western/global imaginary has not been "Indianized" just yet, or a hyper-real India has not quite displaced hyper-real Europe as the imaginary figure of history but, in ways latent and manifest, remains its opposite, paired in a contested yet still enduring structure of domination and subordination. Could it then at least be posited that, as a category of thought, India is ripe for hyper-realization and, for the first time, the global imaginary is under an implicit imperative to brace itself for an imminent arrival of its Indian (cultural) future? The claim made by Balram Halwai, Aravind Adiga's fictional propagandist *par excellence*, that the age of the "white-skinned man" is coming to an end, while the future of the globe is poised to be handed over to the custody of the yellow and the brown man, resonates in light of the recent financial meltdown in America in particular and in the Western world in general. Additionally, it is tempting to interpret the conferring of awards on such cultural products as *SDM* and *The White Tiger* as a sign of the Western cultural sphere's concession that, just as there is taking place a devolving of economic power from the West to the East, the central stage of global popular culture is also shifting from the traditional site of Hollywood to Bollywood.[15] It can be stated provisionally that Bollywood is the preferred mass cultural form via which the rising (and shining) India is articulating its way into the Anglo-American unconscious.[16]

Sans subject matter, *SDM* is not a brown or Indian/Bollywood production; neither can it be labeled an unambiguously white/Western or Hollywood artifact. Its British provenance rests in its geographical site of production, in the fact of the Britishness of its director, of the actor who plays the role of Jamal (Dev Patel), the film's protagonist, and of its screenwriter (Simon Beaufoy), though one only need parse down both Patel and Boyle's ethnic and class composition to understand how they may be held up as synecdoches of the not only browned and blackened but also the hybridized postcoloniality of the EU-ized island nation.[17] Indeed, the fact that a cultural product emanating from a twenty-first century British site of formation could be hybrid and beyond brown or white should not surprise (the way it surprises whenever there is a sighting of brown skin in the landscape of American popular culture). Ever since brown skin crossed the silver screen in the Hanif Kureishi penned and Stephen Frears directed *My Beautiful Laundrette* (1985), and trespassed the spaces of colonial anthropology and history to spaces marked as the present, British popular imaginary has been imploded by a return and rupture simultaneously. In other words, if Boyle's production is hybridly inflected in its locution, not only of modern India but specifically of modern Indian subalternity, then it could be attributed to the fact of its being fashioned in an already globalized Britain that is no stranger to the staging of brownness. It could be argued that in its whiteness, *SDM* is in deep measure fraught with brownness as well.

SDM's "brown" source has an equally elliptical trajectory. The film is a thin, almost tangential adaptation of Indian diplomat cum novelist Vikas Swarup's multi-award winning novel, *Q & A* (2005), which narrates the story (again, one suspects, for the benefit of a primarily Western readership, in artfully contrived digressive form) of the orphan boy Ram Mohammed Thomas's ascent from being a *chawl*-dweller in Mumbai to becoming a billionaire (rupee-wise) through winning a sponsored quiz show (*Who Wants to Win a Billion?*) on TV. In between he has stops as servant in various households (and the job of a waiter in a Mumbai restaurant cum bar) both in the cities of Mumbai and

New Delhi. In the novel, readers are led through a pulsating-with-intrigue (Indian) tale, stylistically modeled (as Swarup says, disavowing elitism) after James Hadley Chase and Alistair MacLean rather than Arundhati Roy.[18] During the course of the novel, Ram encounters a world laden with venality and fraudulence; it is an India where, as critics have contended, Dickens tangles with the Indian reality of assassins, pimps, molesters and sadomasochistic film stars. His movement through India is enabled largely by employment and his interreligious name, born of compromise at the Catholic orphanage where he was raised, which affords him a curious motility. Whether he is a servant or tour guide, altar boy or vagrant, Ram Mohammed Thomas radiates moral clarity while learning the dark side of India's globalizing tilt.

Yet the Indianness of Ram's experience notwithstanding, *Q & A* has been blithely noted by *Guardian* critic Stuart Jeffries, among others, to have an "English" inception. The "slumdog millionaire born in Mumbai's meanest streets was born in London's rather genteel Golders Green," writes Jeffries wryly of the locale where Swarup apparently scribed his way into literary fame via the marvels of Google reach and technology.[19] Jeffries' pointing at the hybridizing potential of the intersection between the subject matter of Indian reality (as in the particular reality of poverty in a globalized India) and the complex optic of London gentility pollinated by the urbane/cosmopolitan chic of Indian diplomatese, throws a hyper–class-cultural twist into the question of who gets to represent the subaltern, famously embodied by the query: "Can the Subaltern Speak?"[20] Through its London birthing, it could be said, the Indian novel contracts globality. In interviews, Swarup has spoken at length about how the choice of London as the site of production mattered. Splaying himself between the spectral context of one nation – India – and the lived metropolis of another – London – Swarup has implicated the English site as indispensable for the conception and completion of his novel because only in London, rife as it is with a culturally enabling ambience, could he have found traction as a novelist, despite being in the midst of a very hectic diplomatic schedule.[21]

Not only does the cultural dynamic of London beget *Q & A* but also the catalyst for the story of the Indian foundling's triumph in the quiz show and his subsequent arrest is the Major Ingram fraud case, where a British army major, Charles Ingram, was charged with cheating his way into winning the British version of *Who Wants to be a Millionaire?*[22] The "coughing major" serves as the muse for Swarup as it sets the writer thinking of transposing the Englishman's predicament onto Indian soil and shifting the subject from British/white to brown subaltern Mumbaikker. This is not to say that the transposition of decorated British ex-army man to Indian subaltern is seamless or literal, or that Ingram reappears in disguise as foundling waiter Ram to get tortured in police custody but, rather, to tease out the complex circuitry of affinity between the real life Ingram and the reel life Ram/Jamal that is hinted at by Swarup, when he wonders aloud (in an interview) the following: if a British major's integrity could be suspect, then how would the integrity of an Indian waiter be perceived? If a white Britisher with proven cultural capital cannot be believed to know all the answers, could one then imagine the plight of a brown waiter who knows the answers, in hierarchy obsessed India?

Just as *Q & A*'s Indianness is compromised by its hybrid or global inception, so too is *SDM*'s genuflection to Bollywood as an informing episteme compromised by its complex affiliation to a kind of globality that is almost the same but not quite white. Director Boyle and screenwriter Beaufoy have both paid copious tributes to Bollywood or, more specifically, to the Hindi cinema of the '70s, as a source from which they have drawn to create the India in *SDM*. Yet Bollywood's presence in *SDM* is diluted. If anything, Bollywood is shown to be a symbol of a mass opiate, a "fix." In a fix-illuminating scene, the young Jamal is ambushed, not by the police but by the jammed lock in one of Mumbai's public latrines, at a moment when a Bollywood superstar alights from his chopper to give *darshan* to a worshipping mob.[23] When Jamal hears of this, he gets as desperate as a wild animal that wants to break out of its cage. In order to court "life," inscribed in a self-autographed image of the superstar, Jamal has to court symbolical death. For nothing, as Gandhi had testified once in a tone of the trademark immeasurable irony that can be labeled "Gandhian," signifies death more voluminously for an Indian subject than human shit. Jamal jumps into an excremental pond, as it were, just as Mark Renton in Boyle's *Trainspotting* (1996) had dug his hands deep inside "Scotland's worst public latrine" to retrieve the butt ends of his "fix." Mired in (human) shit, Jamal appears smiling beatifically at the superstar, as the mob gives way to him in disgust. The superstar, as disembodied fix (we only see his manicured and bejeweled fingers reaching out to accept Jamal's outstretched hands holding a paper on which the star must put his signature) that neither sees nor smells the fixee, signs his name on a crumpled shit-pasted paper displaying his glory image with grand insouciance that Jamal takes as recognition of his presence.

If one contends that the shit-mired materializing of the illicit, therefore illegible, body in public discourse is a perfect visualization of the "speaking" subaltern, then one could say that the subaltern speaks (in this scene) in *SDM*. However, it could be emphatically contended that the subaltern does not speak like the hero of Hindi cinema of the 1970s. In content as much as in form, *SDM* diverts from Bollywood. What really is more sustainedly and deliberatively appropriated from the urn of popular Hindi cinema is a binary logic that governs the film's articulation of the "new" India, a nation that is shown to egress out of symbolical and material darkness into the light of the modernizing project of globalization. Of course, this is not to suggest that the film's depiction of the emergent India is unproblematically or homogeneously virtue invested, for the negative politics of the old economy brood menacingly in the margins, ready to encroach into the light of the new economy. Predatory institutions of child slavery and terrorism loom large; however they are not necessarily implicated with the new economy but shown as disjunctive formations living anachronistically with the new, deserving thus to be terminated rather than tolerated and understood.

The binarity with which an India is posited – before and after the fact of globalization – most strongly manifests itself in the contrast between a temporally anterior Hindi India and its modern anglicized present. Within the Hindi India, there are latent structures of subjugation. Thus is made not only a prototypically interventionist utterance by the American tourist in one of the early scenes of *SDM*, but also a standard (i.e., universal) interventionist gesture as, in a flash, comes out from the pocket of one of the Americans, "real America," crystallized in the form of a crisp Benjamin. At a glance, the scene unfolds like a tableau vivant of how the American (read: Western) sense of compassionate justice endures in the face of global insentience to human (read: non-Western) suffering. The tourists in question are, on the one hand, outraged by an act of violence they have just witnessed – their Indian chauffeur has just pummeled the young Jamal on charges of pilfering – and, on the other, moved to compassion for the powerless young victim. Out of compassion, the woman tries to protect Jamal from further violence and motions to her husband to give him money, to compensate, one can surmise, for the thrashing he has received at the hands of one of his own. While we cheerlead this act of benevolence on, seduced perhaps by the neoliberal belief in the liberatory potential of international capital – in its power to transform, as it were, the subaltern's "life itself" – we also view the seemingly artless action of this old-fashioned giving with skepticism. The transaction – the offering of beneficence by the Americans and the receiving of it by the native – could be said to have taken place between differential structures of transnational privilege and within spatial and temporal constructs that are homogenous and empty, evacuated, that is, of the coordinates of diachronic history.[24]

Yet Jamal's brother, Salim, is culpable; he has committed an act of chicanery: his band of roving, slum dwelling adolescents has indeed marauded; they have vandalized the Americans' car while Jamal, pretending to be an authentic tour guide, has lured the Americans away and the Indian driver, again prototypically, has gone to pee. To put the equation crudely, the Americans have been robbed blind by the brothers and their cohorts, and the Indian driver punishes Jamal for not only stealing from gullible foreigners but for bringing down the name of the nation in the world. He remonstrates in the only way he knows – the Indian way – which is through the terror of physical brutality over the due process of institutionalized legal deliberation. Thus, the Americans are not revolted by the boys' orchestration of the pilfering but by the local manner of dispensing justice; asking the driver to refrain from violence, they value – presumably in the spirit of universal civility and instrumental reason – Jamal's life over that of their car. In one spontaneously combusted stroke of enlightened interventionism, they not only reduce the Indian driver to the status of an unenlightened subhuman but also reward Jamal for opening their eyes to the shocking brutalization of the powerless by the slightly more empowered in the postcolonial state. It could be argued that in this scene, Jamal has sold shining India's dirty secret to the world. Through Jamal, the (mostly Western) audience has a glimpse of Indian darkness, where the big fish eat the small with violent impunity and entrap Indian life within atavistic structures of chaos, despair and violence. Lying terrorized on the ground, Jamal articulates the real condition of the twenty-first century's most impressive GDP status-attaining nation in terms that are severely implicating: "You wanted to see a bit of real India [...] here it is," he says, indignantly pointing a finger of accusation at the driver and eliciting, in the process, the tourists' self-righteously Orientalist intervention.

Thus is articulated the "real India" of real time's global postmodernity, in a relationship of implicit imperial subordination with the "real America." But more significantly, perhaps, the colonial trope of Manichean divisions permeates further, for real India is imagined to be internally dichotomized as well. Filtered through the film's slumdog optic, the topography of Indian modernity is a riven topography, much like the Fanonian landscape of the settler – colonizer.[25] Invoking repeatedly the classic Bollywood – style steep duality of the rich and the poor, the before and the after, the pro and the con (along with a dose of the good and the evil), the movie predicates an architecture of global India on a series of colliding binaries, reproducing not an India that is modern in and of itself but one that has been rendered modern by globalization's transforming agency. The moments of real change, from old to new, poor to rich, sectarian to secular and from Hindi–parochial to English–cosmopolitan, are registered only when extant India is shown to encounter global capital. It is suggested that, without these transformative moments of encounter, originating elsewhere outside the film's framing, India would remain a space as colonially entropic as the African postcolony of Achille Mbembe's formulation.[26]

The film begins in the present of a postglobalized India, in a scene where Jamal is being interrogated in police custody because the authorities want to know how he finagled his way into winning a million rupees at a television quiz show game. In this Indian present, the darkness of child slavery has been replaced by the light of call center-abstracted labor, the slums have been razed to make way for luxury high-rises, and subjectivities are imagined through the diffracting interface of sponsored television shows. As proclaimed by Salim, one of the film's slumdogs who strikes it rich in the nation's imploding globalized (and illicit) economy, India has arrived *in toto* into the eye of global modernity (the center). While this view of progress, from pre- to postglobalization, promulgated by transnational capital, is fraught with both real and epistemic violence, this violence, in a Marxian mode, is also taken to be a necessary concomitant of the process. The progress of India's material domain is repeated also in the inner domain of the film's linguistic register as the nation is seen to ascend idiomatically from a bounded space of Hindi, to a more deterritorialized site of international English, or "Hinglish." If globalization propels the Hindi-India of yore into an English/bilingual India of contemporary imagining, then the transition, in turn, is structurally replicated in the film's appropriation and subsequent universalization of the aesthetic of Bollywood, by which both director Boyle and screenwriter Beaufoy claim (swear, rather) to have been inspired to make Bollywood less singular and opaque and more globally legible, even perhaps translucent. The Bollywood of *SDM*'s staging is thus a translated Bollywood, interpellated by a globalization-induced sheen of market-oriented postmodernity and, by extension, the India that is enunciated through the Bollywoodian form to occupy the globe's center is a translated India.

In other words, what is truly celebrated, or Jai Ho-ed, in the film is not necessarily the emergent modernity of the real India of history, or the India of a specific geographical referent, but an Indian postmodernity that is hyper-realized through global capital's discursive mediation. Or, what is made iconic, rendered into a commodified global imaginary that is measurable, bounded and monetized, is not Indian modernity, Indian poverty/subalternity or the modernity of Bollywood as cultural form in and of itself – a modernity that is distilled through the Indian subaltern's messy, unstable and disjunctive yet autonomous experience of it – but an Indian modernity that undergoes sublation to an extent that a recognition of its newfangledness becomes contingent on a willingness of the oldfangled to transition into the new through the presumed to be stable grid of globalization. India, it could be interpreted, is modern only in so far as it is globalized. One could argue that what is really Jai Ho-ed, or paeaned into global visibility, is the fact of India's amenability to conversion into a hyper-real India whose ideological currency is consistent with the ideology of world market corporate capital.

The fact of Indian transigence is reinforced not only in the imagined nation's breezy, almost unreflective adoption of the call center over the train as the prime symbolic metric of its advancement from industrial-colonial modern to service sectorized global-postmodern, but also in its protagonist, Jamal Malik's labile subjectivity. It can be said that the hybrid, English-speaking, death-defyingly love-questing Jamal, who does not know what Indian rupee note Mahatma Gandhi's face is featured on but knows, through fortuitous street tutelage, that the face of Benjamin Franklin is equivalent to one hundred American dollars, and who fashions his love quest more after Orpheus's quest for Eurydice than after the emperor Shah Jahan's for Mumtaz Mahal, arrives into the film's template of globality as an already globalized subject. Jamal is shown less as a Muslim subject in India and more as a generic Everyman, disinvested of thorny identitarian nodes like that of his Muslim–Indian particularity. Yet the film implicates India in a postcolonial politics that has shades of the genocidal. Jamal himself is rendered an orphan when his mother is killed in an anti-Muslim carnage which, in the film's dark India scenes, is framed as a formation that is specifically engineered by Hindu chauvinism. It could be argued that Jamal's status as an underprivileged, underemployed servant, serving tea to call center workers in metropolitan Mumbai, is on account of his Indian–Muslim positionality in the postcolonial nation. Yet both Jamal and his older sibling Salim remain disengaged politically. Jamal is so cleansed of identity markers bearing the potential to impinge upon his translatability into global capital's subject that, like the nation space upon which his rags to riches destiny unravels, he becomes a radically desubjectivized habitus into which capital can be safely transferred and through which capital can flow unimpeded. In other words, in *SDM* both the body of the protagonist and that of the nation are divested of historical particularities and their attendant complexities.

In emptying India and the Indian–Muslim Jamal thus of the particularities of their respective Indianness/Muslimness, *SDM*, I argue, breaks an implicit promise of enunciating the complex modernities (like that of twenty-first century India) in terms that are non-Eurocentric and non-universalist. This is not to suggest that the film's dwelling on/in India is uncomplicatedly regressive-colonial for, more often than not, the Danny Boyle production glows with a timbre of giddy love for the Indian (slum) life in and of itself (though the everyday "life itself" does not materialize into a site for the production of politically fruitful subjectivities). What primarily disappoints, one can assert, is the fact of mediation itself, for one expects global popular culture artifacts like *SDM*, that seek to represent the Other within the framework of a global rather than a Western episteme, to deliver relatively unmediated articulations, raw and unfiltered positings, even. But, as theorists have argued, it is futile to demand unmediated enunciations, because the fact of mediation is an ineluctable fact of history.[27] It could be said that the history of the representation of the non-West by the West and, to a certain extent, the history of the self representation of the non-West, has invariably been a history of mediation of the former by the latter. Thus, to expect an unmediated enunciation of Indian modernity – under colonial modernity or under global postmodernity – entails a forgetting of the essentially historicist and particularist trajectory of the discursive formations of both modernity and globality. In other words, the term modernity assembles a group of other, particular terms (progress, freedom, autonomy, development and so forth), which have a local history but which have become "North Atlantic universals" through the conjuncture of the Americo–European imperial projects and the world capitalist economy.[28] One can rationalize that *SDM*, despite being touted as one of the current century's most planetarily successful virtual portals into the searing truth of poverty in a globalized India is, after all, a Western meditation on the East, and is thus historically tangled in a filtered offering of Indian modernity. Yet globalization also presages the possibility of a liberation/deliverance from mediation because one imagines the dominant episteme of globalization to be neither Western nor non–Western but one that is produced out of global/transnational heterogeneity and differences. Theoretically speaking, globalization is ideally an agency of neither translation nor Hegelian sublation (*aufheben*); on the contrary, it is an agency of toleration; it celebrates difference through reveling in the unstructured heterotemporality and heterospatiality of multiple modernities and histories. In contrast to the universalizing and disciplinary impulses of imperial sovereignty, the postmodern sovereignty of globalization revels in release, dissipation and liberation through an impromptu inhabitation within hybridized and fragmented subjectivities.

One might then reposit the question: How is millennial India's emerging centrality and, by extension, the centrality of the East troped under the aegis of postmodern sovereignty's politics of difference and pluralism? An answer might be, "problematically." As a paradigmatic text of globality such as *SDM* demonstrates, while the East as an emergent cultural, geopolitical and economic formation is troped under the sign of difference, it is also troped *within* the structure of a sign of the global that is still bound up with the residual–colonial, or residual–Western. As I have argued, postmodern sovereignty simultaneously jibes with difference and mandates a translation of difference into sameness. Drawing from Dipesh Chakrabarty's claim that a category of thought gets translated when it travels from one culture to another, one can contend that an act of transition, from pre- to post-, also entails an act of translation, where the transitioned subject cannot escape being reconstituted by the transitioning agency's ideological apparatus. In *SDM*, India transitions from pre- to postglobal, from peripheral to central, under the sign of an aterritorial and acephalous contra-referent; but in the process of transition, it also gets translated into a postmodern India that is postmodern because it is willing to be global.

In the Hindi India, not only is Hindi literally the *lingua franca* of the masses – and what is spoken is translated into English subtitles for the benefit of the audience – but the poor (with which Hindi India seemingly teems), I suggest, are also invested in Hindi or vernacular subjectivities. The existence of Hindi life worlds implies the possibility of being simultaneously human and poor. The poor of Hindi India revel in their informal/vernacular subjectivities and flaunt them as well. Thus, when the English teacher in a (poorly) state funded municipal school gets furious at Jamal and Salim for coming late to class every day and for never buying the recommended textbooks (especially *The Three Musketeers*, which seems to be a central node of the English curriculum), the brothers laugh in his face and playfully refuse to submit to a broken system of education. The slum children are shown to be at play all the time and, transgressively, they organize cricket matches on patches of land that do not belong to them but to developers. The state, acting at the behest of such developers, chases the children away from the fields and herds them back into the slums. The slum dwellers are thus regularly policed and subjected to statist violence.

Yet the poor do not necessarily cower or think of avenging the injustice of poverty in the mode of a Bollywood drama. Neither do they profess a shame in being poor: the children laugh all the way back to their shanties and the joke is on the potbellied *havildar*, who is too fat to run. The *havildar* ends up being confronted by the matriarch – Salim and Jamal's mother – who fends off state violence admirably by figuratively positioning herself between the agents of violence and the children. In the face of this defiance, both virtuous and nonsensical, the male agent of violence slinks away. The state's attempt to contain and discipline the slumdogs and/or to completely render invalid their citizenship within the state is, it could be said, contested by the pre-English/global inhabitants of the Hindi India in *SDM*. The mode of resistance is vernacular.

But no sooner than capital – in the form of developers, marketers, buyers and sellers, and corporate sponsors of TV game shows – displaces the state as the reigning authority against which the poor of "Hindi" India have to stand up, the modes of vernacular defiance no longer suffice, because resistance in the conventional sense is no longer needed. The new authority, the advent of which coincides with the advent of English as the film's lingua franca, is seemingly plurally inclined, irresistible and does not mind the poor. The poor in English India are not relegated to the status of the subhuman but are, on the contrary, normalized as subjects who have equal opportunity to get rich, provided they believe in the world as one big market. Capital befriends the

English slumdogs, Salim and Jamal, and while Salim seeks a way out of state violence by selling himself to the authority of an international gangster awash in cash, Jamal, too, is borne out of poverty on the back, as it were, of a million rupees won through participating in a television game show sponsored by the local emissary of a multinational corporation. In other words, Jamal, too, has to become a millionaire before he gets Latika, the symbol of his undying love, and India has to become amenable to market induced modernity before it can occupy a position of centrality of the twenty-first century's millionaire nation. Jamal and Latika can Jai Ho the triumph of love and of the nation after the nation has been globalized by integrating its domestic economy with the global one. In an India thus translated, Jamal is celebrated as a hero by the urban poor – whose pastime is not cricketing or rioting but getting hooked to reality TV shows broadcast in a global Hinglish (or "Engdi") – because he has won his lady love *via media* a million rupees cash prize. After he answers the winning question correctly and steps out of the studio in a daze, a crowd of urban poor swoop on him and sweep him off the ground, Jai Ho-ing his dogged yet fortuitous arrival into a form of modernity whose framing parameters are largely economic.

Interestingly, there are remnants of the Hindi India in the form of trains that stand still in the background while Jamal and Latika dance ecstatically to the rhythm of a Bollywood number, composed by the hottest Indian music composer who is also known to be the most global of all Indian pop music artists. What is foregrounded in this crucial song and dance scene is the global, while what recedes to the background is the Indian, represented by immotile technology that has roots in colonial India. The stark contrast between the Hindi background and the global (in the sense that it transcends a monolithic language) displays not just a transition from old to new or from national to global but a phagocytizing of the former by the latter. Stated further, not only is there a discontinuity between the back- and the foreground but, also, within the foregrounded global, the English is prioritized over the Hindi. Or, the Hindi sounds like an attractive – because marketable – accoutrement within the dominant structure of English. Put otherwise, while the film's title – in which two heterogeneous horizons of humanity, the refuse and the cherished, are yoked together with violence – promises a delighting in the concurrence of the high and the low, the central and the marginal, the film ends up performing a conversion of the latter to the former. *SDM*'s triumph lies in the realization of India as post-national global space that is uncoded and deterritorialized, therefore a fecund field of free play for capital. In other words, Danny Boyle's multi-award winning window on the new India is really a window on globalization, acting to transform old India into a new possibility for itself.

Notes

1 India currently boasts 53 billionaires, and the media buzz is that it is projected to be the world's third-largest economy by 2050. India's involvement in strategic infrastructure projects in Afghanistan is also an example of its increasing significance in global geopolitics. More information on the nation's aid to countries like Afghanistan can be found in *The India Defence Review*. Online: http://www.indiandefencereview.com (accessed 1 July 2012).

2 Aravind Adiga, *The White Tiger* (New York: Free Press, 2008), 17.

3 See, for instance, Fareed Zakaria's *The Post-American World* (New York: W. W. Norton, 2008). Zakaria insinuates that, in a post-American world order, paradigms are being greatly shifted and while older, more established Western ones are being challenged, newer ones are emerging from those geographical demesnes of the world that had not too long ago played second, third or, at best, fourth fiddle to the West as economic powers.

4 See Dipesh Chakrabarty's *Provincializing Europe: Postcolonial Thought and Historical Difference* (Princeton: Princeton University Press, 2006).

5 Ibid., 110.

6 In *A Critique of Postcolonial Reason: Toward a History of the Vanishing Present* (Cambridge: Harvard University Press, 1999), Gayatri Spivak writes of the colonial episteme as being essentially an empire of reason that "shuts up" the irrational native episteme (25–7). A global episteme would not only let the native episteme "speak" but would also be influenced by it in turn and alter its own speaking to suit a multipolar world order.

7 See Antonio Negri and Michael Hardt's *Empire* (Cambridge: Harvard University Press, 2000). Hardt and Negri argue that capitalism has entered a new historical stage in which the sovereignty of nation-states is withering away in the face of globalization. A new, global form of sovereignty – Empire – is rising up in its place composed of a series of national and supranational "organisms" united under a single logic of rule. Multinational corporations and global institutions like the International Monetary Fund or World Trade Organization preside over this system alongside nation-states. Empire is not based on fixed boundaries or territorial centers of power. Instead power lies "both everywhere and nowhere" (110). Accompanying this process, they argue, a new form of production based on 'immaterial labor' has become dominant. Instead of producing things, immaterial labor produces "a service, a cultural product, knowledge or communication" (107).

8 Spiritual guru *par excellence* Deepak Chopra has valiantly defended *SDM* against its detractors as a film that gives an "ultimate retort to colonialism" by implicitly stating that the "coolie" and the "wallahs" have more smarts than the sahibs to get the girl and the money by transcending their impoverished material conditions. Chopra credits the "white" Danny Boyle for doing for "brown" Indians what "brown" Indians ought to have done for themselves – creating an onscreen Indian presence that is self-respectful yet real. However, what grabs the reader's attention is Chopra's clinching claim that Boyle dares to be "universal," which means, he says, "that India may dare to be universal one day." See "*Slumdog Millionaire*: Dilemma of a New India." *Huffington Post*. Online: http://www.huffingtonpost.com/deepak-chopra/slumdog-millionaire-dilem_b_170920.html (accessed 1 August 2012).

9 I borrow the concept of anachronism from Chakrabarty's *Provincializing Europe*. In his open view of the present, Chakrabarty forwards the idea of the "timeknot" (47).

He successfully demonstrates through examples that many persons and objects belong not to a single time but to multiple times and that the present is indeed open, including past and future. A more open and expanded understanding of the present is very significant, for such an understanding allows many people to "belong" in multiple time periods, including modernity. The discipline of history is centered round the treatment of change and continuity over time and Chakrabarty insists that much less need change and much more can remain the same in modernization than many presently believe.

10 Unlike previous Western cinematic representations of India, ranging from Richard Attenborough's *Gandhi* (1982) to Roland Joffe's *City of Joy* (1992), all of which could be said to have been constructed under the sovereignty of an older, residual, colonial paradigm of power, the India of *SDM* is represented coevally.

11 I draw the notion of convivial as a representational apparatus from Paul Gilroy's *Postcolonial Melancholia* (New York: Columbia University Press, 2005).

12 See Anandam Kavoori's essay, "Why the Sun Shines on *Slumdog*," (143) included in this volume.

13 See Shakuntala Banaji's "Seduced 'Outsiders' versus Sceptical 'Insiders'?: *Slumdog Millionaire* through its Re/Viewers," for an overview of the deeply colliding opinions on the film (in *Participations: Journal of Audience and Reception Studies* 7.1 (2010)). Regarding claims about *SDM* as "poverty porn," see, respectively, Alice Miles' review in the *Times*, 14 January 2009, and David Denby's in *New Yorker*, 9–16 February 2009.

14 By India, I mean, following Chakrabarty, to implicate not the geographical region of the world we call India but the imaginary figure that is, like the imaginary figure of Europe, being constituted and reconstituted in recent discourses as a figure of burgeoning centrality, not only in the economic sphere but also in the thought sphere; in other words, the new paradigm of power is laboring to reify India and confer on it the status of a potential universal-in-the-making. See the Introduction to *Provincializing Europe*. Also, see Sunil Khilnani's *The Idea of India* (New York: Farrar Straus and Giroux, 1998).

15 Borrowing from Chakrabarty, I use the term Hollywood as a geographically indeterminate term, one that is more an analytic category than a specific site of production (10–15).

16 This is not to claim Bollywood as an authentic Indian product; the provenance of Bollywood itself has always already been contested as hybrid and, with a name that is redolent of a Hollywood derivative, Bollywood has emerged since the 1990s onward as a space of cultural production and expression that is now decidedly global, problematizing the neatness of such categories as Indian cinema, nation, public, culture, identity, politics and our understandings and assumptions of relationships among these categories. Indeed, Indian cinema, although a national cinema, has deterritorialized to an extent that its boundaries are no longer those of the nation-state. However, its transnationality notwithstanding, there is something inveterately Indian about Bollywood; even if that something pertains to a non-Western audience's citing of Bollywood cinema as (emotionally) appealing because it is seen as an alternative to the Americanness of Hollywood in its Third World or postcolonial sensibilities and structures of feeling. See Madhava Prasad, "This Thing Called Bollywood." Online: http://www.india-seminar.com/2003/525/525%20madhava%20prasad.htm (accessed 15 July 2012).

17 While Boyle, whose mother's family is Irish, hails from a working class Northerner background that creates for him a hybrid positionality, giving him a legitimately outsider's perspective on Englishness and English colonialism, Dev Patel is British–Kenyan–Indian, a thrice diasporized entity.

18 See http://www.vikasswarup.net/ for a collection of Vikas Swarup's interviews (accessed 15 March 2012).

19 In an interview, Swarup was asked about the authenticity of the details with which he has described Dharavi, famous in popular imagination as the world's largest slum, in *Q & A*. Swarup's response was tragicomical in its essence: he said he has never been even remotely close to slums, let alone places like Dharavi, and his knowledge of Dharavi was facilitated by Google. "Thanks to Google," Swarup said, "I was able to gather all pertinent information about Dharavi in less than two weeks." Yet critics, especially writing in the Western media outlets, have lavished praise on the authenticity of Swarup's representation of the Dharavi life-world; the "gut-wrenchingness" of eyewitness accounts has been attributed to him. "I'm the luckiest novelist in the world." *Guardian*. Online: http://www.guardian.co.uk/books/2009/jan/16/danny-boyle-india (accessed 3 April 2012).

20 In her essay, "Can the Subaltern Speak?" Gayatri Spivak expresses concern for the processes whereby postcolonial studies reinscribe, co-opt and repeat neocolonial imperatives of cultural erasure, political domination and economic profiteering. Spivak, in other words, asks if the postcolonial critic, by virtue of assuming hegemonically (without the necessary consent) the deluxe right to represent the subaltern of his/her own nation, becomes unknowingly complicit in the task of imperialism.

21 "I am an 'accidental' writer. I used to write in my school days and even won some creative writing contests. But I never thought I would be a novelist and did not write a word of fiction for almost fifteen years. It was only when I was posted in London that I got inspired to try my hand at fiction, motivated by some of my contemporaries in the Foreign Service who had written novels, and by the city of London itself, which is such a vibrant cultural hub," says Swarup in an interview. "I'm the luckiest novelist in the world." *Guardian*. Online: http://www.guardian.co.uk/books/2009/jan/16/danny-boyle-india (accessed 3 April 2012).

22 Charles Ingram, a former British army major and a Mensa member created a national stir when he was accused of cheating (through creating a somewhat intricate "coughing code" with a member of the audience to get to the right answer) in the television show to win a million pounds. Ingram contested the jury verdict of fraud and has since maintained his innocence; defenders of the "coughing major's" innocence have argued that the fraud charges in itself were a hoax pulled by the game's corporate sponsors because they were unwilling to disburse such a large sum. "Charles Ingram." Wikipedia. Online: http://en.wikipedia.org/wiki/Charles_Ingram (accessed 1 August 2012). Swarup footnotes this episode in the police custody scene, where the sponsors of the show discuss the possibility of framing Ram Mohammed Thomas falsely in collusion with the police Commissioner (13).

23 Here we have the ironic insertion of superstar Amitabh Bachchan, a larger than life entertainment entity who has crossed over into the "real" as well, marketing not stories of India but India itself to the world.

24 This scene of the mapping of real India and real America in *SDM* can be seen as temporally and spatially Orientalist in the sense that the Americans' reflexive (and naïve) monetizing of the problem of deep transnational-colonial structures reproduces real India and real America in a relationship of imperial subordination where real America triumphs with a heart that enshrines immanent economy-transcending enlightenment virtues over real India that is at the very same heart, irredeemably dark. The diachrony of Indian history is thereby denied and India is configured as a stable ontological category where darkness is a natural condition of being.

25 Frantz Fanon, *The Wretched of the Earth* (New York: Grove Press, 2004 [1964]).

26 Achille Mbembe, *On the Postcolony* (Berkeley: University of California Press, 2001).

27 In his *Anthropology and the Modern World* (New York: Palgrave Macmillan, 2003), Michel-Rolp Trouillot challenges contemporary anthropologists to question dominant narratives of globalization and to radically rethink the utility of the concept of culture, the emphasis upon fieldwork as the central methodology of the discipline, and the relationship between anthropologists and the people whom they study.

28 Trouillot, *Anthropology*, 220.

Chapter 3

SLUMLORD AESTHETICS AND THE QUESTION OF INDIAN POVERTY

Nandini Chandra

In October 2011, Sushil Kumar, a computer operator from Motihari with a salary of 6,000 rupees, won five crore rupees on *Kaun Banega Crorepati?* (henceforth *KBC*), the Indian version of *Who Wants to Be a Millionaire?*, the original British quiz show which doubles up as a reality show in following the fortunes of its participants. The press repeatedly described him as the real-life Jamal Malik, the hero of *Slumdog Millionaire* (henceforth *SDM*), in what is perceived to be a similar fairytale turnaround. However, in the less than fairytale plot of his life, the money will be used to build a roof on a house where his parents and five brothers live along with their families, to purchase gold jewelry for his wife, to build a library to store his magazines and books and, most importantly, to allow him the freedom to pursue his ambition of becoming an Indian Administrative Service (IAS) officer.[1] This ambition of becoming a civil servant will require him to devote all waking hours to prepare for the fiercely competitive examination called the Union Public Service Commission (UPSC), identified especially in Bihar as the route to supreme symbolic capital and power, above and beyond anything money can buy. The newspapers report that he has already shifted to a cramped paying guest accommodation in a university campus neighborhood in Delhi. He is sharing the room with four or five other immigrants from Bihar, all of whom are preparing for the UPSC.[2] Such slumming and the monasticism of living apart from his wife are considered necessary sacrifices in the bid to pass the exams.

There is nothing unique about Sushil Kumar's story. If one imagines the status of game show winners to be analogous to that of lottery winners, then going by the known statistics regarding the latter category, windfalls rarely bring about a fairytale ending. Far from it, there is danger of being cheated, claims from extended family and real threat to one's life. From the initial publicity to the actual delivery of the money, it is as if one's entrenchment in and subjection to the economy becomes more intensive than it was in a former life of wage earning. Far from being an exit from the depredations of wage slavery, lottery winners are often known to continue to spend a bulk of their winnings in buying more lottery tickets,[3] an addiction built into the fantasy of the exit. In the Indian case, as witnessed with Sushil Kumar, the fantasy and addiction take on a different form. A deliberate and carefully cultivated culture of poverty and hoarding, which is a peculiar feature of middle-class households, gets intensified or activated the moment one comes into money. This means that there is a premium on saving rather than pleasure or exit. The setting of a windfall story in this work ethic dominated, petit bourgeois class reality is meant to precipitate the eclipse of the culture of saving and poverty.

The recent spiral in television-based game shows and talent shows with big money in rewards is to be seen as a culturally appropriate way to inaugurate a credit-based economy in a society that is basically poor. Credit is a crucial component of foreign direct investment (FDI) mandated by the World Trade Organization/ General Agreement on Tariffs and Trade (WTO/GATT), an agreement of which India has been a signatory since the last decade. The new global order under WTO presumes easy and smooth flows of capital, products and labor between different parts of the world.[4] The task of fashioning this unified global order, in which the distinctions between rich and poor countries are supposed to have been effaced, is not possible in reality. It is only by introducing new spending habits based on credit that the pervasive sense of poverty and squalor can be made to vanish, at least from the realm of popular consciousness. This is where the communications industry plays an indispensable role by creating a virtual network of connections, stimuli and rewards, such that the (un)truths of a unified global order are registered through cognitive and subliminal effects.

For too long, the West has looked at India exclusively through the prism of poverty and underdevelopment. The new mediatized and digitalized global reality demands a change of frame. However, before the frame can be changed, the stuff inside the frame needs to be properly repositioned so that it does not spill out. There is an obligation to revisit the old questions of poverty and unemployment in order to be able to jettison them more thoroughly. *SDM* (based on Indian diplomat, Vikas Swarup's novel, *Q & A*) takes up the tropes of gaming and game changing to trace the metamorphosis of a Bombay slum dweller into a millionaire. The particular format is the television reality quiz show, less flashy forms of which have conventionally been the showcase vehicle for public school-educated middle-class boys since the early 1980s, such as the extremely popular Doordarshan-based *Quiz Time*, conducted by Siddhartha Basu. Basu's forte, in a highly successful career as television producer and director, has been quiz shows including *KBC*.[5]

Swarup would have surely grown up watching *Quiz Time*, a must-watch for all civil services aspirants. Unlike the English-speaking class to which the earlier quiz shows catered, *KBC* is clearly for a lower middle-class, vernacular, small-town public. Likewise, in *SDM*, the protagonist is a boy from the slums who taps his street knowledge to win a twenty million dollar reality quiz show. In the quiz, Jamal is unable to answer questions that test his nationalist knowledge but is surprisingly comfortable with those that mark his familiarity with international trivia. For instance, while he knows that Benjamin Franklin adorns a 100 dollar bill, he has no clue about who adorns the 1,000 rupee note. This is obviously meant to suggest the irrelevance of the nation to its most marginalized member but, less obviously, also indicates the nation's redundancy in a globalized neoliberal setup where everything is valued in dollars.

It is important to contextualize the "Cinderella effect" created by these game shows in view of the fact that, unlike the earlier quiz format with modest prizes, the contemporary reality-based quiz show is part of a big corporate sponsorship, dedicated to transformation and the promise of an exit. The defense of an elite culture capital is no longer at stake. In the contemporary calculation of corporate interests, with their rhetoric of the informatization of labor and the generalization of the service industry, the traditional working class has been declared to be an obsolete category.[6] These game shows then direct the bulk of their energy to the unemployed detritus, the reserve army of workers who are offered the promise of an exit from poverty. The solution through reality quizzes becomes paradoxically homologous to the dream of communism, in which the true potential of humanity can be realized only after the abolition of wage slavery. Similarly, love and the promise of happiness in the film can be realized only after the slumdog has become a millionaire, abolishing thereby the prospect of ever engaging in wage slavery.

The Cinderella effect is what critic David Gritten identified while referring to the film as the "first film of the Obama era."[7] Probably what he means by this is that the film engages in an Obama type "yes we can" idealism without averting one's eyes from the painful reality. In other words, the film displays a hard-nosed idealism appropriate to a crisis and recession phase of capitalism. That the film won all the top Anglo-American awards – the Oscars, the Golden Globes, the BAFTAs – is further validation of this facile feel-good factor, which it seeks to capture in a neo-neorealist mode with location shooting and gritty drama. The film was shot in the Nehru Nagar slums near Dharavi. In contrast to the usual social realist or documentary style framing of poverty conventional in Western narratives of India (typically something like Louis Malle's 1969 documentary, *Calcutta*, banned by the Indian government from being broadcast on the BBC,[8] or even the 1988 Mira Nair film *Salaam Bombay*, with its stark portrait of the Bombay slums), we have here a return to a nineteenth-century melodramatic mode reminiscent of Dickens. The Dickensian portrayal is a sentimental but validating look at the lives of the poor and destitute, also congruent with the *filmi* sensibility of Hindi commercial cinema. The centrality of the neo-Gothic structure of the Victoria Terminus station as the transformative point in the film is an embodiment of this Dickensian aura as much as an invocation of the imperial vision. Thus, despite the rhetoric of a united global world in which nation-states have almost dissolved, the film underwrites its strong British credentials. Gritten reports a fierce nationalist campaign among Britishers who felt that *SDM* could have been only made by an English person. Hollywood, in their view, would not have touched a film using a Muslim lead with a barge pole.[9]

As for Bollywood, initially at least, there was a strong knee-jerk reaction. Renowned Bollywood superstar Amitabh Bachchan's blog officially advanced the chauvinist argument that outsiders have no right to depict the seamier side of native life. The way this hyper-nationalist sentiment has been refracted in the international press says something about the film's motivations. For instance, most reports translate Bachchan's statement as the Indian people's "inability to take a brutal look at themselves,"[10] assuming both that the so-called West has a hotline with the underclass, and that Mr. Bachchan is one of the common "Indian people."

Boyle had promised the studio bosses a film in English.[11] Loveleen Tandan, the co-director, took her role as cover-up officer for cultural gaffes seriously enough to insist that the boys from the Nehru Nagar slum speak in Hindi rather than English. Despite her efforts, the film, which is governed by studio dynamics more than being an independent work of art, is full of gaffes. The upper class body language of its avowedly slum-dwelling protagonists is a glaring inconsistency. Again, the part given to Anil Kapoor (the actor who plays the role of the typical Bollywood superstar who hosts *KBC*), in which he treats the working class participant in an exaggeratedly condescending fashion, does not really capture the particular loudness of a Bollywoodian melodrama. While one does not necessarily doubt the potential arrogance of Bollywood superstars, the social skills they acquire in real life over years of proximity to the film industry's laboring force (from the technicians to the spotboys), not to mention their rigorous and necessary training in a facile populism, does not square with the openly snobbish airs of the superstar played by Anil Kapoor. Then again, the use of English when the boys reach adolescence could have been justified by the simple suggestion that they picked it up from the tourist-infested streets of Agra or even from the call center. And while there is an attempt to imbue the film with a self-consciously heroic Muslim profile, the film overwrites it with a totally Hindu concept of destiny. Ironically, even the end credits song, *Jai Ho*, seems to suggest an orchestrated mass pilgrimage to Vaishno-devi rather than the triumph of the Muslim underdog, with its chorus of Jai Hos, a typically Hindu salutation. What these superficial glitches point to is a skewed alignment with the deep structure of Indian reality. But insofar as this reality is constantly changing, there cannot be a privileged insider position either.

The idea of a cultural expert who will identify the lapses in the representation of Indian culture is not simply about getting the language right. As is evident in the above examples, the idea of culture cannot simply be taken to mean a formal criterion that can be ticked off a list, that one either knows or does not. The affect identified as Indian can only be grasped if we sift through the mediations of different artistic forms, as part of a historicized process rather than seeing them in terms of a product. The fact is that even though *SDM* is invested in a neoliberal economy beneficial to the Indian upper class, the Indian bourgeoisie's residual cultural orientation as national and progressive obscures their present transnational and neo-imperialistic affiliations. For instance, Bachchan's response cannot simply be ascribed to false consciousness or hypocrisy. The structure of feeling that he inhabits via his poet father's (Harivansh Rai Bachchan) close proximity to the progressive bourgeoisie (Nehru and the progressive writers) in the nationalist past could very well have led him to a habitual reflex where nationalist pride surfaces in a strangely distorted manner. The film already gestures towards his angry young man avatar of the 1970s. His response is then not merely the response of an individual, but of a collective past and his own institutionalization within it. Culture in this respect is necessarily rendered through memory and an intergenerational class consciousness.[12]

Given this complex intermeshing of a skewed Indian and global context surrounding the film's production and reception, it becomes pertinent to frame the question of the specific nature of Indian poverty raised by the film. The film is hardly unique in addressing the spectacle of the Bombay poor, their dismal conditions of living and defecating, or their great disparity vis-à-vis the Indian rich. But it ultimately serves to crystallize a general consensus achieved in recent years on the disengagement of labor from questions of poverty and wealth creation. Partha Chatterjee's much talked about essay, "Democracy and Economic Transformation," mobilizes the concept of a "political society" to merge the realms of peasant detritus and urban poor with petty entrepreneurs as well as the more shadowy criminal class.[13] His argument reads something like this: since the informal and irregular labor has not been and cannot be integrated into the corporate-style capitalist structures, they not only lose out on the benefits of civil society, but their only salvation lies in being appropriated by governmental structures and schemes. This strange and sly equation of the poor with the criminal class is viciously ideological. While thinking of this class's autonomy from capitalist structures, one cannot afford to forget, especially in the light of recent and ongoing history, that capital is accumulated through forcible dispossession of these very populations, through what is considered to be a judicious use of the government's repressive instruments by agents of "neoliberal growth." This same government, after raping the underclass, is supposed to do double duty as their benign caretaker.

The outcome of dispossession is the army of surplus labor who, by driving down wages, immediately and concretely increase the relative surplus value appropriated by capitalists (the difference between the money spent to buy labor power and the money made by selling the products of labor). Their abstract mediation of the standard value of labor makes them an integral part of a proletarian population, even though they may not possess a revolutionary subjectivity. In contrast to Chatterjee's view, the film, in its neoliberal optimism, sees the unskilled immigrant poor as immediately appropriable within the interstices of corporatized service industries instead of being the target of government schemes. However, the film ultimately participates in the denial of the potential usefulness of the work they do and its lack of reward. Like Chatterjee, it also insists on placing them outside the purview of the juridical civil state, where law and order do not prevail in the same familiar way, thus surrounding their lives with a mystique that films like Boyle's can successfully unravel for a neoliberal audience.

The film then endows the poor with humanity and dignity. From a neoliberal vantage point, the poor cannot be seen through what are perceived as "instrumentalist" categories of labor or class. They are instead seen as denizens of a shadowy, illicit realm, which can be made comprehensible only by integrating it within certain humanist tropes like love and freedom. It is remarkable that the topography of the places where the poor live is seen largely through aerial shots – mountains of garbage, huge green forests of wasteland, rivers of feces. The little boys, as they jump back and forth through this panoramic natural landscape, acquire the characteristic of lotuses blooming in mud. These distant shots have the advantage of lending perspective, especially as the boys return to the city as mature English-speaking individuals, who know how to take care of themselves. The shit-smeared scene in the beginning and the scene where a massive bogeyman-type figure gouges out the eyes of little children with a spoon are, on the other hand, tightly framed to communicate the horror of the other world, which may be packaged for a poverty tour (like the one where Shantaram took Madonna by the hand and led her through the giddy lanes of Dharavi).[14]

The slum, the common tank where the mother is felled by one swoop of the Hindu fundamentalist sword, the brothel, the child labor, the exploitative policemen, the curious schoolmaster in a *dhoti*, and the mafia bosses are all stops on this guided tour. Even though equally commodified, the poverty one finds in more popular Bollywood fare represents the *chawl* (shared home of the hardworking poor) more heterogeneously. The same space can be imbued with a variety of signifiers depending on whether it is a crime drama, a social comedy or a new age thriller. *SDM* however tries to bring us the sprawl of the slum in a single sweep, an expansive and oppressive microcosm without an outside.

If there are overlaps to be found in Bollywood, we will find them in the aesthetics of the new, so-called independent cinema, which likewise celebrate the resources of the underdog or the lower middle-class entrepreneur. In them too, we find an echo of the severe eschewal of the institutions of state and civil society, as opposed to the older Bombay cinema in which the state ultimately inserted itself as the benefactor of the oppressed. *SDM*, invested in showing that real harmony is ultimately produced by a direct interaction between capital and labor, makes the state and civil society completely redundant. The context is one where capital will always be benefiting labor and not the other way around. This is probably an acknowledgement of the fact that, under the present phase of free market enterprise, the Indian state has subordinated itself so completely to capital that it need not even appear as a separate entity. While it is true that the police initially torture Jamal at the television producer's behest, they are not persuaded by the market's impartial logic. Only after a lapse of time does the inspector come round to Jamal's version of the story, and escorts him to the media room: a display of faith in corporate capital's benevolent intentions. But while Bollywood is equally welcoming of foreign capital, a non-Bollywood production like *SDM* takes on more immediately imperialist overtones. The rhetoric of good will and benevolence strives to conceal the conditions of its production, encapsulated by a patchy realism which seems to suggest that its real commitment is to the true heart of India, rather than to a magic realist Bollywood imaginary which it uses merely as the scaffolding for its conventional plot's unfolding.

The direct connectivity of India with an international public via tourism, call centers, media and other service industry networks makes the proximity of its population to foreign capital extremely clear. The absence of an organized labor force or any political platform in the film makes it possible to suggest that capital is free of any vested interest, and imbued with the most benign intentions. The film is produced by Celador Films, the very company which originally created the *Who Wants to Be a Millionaire?* contest. For all its self irony, and the rhetoric of redeeming the wretched of the earth, one would never guess that the film was a promotion of the philosophy of gambling. In fact, TV game shows encourage the contestants to think of themselves as obligated to the judges and alternatively make them feel entitled to disproportionately large sums of the prize money in a caricature of the deserving or meritorious poor. At the same time, the ruthlessness with which the contestants are evicted draws brief attention to the studio producers' less than benign intentions as business entrepreneurs, only to deflect it to a professional ethic, which seeks to dignify its lottery or gambling mode. Needless to say, there has been an unprecedented rise in singing, acting and dancing schools since the growth of reality talent contests on Indian television, in turn inspired by the big money in the corporate-sponsored showbiz industry, which makes the aspirations of the contestants less illegitimate perhaps. The dynamics of reality television get enacted when little Jamal is propped up to be a singer by the beggar kingpin Maman, and the little fellow really thinks his time has come. In the spirit of entitlement of reality television contestants, he demands a fifty rupee note from him before he sings his piece, announcing that he is, after all, a professional.

The extension of the entrepreneurial ethic to the informal service class makes even contractual labor conditions of *chai wallahs* seem like a welcome novelty. The hotel kitchen seems like a refuge of freedom for the canny child waiter, who gets plenty of time off even as Salim complains of the utopian life they have left behind stealing tires in the by-lanes of Agra. The tourist industry seems like a utopia of castoffs and gullible "whities" waiting to be ripped off by these wily, self-appointed guides. In short, the film tries to show that for those who can think on their feet, access to wealth is not a problem. Child labor is not really seen as exploitative but as enabling the education of budding young adults. In fact, we hardly perceive their contribution in terms of real labor. They are seen as gaining from or indeed "gaming" rather than giving to the system, sabotaging, picking up the leftovers, staying in empty hotel rooms, stealing. Their labor is forever in the background. What is in the foreground is the readymade wealth they are continually grabbing. Wealth is seen not as something created by labor but as always already there to be accessed, like the twenty million rupee game show prize, a clear repudiation of the true dynamics of labor and class.

It is well known that substantial amounts of income invested in gambling activities all over the world come from the poor. The gambling industry works predominantly on the backs of gambling addicts in low-income neighborhoods.[15] Studies have shown how the funding for these peoples' gambling habits (as much as that for the various micro-credit schemes that target them) comes from their cutting back on basic needs, in the case of the extreme poor, on food and health care. Far from bringing in pots of gold, the people who gamble chip even their subsistence income away.

The idea of a slumdog millionaire is, very simply put, an attempt to aid this process of destitution. The idea is to deflect the reality principle in such a way that it severs the imagination from the historical structure of debt and poverty. Irrespective of who the film is intended for, whether the petit bourgeois, aspirational subjects of former colonies or the imperial elites of the metropolis, the film succeeds in prizing loose the hoarding tendency, and embedding instead the lessons of commodity fetishism. The splitting into the good brother, Jamal, who stakes everything for love versus the bad brother, Salim, who literally embraces commodity fetishism (he is sprawled in a bathtub full of cash) is further meant to deflect us from the overall commodity fetishism advanced by the film. This is embodied by deploying the poor in the service of a fantastic narrative where money has turned into an absolute principle – it can be spent, burnt or submerged, delinked as it is from any concrete use value or real memory. What is remarkable is the fact that, while the film deploys the denizen of the slum (the lumpenproletariat), the game show usually targets a member of the lower middle class, who has a basic school or college degree, in other words, the informatized worker. The challenge is to symbolically stem the tide of proletarianization that might sweep both the lumpenproletariat and the petit bourgeoisie, by creating cultural barricades that will prevent them from going over to the other side. Jamal Malik and Sushil Kumar are obviously bereft of any revolutionary class consciousness. Yet insofar as the real life slumdog refuses to accept the resolution provided by the film – sticking firmly to a peasant ethic of subsistence and caution – there is an implicit refusal of the neoliberal plot of speculation and consumerism.

Notes

1 Shivani Naik, "Motihari Millionaire," *Indian Express*, 13 November 2011.
2 Divya Pal, "Kaun Banega Crorepati 5 Winner to stay in Delhi," *Times of India*, 7 November 2011. Online: http://articles.timesofindia.indiatimes.com/2011-11-07/tv/30366787_1_sushil-kumar-din-ka-upsc-exams (accessed 7 November 2011).
3 "Lottery Winners: Stories of Big Lottery Winners." Lottery Winners. Online: http://www.biglotterywinners.com/2011/10/list-of-black-lottery-winners.html (accessed 10 October 2011).
4 India has been a WTO member since 1 January 1995. World Trade Organization. Online: http://www.wto.org/english/thewto_e/countries_e/india_e.htm (accessed 15 January 2012).
5 Siddhartha Basu's career as a quizmaster is a classic example of small enterprise becoming corporate in neoliberal India. From modest beginnings in intercollegiate quizzes to *Quiz Time*, *Mastermind India* and *KBC*, owned by his company Big Synergy, an affiliate of the Big Reliance Entertainment India Ltd. since 2007, the petit bourgeois has indeed become a big bourgeois. "Siddhartha Basu," Wikipedia. Online: http://en.wikipedia.org/wiki/Siddhartha_Basu (accessed 15 January 2012).

6 "The rejection of the organized working class in favor of those in the margin of the labor market as the new subject of revolutionary politics," or the celebration of "informatization as an exhilarating sign," are moves in a new New Left that often coalesce with the enthusiasts of the new global order. Alex Callinicos and Timothy Brennan quoted in *Debating Empire*, edited by Gopal Balakrishnan (New York: Verso, 2003).

7 David Gritten, "Slumdog Millionaire: The first film of the Obama Era," *Washington Post*, 12 January 2009. Online: http://www.telegraph.co.uk/culture/film/4224827/Slumdog-Millionaire-the-first-film-of-the-Obama-era.html (accessed 15 January 2009).

8 The Indian government banned the BBC from filming in India for several years after they fell foul of Malle's fascination with poverty. "Louis Malle," Wikipedia. Online: http://en.wikipedia.org/wiki/Louis_Malle (accessed 10 November 2011).

9 Gritten, "Slumdog Millionaire."

10 Blog post, "Slumdog Millionaire could only have been made by a westerner," *Guardian*, 15 January 2009. Online: http://www.guardian.co.uk/film/filmblog/2009/

11 John Jurgensen, "The Co-Pilot of 'Slumdog,'" *Wall Street Journal*, 10 January 2009. Online: http://online.wsj.com/article/SB123146019434866263.html (accessed 14 January 2009).

12 The concept of "structure of feeling" is Raymond Williams' theoretical contribution to understanding the cultural response of a new generation to subtle but significant changes in the historical field. It is primarily seen as an analytical tool to discern "a pattern of impulses, restraints, tones, for which the best evidence was often the actual conventions of literary or dramatic writing." But pertinent to my discussion is the meaning of the concept as that which is not fully articulated— "all that comes through as disturbance, tension, blockage" —almost like a temporal distortion. See the section on "The Long Revolution," in *Politics and Letters: Interviews with New Left Review* by Raymond Williams (New York: Verso, 1981), 168.

13 Partha Chatterjee, "Democracy and Economic Transformation in India," *Economic and Political Weekly* 43.16 (April 2008): 19–25.

14 When pop star Madonna visited Bombay in 2007, she was taken to Dharavi by the author of *Shantaram*, Gregory David Roberts. Online: http://www.stargold.in/features.aspx?aid=4124&page=7 (accessed 15 January 2012).

15 "Lotteries: The Effects of Lotteries." Library Index. Online: http://www.libraryindex.com/pages/1608/Lotteries-EFFECTS-LOTTERIES.html (accessed 6 October 2011).

Chapter 4

WATCHING TIME: *SLUMDOG MILLIONAIRE* AND NATIONAL ONTOLOGY

Lakshmi Padmanabhan

> The child is special now. This is not an ordinary child, this is an Oscar child.[1]

In 2009, the *Sunday Times* reported that one of the child actors of the film *Slumdog Millionaire* (hereafter *Slumdog*), Rubina Ali, was to be illegally sold to pay for her family's livelihood. Rubina's uncle described her as an "Oscar child," justifying the higher price they had asked for, and permanently marking her body as a part of the film she had acted in the year before. This link made between Rubina and *Slumdog* materially embodies the links that I will trace through this chapter. Using Amit Rai's arguments on media assemblages and Brian Massumi's arguments on ontology and temporality, I trace the multiple subjectivities and temporalities of *Slumdog* as a media event. I argue that reading the film's fractured temporalities allows for an understanding of how the nation functions within the filmic time-space.

Two terms recur through this chapter that merit definition. The first is the "media assemblage." The idea of the assemblage builds on the work of several philosophers, particularly Gilles Deleuze and Henri Bergson. As Jasbir Puar explains in her work, *Terrorist Assemblages: Homonationalism in Queer Times* (2007), the assemblage, as a series of dispersed but mutually implicated and messy networks, draws together enunciation and dissolution, causality and effect and organic and nonorganic forces.[2]

And later, "assemblage here points to the inability to clearly delineate a temporal, spatial, energetic, or molecular distinction between a discrete biological body and technology."[3] Amit Rai conceives of the media assemblage as the constantly "becoming" or emerging combination of bodily sensation, affect, capital flows, viewing practices and networks of circulation that films are imbricated within, in his *Untimely Bollywood: Globalization and India's New Media Assemblage* (2009).[4] In this chapter, I use the assemblage as the guiding principle for my method of analysis. I map out sections of the media assemblage that is *Slumdog* in order to illustrate the constantly emerging networks that it encompasses. The second term requiring explanation is "duration." By duration, I refer to Amit Rai's reworking of Gilles Deleuze's concept. Rai explains duration as "both the nested temporalities that are lived through the assemblage, and the duration it has as an entity in its own right."[5] For film analysis, this definition would include the duration of the film's running time, shot lengths and sequencing as well the duration of its continued circulation in the public sphere.

The goal of this chapter is to attempt a form of film analysis that takes into account what representations do, as opposed to what they mean. This is particularly relevant to *Slumdog* because of the conflicting nationalist discourses that it has been linked to in various media. For example:

> In many respects, *Slumdog Millionaire* could only be British. It is technically adept in a manner that still eludes India's Bollywood cinema; Boyle is at the top of his form. Its subject matter is too foreign and remote to have been initiated by Hollywood; we British are not quite so insular in our world-view. And would any US studio bigwig approve a film with a Muslim hero?[6]
>
> One look at *Slumdog Millionaire*, and you know that its spirit and soul is [*sic*] flagrantly, proudly Indian: the Empire has been finally, overwhelmingly trounced.[7]
>
> Just days after Barack Obama, a self-described "mutt" because of his mixed racial heritage, took office as our new president, the motion picture academy honored its own cinematic mutt, *Slumdog Millionaire* giving the film 10 Oscar nominations, including one for Best Picture.[8]

The common thread that runs through the articles from which these quotes are cited is the ease with which the film is folded into a national media assemblage, whether British, Indian, or American. Each of these writers insists on tying the film to a specific national idea through its appropriation into a linear history. Each attempt at narrating *Slumdog*'s origins highlights a moment in which the film is attached to larger historical narratives of a nation. In this sense, *Slumdog Millionaire* serves as an example of globalized cultural production, not only because it is a multicultural film, but because it highlights the tenuous nature of national histories.

Slumdog's nationalist narratives are built on both spatial and temporal histories. For example, its appropriation of Indianness functions through the emphasis on the location of the film – "The story is universal, but it could have only been made in Mumbai"[9] – and the authentic materiality of the bodies – "Ms. Tandan ended up hiring real kids, some of them from the Mumbai slums, to play the three lead child characters."[10] Such a narration is also contingent on moving back through time to build a retrospective filmic genealogy for *Slumdog Millionaire*, as Amitava Kumar builds in his article for *Vanity Fair*.[11] These conflicting genealogies for *Slumdog* are specifically linked to the national. For example, Amitava Kumar argues that the Indian film industry had already produced the forerunners to *Slumdog*, and Shubra Gupta links *Slumdog*'s success to its setting of Mumbai and India as a nation, while in David Gritten's narration, India does not possess the technical capability to produce such a film but the UK does and hence only the British could have made it. This backward movement – the rearranging of the past to make the present the teleological end of the genealogy – is a move that makes apparent the unstable origins of media objects and representations, since we can see history repeatedly rewritten and are therefore losing the status of a singular truth about the origins of the media object. By co-opting *Slumdog* into whichever national film history the writer subscribes to, he/she mirrors the ways in which the national histories are narrated.

As these quotes indicate, there are lengthy conflicts around media objects about the specific meaning of their representation. One of the conflicts about *Slumdog* was whether it was a "good" representation of Indians.[12] As Amit Rai notes in his work *Untimely Bollywood*,

> for too long, representation has been thought in terms of an actualized product of given hierarchies of power. But what if representation is an event that performs anew with each repetition and with each new scene of circulation being an unpredictable but patterned trajectory?[13]

The aim of the paper is to trace some of the trajectories of the film, to highlight the many linked bodies, and times, that are united within the assemblage that is *Slumdog*. By looking at the film as an event, I argue that the filmic assemblage makes apparent the ways in which the nation is changing – just as *Slumdog* is constantly in circulation and gains new meaning, the India that it represents also changes.[14] Through the chapter, I use temporal analysis to highlight these changes. As Brian Massumi argues in his work *Parables for the Virtual: Movement, Affect, Sensation* (2002), to understand change, we must understand temporality since change can only be mapped over time.[15] As Elizabeth Grosz observes in her work, *The Nick of Time: Politics, Evolution, and the Untimely* (2004):

> Time is neither fully "present," a thing in itself, nor is it a pure abstraction [...] It is a kind of evanescence that appears only at those moments when our

> expectations are (positively or negatively) surprised. We can think it only if we are jarred out our immersion in its continuity.[16]

My analysis follows the temporal moves that the film makes in order to highlight the moments of temporal disjuncture and change in both the film and the idea of nation that *Slumdog* illustrates.

The Present is not Enough

Brian Massumi, in his work, *Parables for the Virtual* (2002), argues for an understanding of being that is constantly in movement – a process. This process is how Massumi sees the body existing in the world, with the subject positions that bodies occupy only being residues or retrospective orderings of these bodies. This analysis emphasizes the coherence of the body over time as the way in which to understand being. In *Slumdog*, we see an illustration of this being in process, where each of the main characters in the film literally changes into a different person with the passing of time, while still held together under the auspices of a single character. By casting three people to play each character, we see the way time lends coherence to an otherwise disparate group of bodies, i.e., it is only through acknowledging the passage of time and the process of aging that we know they are ostensibly the same character. Hence, the character of Jamal is primarily a temporal construct.

While the title credits of the film list Dev Patel as the actor who portrays Jamal, over the course of the film, we are introduced to two other people – Ayush Mahesh Khedekar ("Young Jamal") and Tanay Hemant Chheda ("Middle Jamal") – that create the unified subject of Jamal Malik. Through the film narrative, we see them embody the growth of the subject into different people as they move through the time-space of the film. Roughly forty minutes in, we are provided with a short sequence in which the youngest protagonists – Ayush Khedekar as Jamal and Azharuddin Mohammed Ismail as Salim – work and travel on various trains through the north Indian countryside by selling assorted goods such as whistles and fruit in order to pay for food. Along with breathtaking imagery of the two children on top of the train traveling through the desert, we have M. I. A.'s hit single, "Paper Planes," as the soundtrack to the montage. The song is off her second album, *Kala*, which was released in 2007, and serves as a trajectory for the film that we shall briefly trace in the next section. However, during the sequence, we see the two kids stealing food from passengers through the window and illegally climbing to the roof of the trains in order to travel for free. During one such theft, Young Jamal (Ayush Khedekar) is hanging off the side of a train with rope held by Young Salim, and reaching into a train compartment to steal some bread from a family (Fig. 4.1).

Figure 4.1. Jamal and Salim stealing food from the train compartment.

Unfortunately, they are caught in the act and Jamal is tugged off the train by one of the family members, closely followed by Salim. As a result, they fall away to the side of the track and tumble down a slope. The duration of their fall (about eighteen seconds in the film) lasts longer than most of the earlier montage and, once the dust from their fall clears, both characters appear to have grown, into Tanay Chheda as Middle Jamal and Ashutosh Lobo Gajiwala as Middle Salim. In those eighteen seconds, time is concentrated – the passing of years into the moments of a fall, arriving at the present. This temporal jump – the compression of time – makes apparent the abrupt shift in the time of the film. This sequence, by almost erasing the process of "becoming," in the dual sense of becoming Middle Jamal from Youngest Jamal and in the Deleuzian sense of "becoming beyond or without being," in fact highlights this absence, drawing attention to the passage of time, and linking these two bodies under the same character.[17]

The passage of time for these characters also runs parallel to the changing times of the nation. Jamal's character is repeatedly linked through the narrative and dialogue to India's globalization. Middle Jamal makes such an observation linking himself to the nation during his stint as a tour guide at the Taj Mahal. In a short sequence about halfway through the film, Middle Jamal is guiding an American couple in the outskirts of Agra. We have a moment where the impeding future seems to be hinted at, where Jamal is taking the couple through a "dhobi ghat" – an area, usually on the banks of a river, which is used to wash clothes by the washermen from the area. The camera pans over a large area filled with people washing clothes and drying them out, as Jamal describes the function of the dhobi ghat, selling the spectacle of poverty to the tourists. In that moment, we see an address to the film's future dissidents who accuse *Slumdog* of trafficking in "poverty porn."[18] As the scene continues, we see Salim strip the tourists' car of its movable parts, leaving it standing on bricks when the American couple returns from "taking a good look" at the dhobi ghat. When the driver begins to beat up Jamal, accusing him of cheating the couple, Jamal remarks, "you wanted to see a bit of the real India? Well, here it is." The tourist responds, "well, here is a bit of the real America, son!" and gives him a $100 bill. This repeated linking of the "real India" with Jamal's narrative and through his character highlight the allegorical frame of reference through which the film appears to narrate his story as the story of a "real" Indian – a fact that Prem Kumar, host of *Who Wants to Be a Millionaire?*, observes by pointing out that he's a chai wallah from amchi Mumbai (a tea-seller from our own Mumbai) while introducing him to the audience in the opening sequence of the film.

As Jamal narrates his reason for knowing the answer to the question "Which American President is on the $100 bill?" he begins with the phrase, "Bombay had turned into Mumbai," as the scene changes from his seat in the police station to Middle Jamal and Middle Salim walking through the outskirts of Mumbai. This rather unremarkable linguistic change – Bombay to Mumbai – involved, in its becoming, a national push by major political parties in various metropolitan cities to move away from the anglicized names that marked colonial rule and towards Indic nomenclature. While the Shiv Sena had pushed for the change in Mumbai when they came to power in 1995, similar changes occurred in Chennai (Madras), Bengaluru (Bangalore) and Kolkata (Calcutta) that began in the late '90s and continued into the new century. The politics of this renaming simultaneously involved the restructuring of Indian urban spaces by a newly globalized culture, rising fundamentalism and rapid economic growth. Jamal, just like the city and nation around him, is affected by this changing socioeconomic climate. We see him grow from a street kid in the slums of Mumbai to the individual who captures a whole nation's interest. He moves across the country, earning his way with small jobs and petty theft to becoming a tour guide at the Taj Mahal, where he speaks English and earns his income in US dollars. Eventually he moves on to serving tea at call centers and even passes for one of the call center employees. Through the film, we are also provided with views of his slum as it changes – from the tightly packed rows of huts of his childhood, we see the area giving way to a high-rise office building. In each of these instances, we see the fractured subject that is Jamal repeatedly linked to the changing times of the nation, and the interplay between his temporally split narrative and that of the nation is brought to stark relief in these moments when Jamal's story and India's development are overtly linked.

Becoming National

In this section, I explore a few examples from the film that illustrate the moments in which the film inserts itself into an Indian time-space. Building on the previous section's temporal analysis of the narrative, I use this section to highlight the fact that the film's claims of national belonging also occur stylistically by examining the formal aspects of the film that reflect the fracturing of national time-space.

An early instance of this argument is seen when Young Jamal goes to great lengths to get Amitabh Bachchan's autograph. In the sequence, his brother locks Young Jamal in the toilet when they hear Bachchan's visit being announced. We are then provided a quick montage of Bachchan's earlier films in order to orient the viewer to his popularity, before returning to Jamal, who opens up a folded photograph of the actor that he carries with him everywhere. This reference to Amitabh Bachchan's celebrity status in Indian film emphasizes *Slumdog*'s origins in Bollywood and its ties to the Indian film audience. By taking up the task of explaining Amitabh's popularity, *Slumdog* implies that it is aware of Bollywood's trends and is therefore connected to the Indian film audience. However, an appearance by Amitabh Bachchan in a Bollywood film would hardly require a montage of his work to explain his popularity. And by including the montage, the film illustrates that it is speaking to several different national and transnational audiences – to the Indian audience by its acknowledgement of Bachchan's popularity, and to an international audience from its explanation of Bachchan to its viewers. This double movement – into Indianness and out of it – is brought into stark relief as the scene continues with Young Jamal jumping into the feces below the toilet in order to escape the toilet and reach Bachchan in time for an autograph.

Watching this sequence, the audience is made aware of their own potential decision when faced with the choice of missing Bachchan's autograph or wading through the feces. Despite being a dramatic exaggeration of such a choice, an audience that is intimately acquainted with Bollywood and Bachchan could affectively connect to the decision Jamal makes by jumping into the feces while a viewer who does not possess the same sense of affective belonging to Indian media would find it far more difficult to comprehend. Having no real tie to Bachchan, the decision to wade through excreta for a simple autograph appears excessive and unrelatable. What the film fails to do in including the montage of earlier films starring Bachchan is convey the sense of affective belonging that is tied to Bachchan as a celebrity and Bollywood as a phenomenon in Indian society. This excess – the sense of affective belonging that is formed in a particular time-space (and this may vary from the diasporic child watching Amitabh Bachchan along with his/her parents as an act of nostalgic longing for the homeland, to an Indian audience waiting in line for the "First Day First Show" tickets) – is the moment at which we, the audience, become national, i.e., belong to a nation.

David Martin-Jones, in his work, *Deleuze, Cinema and National Identity*, invokes Deleuze's concept of the "time-image" that deterritorializes the narrative of a film. Deterritorialization entails the "displacement of narrative into multiple labyrinthine versions."[19] Its opposite, "reterritorialization," entails the "constraining of a narrative into one linear timeline."[20] Martin-Jones highlights ways in which specific films formally illustrate the deterritorialization/ reterritorialization of national identity through the filmic narrative. While he uses this framework to analyze films from the US, South Korea and Italy, his arguments extend the scope of the Deleuzian concepts to the politics of national cinemas in general. He draws together disparate films including *Saving Private Ryan* (Steven Spielberg, 1998), *Peppermint Candy* (Lee Chang-dong, 1999) and *Sliding Doors* (Peter Hewitt, 1998), that form a genre that he characterizes by their "aberrant time schemes and their focus on memory and character identity as the filter through which to examine national identity."[21] I extend this argument to *Slumdog* since it would fall into the genre that he refers to, in order to highlight the moments at which the film becomes national. By arguing that the film is still becoming national, i.e., that it is not quite there yet, we can see the ways in which the film negotiates multiple national time-spaces without fully re-inscribing a single national identity.

The opening sequence of *Slumdog* begins with "Mumbai, 2006, Jamal Malik is one question away from winning 20 million rupees. How did he do it?" followed by dissipating smoke, revealing a close-up shot of a young man's face. In the following rapid series of cuts, we are taken to an overhead shot of falling money into a bathtub, the set of the Indian version of *Who Wants to Be a Millionaire?* and back to the smoke-filled screen. The sequence provides no clues about the temporal order of these spaces, with the transitions occurring through dialogue rather than linear shot editing. The first transition occurs when the young man is seated opposite an older gentleman, who is interrogating him. The latter's only utterance is the word "name," as he slaps the young man, and the scene cuts to a shot of falling money, and then to a darkened scene as a voiceover ensues, welcoming the audience to *Who Wants to Be a Millionaire?* while, backstage, we notice the same young man, as he steps into the center of the set. He is introduced as Jamal Malik from Mumbai, thus answering the question posed in the previous shot. Next, on the set of the game show, the host (Anil Kapoor) asks Jamal to tell us a bit about himself, when the scene cuts to Jamal being dunked into a bucket of water by his interrogator and stating that he worked at a call center in Juhu.

In the first few minutes, the linearity of the filmic narrative is questioned by the lack of temporal grounding. Both the sequence in the police station and the one on the sets of the game show appear to be occurring simultaneously. The viewer is presented with a deterritorialization of time where both narratives – of the interrogation and the game show – occur simultaneously with the same character, Jamal, being present in both. The importance of this deterritorialization lies in its ability to cause a crisis of truth as a single entity. By giving the present no causal relation to the past, this sequence makes apparent the multiple potential presents that are contained in any moment. This temporal fracture serves as a moment in which the film can no longer be viewed as a simple linear narrative but is, in its very form, a collection of narratives rather than a discrete object.

A similar deterritorialization of narrative time occurs at the end of the film when Jamal and Latika finally meet on the tracks of the platform and share their first kiss. The film seems to end with that kiss, and the credits begin to appear on the screen. However, as the credits are rolling, a dance sequence begins on the platform of the train station to the tune of "Jai Ho," with a large group of dancers lined up behind the actors. Shots of their dance are interspersed with the end credits. At the end of the dance, we see Jamal and Latika walk off into the distance. This song and dance sequence appears to have little connection with the movie itself and is not in keeping with the tone of the rest of the film.

This dance sequence, while very common in mainstream Indian film, is far less predominant in other national film industries including those of the UK and the US. This step appears to be an attempt by the film to insert itself into the genre of Bollywood cinema. As Lalitha Gopalan explains in *Cinema of Interruptions*, Indian cinema is often characterized by such sequences that take the audience out of the narrative diegesis and into the realm of cinematic pleasure.[22] More importantly, this song sequence splits the duration of the film itself into two endings – the first where Jamal and Latika kiss on screen before the end credits, and the second when they walk into the distance. These endings, much like the opening credits of the film, destabilize the discreteness of the film's duration. Understanding this film as a *constellation of interruptions*,[23] as Gopalan terms it, breaks up the linear narrative of the film as a form and highlights the filmic assemblage – a collection of fractured, interrelated media that are not limited to a single narrative arc. The following section highlights this more clearly by examining the filmic assemblage of *Slumdog* beyond its internal fissures.

Becoming Transnational

> All the predicates that can be stated of a thing – all the "accidents" that might befall it (even those remaining in potentia) are of its nature? If so, "nature" changes at the slightest move. The concept of nature concerns modification not essence.[24]

So far, I have explored the temporal moves within the form and narrative of the film. In this section, I outline some spatiotemporal links that the film has with other media objects and bodies in order to illustrate the larger networks of capital and affect that *Slumdog* participates in. In *Parables for the Virtual*, Massumi begins to outline a theory of the social that would account for the movement of bodies through space and time, something that he sees as currently lacking in a cultural theory that is focused on positionality and subjects as the site of analysis. Building on Henri Bergson, a French philosopher of temporality, Massumi argues that ontologically, the body is always in movement, and any coherence that a "body" or a subject may have is only provided retrospectively. Such a conception of ontology has several consequences for a theory of identity and media forms. In the case of *Slumdog*, by tracing the trajectories of the different bodies and media associated with the film, we begin to form a picture of *Slumdog*'s constantly evolving networks of relations that extend beyond the immediate storyline and running time. These networks that emerge as *Slumdog* circulates within them illustrate that we must understand the film as a constantly emergent form that is not solely bound to the narrative representations that it contains. This is materially embodied in the link I first cited in the introduction to this chapter, where Rubina Ali's material value is linked to the film. The trust set up by the film's producers to pay for the child actors when they come of age also extends the influence of the film far into the future.[25]

Similarly, tracing the audio for *Slumdog*, particularly M. I. A.'s "Paper Planes," we find it featured in the trailer to *Pineapple Express* (2008) and sampled on the track "Swagga Like Us," by rappers T. I., Jay-Z, Kanye West, and Lil' Wayne, while also being on the soundtrack for the film and eventually remixed several times.[26] According to Ben Thompson of the *Guardian*, the song "turns globalization inside out."[27] The song's association with the film and subsequent popularity allow us to map the networks of capital that it circulates within, connecting the UK production company, Celador Films, with a US production company, Fox Searchlight, that produce a film set within the Indian economy, which employs actors from disparate regions of the world including the slums of Mumbai, the Indian diasporic milieu of London, and Bollywood. Similarly, its affective flows move from the 2009 Grammy stage where M. I. A. performed "Paper Planes," to the slums that Rubina Ali (Latika) lives in, to the Oscar's main stage, then to the multiple sites of viewing through YouTube, and the movie theatres in India, letting us map the changing diagrams of spatio-temporal relations.

Each of these spaces and times that the film is connected to broadens the media assemblage that *Slumdog* consists of. By analyzing this film as an assemblage – a collection of "messy networks" as Puar notes[28] – we move the field of analysis from the representational to ontology. This shift allows us to mark the constantly changing or emerging ontology of the film and moves away from a theory of film that sees it as a static media object with a single narrative and clear duration. One direct conclusion from these maps is the extent of transnational circulation that occurs with the media object. *Slumdog*'s transnational maps of capital and affect clearly illustrate the fact that any claims of national ownership that are made of it can never fully encompass all the relations of capital and affect that it possesses and will create in the future. This chapter has undertaken a temporal analysis *Slumdog Millionaire* to highlight its emerging media assemblage. As a transnational film *Slumdog* may not be the first, but it serves as a particularly strong example of the multiple national contexts that media objects circulate within and this chapter has attempted to map out some of its changing contexts and times.

Notes

1 Quoted in Rhys Blakely, "Rubina Ali's Family Brawl after Father Denies Offering *Slumdog* Actress for Sale," *Sunday Times*, 20 April 2009. Online: http://www.thetimes.co.uk/tto/news/world/asia/article2610127.ece (accessed 15 August 2012).

2 Jasbir Puar, *Terrorist Assemblages: Homonationalism in Queer Times* (Durham, NC: Duke University Press, 2007), 211. Puar builds on Deleuze and Guattari's discussion of assemblages in *A Thousand Plateaus: Capitalism and Schizophrenia* (Minneapolis: University of Minnesota, 1987). In it, Deleuze and Guattari explain the components of an assemblage: "on the one hand it is a *machinic assemblage* of bodies, of actions and passions, an intermingling of bodies reacting to one another; on the other hand it is a *collective assemblage of enunciation*, of acts and statements, of incorporeal transformations attributed to bodies" (88, emphasis in original).

3 Puar, *Terrorist Assemblages*, 217.

4 Amit Rai, *Untimely Bollywood: Globalization and India's New Media Assemblage* (Durham, NC: Duke University Press, 2009), 18–19.

5 Ibid., 5.

6 David Gritten, "Slumdog Millionaire: The first film in the Obama era," *Telegraph*, 12 January 2009. Online: http://www.telegraph.co.uk/culture/film/4224827/Slumdog-Millionaire-the-first-film-of-the-Obama-era.html (accessed 15 August 2012).

7 Shubra Gupta, "Movie Review: *Slumdog Millionaire*," *Indian Express*, 22 January 2009. Online: http://www.indianexpress.com/news/movie-review-slumdog-millionaire/414049/2 (accessed 15 August 2012).

8 Patrick Goldstein and James Rainey, "Oscar Special: Slumdog Still Hollywood's Sweetheart." *Los Angeles Times*. 22 January 2009. Online: http://latimesblogs.latimes.com/the_big_picture/2009/01/oscar-nominatio.html (accessed 15 August 2012).

9 Gupta, "Movie Review: *Slumdog Millionaire*."

10 Somini Sengupta, "Extreme Mumbai, Without Bollywood's Filtered Lens," *New York Times*, 11 November 2008. Online: http://www.nytimes.com/2008/11/16/movies/16seng.html?pagewanted=1&adxnnl=1&adxnnlx=1299819049-QBVV2M8pb389Fkbhcsdfog (accessed 15 August 2012).

11 Amitava Kumar, "Slumdog Millionaire's Bollywood Ancestors," *Vanity Fair*, 23 December 2008. Online: http://www.vanityfair.com/online/oscars/2008/12/slumdog-millionaires-bollywood-ancestors.html (accessed 15 August 2012).

12 Mark Magnier, "Indians don't feel good about *Slumdog Millionaire*," *Los Angeles Times*, 24 January 2009. Online: http://articles.latimes.com/2009/jan/24/world/fg-india-slumdog24 (accessed 15 August 2012).

13 Amit Rai, *Untimely Bollywood*, 3.

14 While in this chapter I examine the Indian nation, one could extend this theoretical framework in comparison to other nations and to the definition of nation itself.

15 Brian Massumi, *Parables for the Virtual: Movement, Affect, Sensation* (Durham, NC: Duke University Press, 2002), 1–6.

16 Elizabeth Grosz, *The Nick of Time: Politics, Evolution, and the Untimely* (Durham, NC: Duke University Press, 2004), 5.

17 While several philosophers have used the term in different ways, for this chapter, I use "becoming" to indicate the state of perpetually emerging into materiality without becoming actualized. Puar, in *Terrorist Assemblages*, and Rai, in *Untimely Bollywood*, both utilize the term in this sense by drawing from Deleuze and Guattari's work in *A Thousand Plateaus* (see note 2). As Massumi explains, "the challenge is to think that process of *formation*, and for that you need a notion of a taking-form" (9, emphasis in original).

18 Alice Miles, "Shocked by Slumdog's Poverty Porn," *Sunday Times*, 14 January 2009. Online: http://www.thetimes.co.uk/tto/law/columnists/article2048284.ece (accessed 15 August 2012).

19 David Martin-Jones, *Deleuze, Cinema, and National Identity* (Edinburgh: Edinburgh University Press, 2006), 4.

20 Deleuze forwarded two types of images within cinema in his books *Cinema 1* and *Cinema 2*. As Martin-Jones explains, the movement-image generally consists of "an unbroken, linear narrative, based upon the continuity editing rules established by the Hollywood studio system," while the time-image generally consisted of films that experimented with non-linear time, often providing multiple, labyrinthine views on time (4).

21 Martin-Jones, *Deleuze, Cinema, and National Identity*, 3.

22 Lalitha Gopalan, *Cinema of Interruptions: Action Genres in Contemporary Indian Cinema* (London: British Film Institute, 2002).

23 Ibid., 3–4.

24 Massumi, *Parables for the Virtual*, 7.

25 Barney Henderson and Dean Nelson, "Slumdog child stars miss out on the movie millions," *Telegraph*, 26 January 2009. Online: http://www.telegraph.co.uk/news/worldnews/asia/4347472/Poor-parents-of-Slumdog-millionaire-stars-say-children-were-exploited.html (accessed 15 August 2012).

26 "Swagga Like Us." Perf. T. I., Jay-Z, Kanye West, M. I. A, Lil' Wayne. *51st Grammy Awards*. Los Angeles: CBS, aired. 8 February 2009. Television.

27 Ben Thompson, "MIA's Paper Planes turns globalization inside out." *Guardian*, 15 June 2011. Online: http://www.guardian.co.uk/music/2011/jun/16/mia-paper-planes (accessed 15 August 2012).

28 Puar, *Terrorist Assemblages*, 211.

Part Two

SLUMDOG AND THE SLUM

Chapter 5

SLUMDOG MILLIONAIRE AND EPISTEMOLOGIES OF THE CITY

Ulka Anjaria and Jonathan Shapiro Anjaria

What the hell can a slumdog possibly know?

—Police Constable, *Slumdog Millionaire*

The swirl of excitement, commentary and controversy surrounding the film *Slumdog Millionaire* (dir. Danny Boyle, 2008) in India and elsewhere calls for a careful analysis of the possibilities and pitfalls of transnational cultural production. Alternatively seen as a celebration of urban India's global coming-of-age, an affront to cultural sensibilities, a sign of neoliberal hegemony or superficial cinematic diversion, *Slumdog* has become one of the most controversial films to sweep the Academy Awards, winning eight out of its ten nominations. The film has spawned hundreds of news articles, reviews and blog entries, along with vigorous academic debate – of which this current volume is just one example. Out of this discourse, a majority of the voices have been somewhat cynical about the film's success. Many critiques come from a well-founded mistrust of the politics of popular culture and an awareness of the largely racist and imperialist history of cross-cultural representations of India and the East in Western film, media and literature. These critiques rely on a generalized skepticism of the political potential of melodramatic film. However, what most critics have overlooked is how Boyle's film offers a possibility for rethinking the relationship between popular cinema and the contemporary Indian urban experience precisely through its fantasy plot. This necessitates revising long-held assumptions within literary and urban studies, such as the monoglossia of filmic texts and the necessarily conservative

A version of this paper was published in *Economic and Political Weekly* 45.24 (12 June 2010): 41–6. Thanks to Ajay Gehlawat for comments on an earlier draft of the paper.

politics of melodrama and fantasy, along with reconsidering Boyle's longer engagement with the aesthetics of urban life.

On one hand, with its gritty view of Mumbai's underbelly, *Slumdog* wades into a troubling history of Western representations of India. Many critics along with prominent individuals such as Indian film icon Amitabh Bachchan have criticized the film, if not dismissed it outright, for its rehashing of old stereotypes of urban Indian squalor and backwardness.[1] Like most Western representations of urban poverty, they claim, *Slumdog* creates a sense of a troubled place out there, disconnected from the world of the viewer and thus unnuanced in its political vision. In this sense, the film is part of a lineage inhabited by such works as *Salaam Bombay!* (dir. Mira Nair, 1988) and *City of Joy* (dir. Roland Joffé, 1992) which, as Vincent Canby put it in his *New York Times* review of Joffé's film, represents an "India [that] exists to be a vast, teeming rehab center where emotionally troubled Americans can find themselves."[2] For its own representation of slums, poverty and the violence of urban life, *Slumdog*'s popularity and critical reception might be seen as signs of how ingrained such static visions of otherness remain in global cinema.

At the same time, critics are not just skeptical of *Slumdog*'s content but its form. The film's melodramatic elements – its happy ending, its "implausible romance," its reliance on coincidence and its eschewal of indeterminacy – signal to many a problematic lack of commitment to realism.[3] From this perspective, the film is so committed to resolving contradictions, neatly tying up loose ends and celebrating some sort of abstract human victory ("love conquers all") that it sacrifices the complexity and materiality of the worlds it represents. This is the view that criticizes *Slumdog* for being a "feel good" film and one explicitly full of "sentimentality."[4] The assumption here is that realism is the only mode capable of depicting the lived experiences of the city and the tensions of social change, and of challenging hegemonic ideological frameworks.[5]

Yet critiques of the film's representation of the Indian city and its lack of realism suffer from an insufficient language from which to read and interpret melodramatic films and to see how images of slums, poverty and violence might function within fantasy plots. Popular film does not have a straightforward relationship with dominant ideology. Instead, the meaning of cinematic representation is mediated through the various parts of which it is constituted, so that plot, genre and aesthetic conventions exist in a dynamic relationship with ideology, at times supporting it, while at other moments undercutting it as well.[6]

In this paper we show how, despite its eschewal of realist conventions, *Slumdog* offers a theory of urban navigation which questions dominant narratives about the all-encompassing power of globalization. It does this by asserting the importance of an alternative realm of knowledge outside of the formal domains of the state. We suggest that attention to the specific authorial and generic histories out of which *Slumdog* emerges complicates a reading of the film in terms of familiar East-West encounters, and shows the film to in fact engender a critical perspective on the Third World city. By constructing a fictional world where the ability to move around and through the city is privileged over institutionalized knowledge (cf. Howell, McFarlane), *Slumdog* offers a reconsideration of the problem of the Third World city in the context of intensified transnational connections.

This paper thus responds to the overdetermined ways in which critics tend to treat melodramatic films as cultural forms always, from the outset, to be viewed with suspicion. As we show, situating a film like *Slumdog* within specific aesthetic histories has the potential to illuminate certain epistemological positions that exist within it, which a prejudice against its formulaic qualities has the potential to foreclose. We suggest that popular aesthetic forms work not only by providing a total picture of an already existing reality but also by conveying an immanent reality or one that is potentially possible. This becomes relevant in contexts such as the fast-moving, Third World megalopolis, in which possibility is a concrete sensibility that infuses and even constitutes the experience of daily life.

Slumdog's Urban Vision

Slumdog Millionaire follows its protagonist, Jamal Malik, along his journey from boyhood to adolescence as he moves from Mumbai's slums to locales around India, and back to Mumbai. There, he works at a call center and finally wins a seat as a contestant on *Who Wants to Be a Millionaire?*, a game show in which he is so successful at answering the questions that he is accused of cheating and is, ultimately, arrested by the show's host. On one hand, Jamal's journey through Mumbai's underbelly is marked by encounters with abusive teachers, anti-Muslim rioters, child beggar gangs, construction mafias and brutal police officers. At the same time, the arc of the plot – what brings these diverse experiences together – is Jamal's decade-long search for his childhood love, Latika. What motivates him to compete in the quiz show is not the financial reward, therefore, but the possibility of being reunited with Latika who, he knows, is an avid fan of the show. The two narratives come together in a series of flashbacks: as Jamal is interrogated by the constable who arrested him, he recalls the experiences in his past which led him to the correct answers.

Critics have generally taken Jamal's winning of *Millionaire*'s top prize amidst a new urban landscape of call centers, consumer spectacles and luxury high-rises to represent a break from the past, a neoliberal optimism, a celebration of values such as individual perseverance and an embrace of a globalized free-market capitalism.[7] As Anand Giridharadas wrote in his jubilant review of the film, *Slumdog* presents "a land of self-makers, where a scruffy son of the slums can, solely of his own effort, hoist himself up, flout his origins, break with fate."[8] Other writers, less enthusiastic about the effects of liberalization, have read Jamal's success in the new consumerist city as a one-sided version of globalization, in which the dominant narrative of rags-to-riches overshadows the systematic exclusion of the poor from its benefits. From this perspective, *Slumdog* "sells a certain dated type of globalism in which the boom times are infinite" and the productive contributions of the poor are invisible.[9] Ironically, and despite these disagreements, critics from both camps understand the film to ultimately be about neoliberal globalization and, moreover, assume globalization to produce not only new landscapes but new risk-taking, profit-maximizing and individualistic urban subjects as well. The fantasy aspect of the story is seen to strip the complex issue of globalization of its contradictions and nuance, leaving a partial and politically compromised parable in its wake.

However, such a reading privileges the narrative arc of the film (Jamal's success on the game show) over attention to the complex moral landscape in which its story is situated. In the scene when Jamal and Salim reunite as adults, for instance, a very different vision of urban reconfiguration emerges. Here, the brothers stand in the skeleton of a half-built luxury apartment building high above the city. In the background is not the older city but the new urban frontier – grassy hills on one side and a Disneyesque neoclassical residential fantasy on the other. His gaze moving swiftly from a small slum to an adjacent sea of glittering new apartment buildings, Salim turns to Jamal and says, "that used to be our slum. Can you believe that, huh?" The camera pans across the new landscape of high-rises – some finished, many unbuilt – as Salim says coolly, "we used to live right there, man. Now, it's all business. India is at the center of the world now, *bhai*. And I [...] I am at the center of the center. This is *all* Javed-*bhai*'s" (Fig. 5.1). Although critics have read this scene as celebrating globalization, it is significant that the words are spoken by Salim, whose morality is severely compromised. Moreover, by registering Mumbai's new globalized spaces as the personal property of Javed, the local mafia don, Salim demonstrates how the new consumer spectacles of the city overlap with, and are enabled by, already existing informal and unofficial knowledge and networks of power, some of which are premised on the very kinds of brutal violence from which Jamal has struggled to escape. From this perspective, the slum and the high-rise apartment building, despite their radically divergent outward physical appearances, are represented as built on the same informal networks of authority.

Figure 5.1. Salim and Jamal looking out over the new urban landscape.

By introducing Salim (backed by Javed) as a paradigmatic entrepreneur within Mumbai's rise to global status, the film not only satirizes claims of globalization's democratic core but, more importantly, identifies a new kind of subject: the urban navigator, the individual who works his/her way through the underbelly of the transforming city, seeking out a path for survival by mobilizing whatever opportunities and limitations are thrown in his/her path. This character is not, of course, unique to *Slumdog*; a similar figure is elaborated, for instance, in Balram of Aravind Adiga's 2008 novel, *The White Tiger*. The urban navigator might be seen as a minor counterpart to the more powerful, well-connected "urban specialist" described by Hansen and Verkaaik, and embodied in *Slumdog*'s Javed.[10] Although he is Salim's moral inverse, Jamal also travels along a similar route and, from the very beginning, his success within the narrative is also premised on deftly navigating both the innocent and the violent landscapes of the city. Salim and Jamal are thus not merely victims of their underdeveloped circumstances – of poverty, violence, and corruption – but offer two different models of how to mobilize these conditions to their respective advantage.

Dystopic Narratives

The aesthetic resources out of which the figure of the urban navigator is constituted do not come only from the urban Indian context but emerge out of the particular filmic eye of *Slumdog*'s director, Danny Boyle. The connection is evident in Boyle's 1996 film, *Trainspotting*, which can be read as a proto-text for *Slumdog*. As an indictment of the social decay of post-Thatcherite capitalism, *Trainspotting* follows the aimless wanderings of a group of young men whose only release from their stifling environment comes in the form of heroin. Set in a depressed suburb of Edinburgh, Scotland, "with its run-down council estates, dilapidated flats, seedy betting shops, appalling toilets, smoke-filled pubs and loud clubs," the film constructs a bleak geography of social alienation and meaninglessness, symbolized through the eponymic activity of trainspotting, which "is intended to be a metaphor for shooting heroin and the obsessional, senseless nature of the addict's life."[11] As such, the film offers a representation of "the voice of the disaffected, the postmodern, postindustrial Scottish junkie-as-critic."[12]

What Boyle brings to the oft-told story of post-industrial Britain is a disturbing aesthetic comprised of a disjointed material world that is itself a product of social alienation. *Trainspotting*'s visual expression is thus a sickened, dilated filmic gaze in which even a baby appears grotesque, like a doll in a horror movie (Fig. 5.2). Moreover, classic interior spaces associated with domesticity and a refuge from the harshness of the urban landscape are represented by way of a disruptive malleability. For instance, the protagonist Renton's withdrawal-induced hallucinations are expressed in the morphing of the interiors of his room. Another character, Spud, his body already distorted by his social marginality, is also subject to such hallucinations: the way the plate of fry-up erupts into the frame to emphasize its nausea-inducing effect on a hungover morning; or the "exaggerated distances in [his] [job] interview."[13] The most iconic of the film's scenes is perhaps where Renton descends deep into his excrement-filled toilet bowl to find the heroin suppositories he had accidentally excreted. The setting is so filthy that Renton wretches as he reaches into the toilet bowl but, as he pushes through he finds that he can enter the bowl itself and swim through the plumbing to find what he had lost (Fig. 5.3). The scene suggests a kind of dystopic parody on urban transcendence, and the accompaniment of Brian Eno's "Deep Blue Day" – a surreal and haunting melody manifestly unsuited for this unpalatable journey down the toilet pipes – only underlines its absurd banality.

Using the same filmic eye in *Slumdog*, Boyle offers a significantly different urban vision from this post-industrial dystopia. In *Slumdog*'s opening sequence, for example, as in *Trainspotting*, the malleability of space reflects particular locations of underprivilege in the city. Beginning with a group of policemen chasing slum boys off an airport tarmac, the camera alternates between the policeman's gaze as they turn into the winding alleyways of the adjacent slum and the boys' gazes as they look back at the policemen to monitor their pursuit. But as the chase gains energy, the camera tilts upwards at times to be caught in the sunlight, or veers to the side to explore a woman dyeing clothes over

Figure 5.2. Images in Boyle's *Trainspotting* bend to reflect the distorted minds of its protagonists.

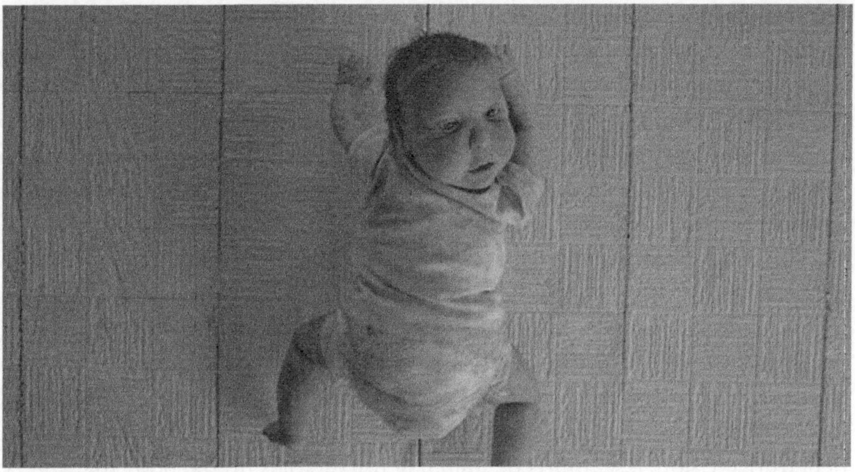

Figure 5.3. A dystopic parody on urban transcendence – Renton descends into the toilet bowl.

a sewer pipe, or a man working on wires, before panning back to the boys' escaping forms. The momentary arresting of the viewer's gaze with these images heightens the contrast between "insider" and "outsider" – with the boys on the one hand, clearly aware of every turn and cranny in the maze-like slum structure, and the viewer and the policeman, unwittingly brought together by their shared ignorance, on the other. Early in the film, therefore, the ability to move in space is linked to the knowledge of the details of urban space, with the panting obesity of the policeman as only an exterior manifestation of the state's ignorance of the intricate, inhabited mazes of city (slum) life.

This spatialization of the police chase inverts conventional hierarchies between police and suspect, and the state and its subjects more generally. Ranjani Mazumdar describes a police chase scene in the film *Black Friday* (dir. Anurag Kashyap, 2004) in which police similarly follow a suspect "through squalor, wires, alleyways, water pipes, underground tunnels, train tracks, and more."[14] But here, "[t]he chase exists [...] as a marker of this desire for a penetrative vision, a scanning of spatial density to pick up the body that will be brutalized for more testimony and confession. No matter how dense the space is, the cops manage to penetrate the layers and the camera strives to capture this process of unraveling."[15] Unsurprisingly then, in *Black Friday*, the extended chase ends in the capturing of the terrorist, where he is "finally picked up, slapped, and taken away for what is perhaps the most brutal form of police torture."[16] Here the camera works alongside the violent and panoptic eye of the state. This marks a significant contrast to the chase scene in *Slumdog*. By presenting the policemen as outsiders, by refusing them the penetrating vision of the camera and the state, and by eclipsing any eventual capture, Boyle's film tells a very different story of the relationship between power and urban navigation.

But it is the transformation of Renton's journey through the pipes of his toilet in *Trainspotting* into a jubilant scene in *Slumdog* that most clearly highlights the contrasting cinematic visions of Boyle's two urban landscapes. Jamal, in the midst of relieving himself in a communal latrine, hears about the impending arrival of Amitabh Bachchan's helicopter. Knowing he desperately wants to see this film hero, his brother torments Jamal by jamming shut the latrine door. With no other option, Jamal holds his nose and jumps into the excrement-filled swamp below the row of latrines and makes his way, covered in feces, to witness Amitabh Bachchan's landing. Clear differences with the parallel scene in *Trainspotting* emerge: while *Trainspotting*'s brief respite from the dystopic reality of post-industrial urban decay serves to highlight the squalid physicality of inhabiting the city (with Renton's squelching footprints as a literalized trace of this oppressive stasis), Jamal's much more deliberate path through the mass of urban waste leads him straight to the feet of a much more

Figure 5.4. A feces-covered Jamal navigating through the crowd to reach the star.

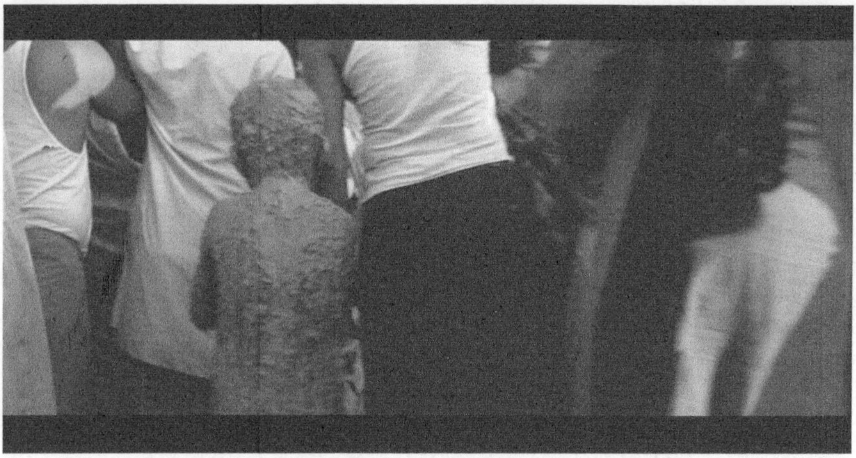

fantastical creation: the biggest star in Hindi film history. This juxtaposition of the most sordid physical manifestation of urban marginality (the open latrines) with the powerful momentum of navigation is here literalized in the way in which Jamal's path through the crowd of onlookers opens up for him merely by dint of his excrement-covered body (Fig. 5.4): here, in a repetition of the movement we saw earlier in the slum chase scene, feces becomes a parodic commentary on mobility by way of under-travelled routes. These scenes serve as crucial indications that, despite its setting in the so-called Third World, *Slumdog* is not in fact a film about the "most wretched, miserable, servile, pathetic trash that was ever shat in civilization," as Renton describes his own world in *Trainspotting*;[17] rather, it is about the productive mobilizations of marginality (here symbolized by shit) for navigating urban life.

In a way, then, *Trainspotting*'s Scotland fares much worse than *Slumdog*'s Mumbai in Boyle's filmic vision. Boyle recasts *Trainspotting*'s alienation, stagnation and immobility into a vision of knowledge, navigation and momentum. Whereas both films focus on capitalism's underside, Scotland lacks Mumbai's redemptive possibilities. With a sense of suffocation and subterranean squalor a guiding topos, *Trainspotting* paints a bleak, static and even decaying picture of the post-industrial urban Scottish landscape. By contrast, *Slumdog* represents less a meditation on urban dystopia than an experimental expression of urban possibility.

Yet critics have failed to recognize this continuity with Boyle's earlier work and instead highlight what many see as *Slumdog*'s dystopic perspective on the city which emphasizes its dysfunction – in which, for instance, the coexistence of "cooking and child-rearing and defecation [as] semi-public activities" indexes a world "where it would be hard to develop the mental independence to question an arranged marriage or abuse by the better-born."[18] In one of the more informed critiques of the film, urban researchers Matias Echanove and Rahul Srivastava argue that *Slumdog*'s representation of the Indian slum ignores its ethos of activity, and paints a negative – and ultimately inaccurate – picture instead:

> Its depiction as a slum does little justice to the reality of Dharavi. Well over a million "eyes on the street," to use Jane Jacobs's phrase, keep Dharavi perhaps safer than most American cities. Yet Dharavi's extreme population density doesn't translate into oppressiveness. The crowd is efficiently absorbed by the thousands of tiny streets branching off bustling commercial arteries. Also, you won't be chased by beggars or see hopeless people loitering – Dharavi is probably the most active and lively part of an incredibly industrious city. People have learned to respond in creative ways to the indifference of the state – including having set up a highly functional recycling industry that serves the whole city.[19]

Here Echanove and Srivastava articulate an essential fact about Mumbai slums that is rarely conveyed in the international press: their centrality to the economic and social life of the city. And yet, in their justified desire to make this argument, the authors overlook the fact the slum they describe – of beggars, hopelessness, loitering and oppressiveness – never appears in *Slumdog*. The imagined slum of *Slumdog* is the opposite: full of energy, industry and life. The terrible violence that does occur in the film – the anti-Muslim pogrom that forces Jamal to go on the run, for instance – is instigated by outside forces, and the film's most graphic violence (the eye-gouging scene) takes place in an orphanage on the city's outskirts. By contrast, the slum itself is constituted by a powerful and energetic spatial politics that is even strong enough, however momentarily, to contest the invasive arm of the state.

This is not, by contrast, the case with *Q & A*, the novel by Vikas Swarup on which *Slumdog* is based. In Swarup's novel, the slum does indeed take on dystopic form, much as described by Echanove and Srivastava. In a representative passage, *Q & A*'s narrator writes:

> I am not alone in Dharavi. There are a million people like me, packed in a two-hundred-hectare triangle of swampy urban wasteland, where we live like animals and die like insects [...] Dharavi is not a place for the squeamish [...] Dharavi's grim landscape of urban squalor deadens and debases us. Its open drains teem with mosquitoes. Its stinking, excrement-lined communal latrines are full of rats, which make you think less about the smell and more about protecting your

> backside. Mounds of filthy garbage lie on every corner, from which ragpickers still manage to find something useful. And at times you have to suck in your breath to squeeze through its narrow claustrophobic alleys. But for the starving residents of Dharavi, this is home. Amid the modern skyscrapers and neon-lit shopping complexes of Mumbai, Dharavi sits like a cancerous lump in the heart of the city.[20]

The fact that Boyle reinterprets Swarup's representation of the slum from a cancer which stifles and slowly kills the city to a space of energy and possibility is essential to his urban vision. In fact, it is this sense of possibility, initiated in these early scenes, that occupies the central thematics of the story as the film progresses. As we will see, the sporadic urban navigation of the young boy will find form in the logic of the quiz show, played and won by the young man.

Knowing the Questions and the Question of Knowing

The game show is the central plot element of *Slumdog* and, as such, the site at which the film's concern with navigating the city emerges and develops most fully. The game show is also the part of the film that seems to epitomize its most melodramatic elements, as it offers a narrative of "rank implausibility" based on the unlikely fact that Jamal knows the answer to almost every question the show asks of him.[21] Whereas most critics have used the quiz show as a reason to dismiss the film, seeing the plot event as another form of urban navigation pushes us to see how in fact even an "unrealistic" story might illuminate questions of central relevance to the problematics of urban India.[22]

Part of the misreading of the quiz show among critics emerges from the assumption that a show such as *Who Wants to Be a Millionaire?* tests knowledge that would never be accessible to someone like Jamal, largely excluded from schools, universities and other institutions of knowledge. By this token, his success on the show can only be an element of pure fantasy. But close attention to how such quiz shows actually work questions this assumption. Quiz shows in fact appeal to wide audiences precisely because they "reduce the value of knowledge to the memorization of fragmented and desultory facts and their rapid recall under pressure."[23] In this way, "by mixing different topics in one series of questions, [they] […] dismantle hierarchical bodies of knowledge into miscellaneous fragments."[24] Moreover, in standard quiz shows, as the questions increase in value, they move progressively from specialized to general knowledge – the latter drawn from a repertoire "so large that exhaustive revision is impossible."[25] In other words, the easiest questions are the ones that rely most upon formal education, whereas the most difficult ones rely on the most general (and thus more random) kinds of knowledge that would have to be "acquired incidentally and over a very long period."[26] To win the top prize in such a show, a contestant must have luck – not luck in the sense of randomly guessing the correct answer but the peculiar luck of having randomly encountered the piece of trivia somewhere in his/her past. The site of such an encounter is most likely in the informal sphere, rather than through educational training. In this way victory on a quiz show – like urban navigation itself – requires a mix of formal and informal knowledge, but cannot be gained in any one domain alone.

Thus Jamal, as someone who has had little formal education but a wealth of experience in the informal realm, finds the earlier questions more difficult than the supposedly harder ones. For instance, he is compelled to use an audience poll for the second question, which is simple by formal standards: "A picture of three lions is seen in the national emblem of India. What is written underneath?" Jamal answers correctly only because the audience votes overwhelmingly for the correct answer – "The Truth Alone Triumphs." He explains the irony to the constable who ridicules him for not knowing the answer to such an easy question:

Constable: My five-year-old daughter can answer that question, but you couldn't. That's strange for a millionaire genius. What happened? Your accomplice nip out for a piss?
Jamal: How much is pani puri at Harish's stall in Chowpatty?
C: What?
J: One plate. How much?
C: Ten rupees.
J: Wrong. Fifteen since Diwali. Who stole Constable Verma's bicycle outside Santa Cruz station last Thursday?
C: You know who that was?
J: Everyone in Juhu knows that. Even five-year-olds.

Here, knowing the cost of daily items and the culprit behind a bicycle theft calls into question society's valorization of formal over informal knowledge. Jamal presents a scenario in which informal knowledge is valuable to the policeman, and thereby destabilizes the hierarchy between them. The fortuitous aspect of the game show for Jamal, then, is not that he unrealistically knows all the answers to the questions, but that the institutionalized knowledge tested by the game show coincides – with the exception of a few early questions, such as the national emblem one – with the "intersubjectively valuable" knowledge he has picked up from his life outside the formal domains of urban habitation.[27] The picture on a $100 bill, the tool Lord Rama holds in his right hand, the name of the blind *bhajan* writer – these bits of trivia are known to Jamal because he has undergone experiences that enabled him, often in dystopic ways, to learn them. This is the plot manifestation of the aesthetic premise we saw developed earlier: the ability to mobilize undertravelled pathways in order to navigate an otherwise hostile urban landscape. This skill is double-edged: Jamal has paid a harsh price for the knowledge of these answers, and at one point he admits, although describing how he answered a quiz question correctly, "I wake up every morning wishing I didn't know the answer to that question." But even such negative experiences are seen as part of the rich lived experience of the city by its underclass, dismantling traditional hierarchies of knowledge. As the constable demurs, "doctors, lawyers, PhDs couldn't answer these questions, but you could?"

Thus while critics see Jamal's unrealistic success on the show as ideologically overdetermined, as a means of celebrating the new possibilities brought by globalization and neoliberalism, they overlook the significant fact that Danny Boyle uses the game-show format to show how Jamal navigates the violent urban landscape by mobilizing particular forms of knowledge disavowed by the neoliberal state. In this way, the fantasy of *Slumdog* lies not simply in his victory on the game show, but in a utopian space where the knowledge gained from living in the city's underbelly has actual monetary value. The unrealistic aspect of its ending is not in Jamal winning the top prize or achieving a rags-to-riches fantasy but, instead, in a fictional world where lived knowledge of the city can achieve the same cultural validation as its institutionalized counterpart. This world does not exist, but by outlining its contours the film makes clear its investment in a more democratic urban landscape, precisely through its unrealistic plot and structure.

Ironically, critics who interpret the game show narrative as unbelievable end up aligning themselves with the constable and the morally corrupt game show host, both of whom refuse to believe that Jamal could actually know the answers to such difficult questions. The constable's disgust – "What the hell can a slumdog possibly know?" – is unwittingly replicated in critical views that dismiss Jamal's knowledge as an unrealistic plot device. Indeed, besides knowledge, the constable's violent words enact a closing down of possibility itself, collapsed into the term's most limited adverbial form: "possibly" as something doubtful, worthy of surprise and shock, rather than as something potential, on the horizon, imminent. And by denying non-realist forms any access to representing truth – including the truth of the possible – the critics make the same mistake.

Conclusion

The prejudicial view that only through realism can a work of art offer a meaningful interpretation of the city is based on a misunderstanding of the way genre works. Reliance on formulaic or unrealistic elements does not, in fact, preclude engagements with the struggles of "real" people, but puts those struggles in relief by offering a way to read them within larger social paradigms. Here, those paradigms are epitomized by the game show, and it is only by energizing them with the logic of urban navigation that Jamal can emerge victorious by the end of the film. It is significant, in this regard, that in the same year as *Slumdog*'s Academy Award wins, a film about rural Indian children receiving surgery to fix cleft palates won the Oscar for best documentary short. The film, entitled *Smile Pinki* (dir. Megan Mylan, 2008), was marketed as "A Real-World Fairy Tale," as it showed "a journey from isolation to embrace" through the story of a young disfigured girl whose life is changed when she receives the simple rehabilitative surgery.[28] Indeed, critics have pointed out the fallacy of documentary happy endings as well – another example being the 2004 Oscar-winning documentary *Born Into Brothels*.[29] Yet these critiques are directed primarily at the "fictionalization" of true stories, of making actual lives aesthetically pleasing for the sake of art. The assumptions behind this criticism are clear: the less fictionalized a story, the more true. This is the epistemological standpoint that views *Slumdog*'s utopic landscape with suspicion. In many ways, *Slumdog* is the converse of *Smile Pinki*: it is, if anything, a fairy-world real tale – in which truth is accessed precisely through its fantasy. Though founded upon a highly improbable circumstance, the film nevertheless tells us something about the contemporary urban world.

Notes

1 "Bollywood icon Amitabh Bachchan rubbishes Slumdog Millionaire," *Guardian*, 14 January 2009. Online: http://www.guardian.co.uk/film/2009/jan/14/amitabh-bachchan-rubbishes-slumdog-millionaire (accessed 4 October 2011).

2 Canby, "Patrick Swayze Down and Out in Calcutta," *New York Times*, 15 April 1992. Online: http://movies.nytimes.com/movie/review?res=9E0CEEDC1F3DF936A2575 7C0A964958260 (accessed 16 March 2010). Poonam Arora similarly writes of *Salaam Bombay*, "Despite the veneer of documentary realism, 'Bombay' as locale functions merely as a representative, and therefore interchangeable, Third World city anywhere, and Chaipau, as protagonist, functions as any oppressed Third World subject" ("The Production of Third World Subjects for First World Consumption: *Salaam Bombay* and *Parama*," in *Multiple Voices in Feminist Film Criticism*, edited by Diane Carson, Linda Dittmar, Janice R. Welsch. Minneapolis: University of Minnesota Press, 1994), 294–5.

3 Shakuntala Banaji, "Seduced 'Outsiders' Versus Sceptical 'Insiders'?: *Slumdog Millionaire* Through Its Re/Viewers," *Participations* 7.1 (2010): 15.

4 See Vrinda Nabar, "Slumdog Millionaire Bizarrely Plausible?" *DNA*, 10 January 2009. Online: http://www.dnaindia.com/opinion/main-article_slumdog-millionaire-bizarrely plausible_1220495 (accessed 7 May 2010); and J. M. Tyree, "Against the Clock: *Slumdog Millionaire* and the *Curious Case of Benjamin Button*." *Film Quarterly* 62.4 (2009): 34.

5 A related prejudice is in favor of the purity of genre, leading some critics to decry *Slumdog* for "want[ing] to have it both ways by allowing images of actual horror to seep into a Bollywood-like dream and then letting us off the hook by suggesting not only that true love conquers all, but also that personal decency might well result in a multimillion-dollar payday [...] There is a contradiction between what the film tells us about how the universe operates and what it shows us about abject poverty" (Tyree, "Against the Clock," 36). Likewise: "A slippery and self-conscious concoction, *Slumdog* has it both ways. It makes a show of being anchored in a real-world social context, then asks to be read as a fantasy. It ladles on brutality only to dispel it with frivolity" (Dennis Lim, "What, Exactly, Is *Slumdog Millionaire*?" *Slate*, 26 January 2009. Online: http://www.slate.com/id/2209783/pagenum/all/#p2 (accessed 7 May 2010)).

6 We discuss in more detail the relationship between textual elements, generic conventions and social critique in "Text, Genre, Society" (Anjaria and Anjaria, "Text, Genre, Society: Hindi youth films and postcolonial desire," *South Asian Popular Culture* 6.2 (2008): esp. 126–131).

7 Nandini Chandra, "Slumlord Aesthetics and the Question of Indian Poverty," included in this volume; Bernard Beck, "Angels With Dirty Faces: Who Invited *Slumdog Millionaire* and *The Visitor*?" *Multicultural Perspectives* 11.3 (2009): 149.

8 Anand Giridharadas, "Horatio Alger Relocates to a Mumbai Slum," *New York Times*, 17 January 2009. Online: http://www.nytimes.com/2009/01/18/weekinreview/18giridharadas.html (accessed 27 January 2012).

9 Tyree, "Against the Clock," 35; Chandra, "Slumlord Aesthetics," included in this volume.

10 Thomas Blom Hansen and Oskar Verkaaik, "Urban Charisma: On everyday mythologies in the city," *Critique of Anthropology* 29.5 (2009): 16. Howell makes this point in a different context, discussing "the urban detective, who is really a kind of active flaneur able to conquer the physical and epistemological anxieties of the city not merely through a voyeuristic illusion of intelligibility, but also through the active creation of order, the mastering of the urban environment" ("Crime and the City Solution: Crime fiction, urban knowledge, and radical geography," *Antipode* 30.4 (1998): 361).

11 Murray Smith, "Transnational Trainspotting," in *The Media in Britain: Current Debates and Developments*, edited by Jane Stokes, Anna Reading (Houndmills: Macmillan, 1999), 224; Bert Cardullo, "Fiction Into Film, or Bringing Welsh to a Boyle," *Literature/ Film Quarterly* 25.3 (1997): 159.

12 Grant Farred, "Wankerdom: *Trainspotting* as a rejection of the postcolonial?" *South Atlantic Quarterly* 103.1 (2004): 217.

13 Smith, "Transnational Trainspotting," 223, 225.

14 Ranjani Mazumdar, "Terrorism, Conspiracy, and Surveillance in Bombay's Urban Cinema," *Social Research* 78.1 (2011): 154.

15 Ibid.

16 Ibid.

17 Quoted in Smith, "Transnational Trainspotting," 219.

18 Giridharadas, "Horatio Alger."

19 Echanove and Srivastava, "Taking the Slum Out of 'Slumdog,'" *New York Times*, 21 February 2009. Online: http://www.nytimes.com/2009/02/21/opinion/21srivastava.html (accessed 27 January 2012). In an argument similar to that of Echanove and Srivastava, Mitu Sengupta argues that *Slumdog* misrepresents the slum "as a feral wasteland, with little evidence or order, community or compassion. Other than the

children, no one is even remotely well-intentioned. Hustlers and petty warlords run amok, and even Jamal's schoolteacher is inexplicably callous. This is a place of sheer evil and decay" ("A Hollow Message of Social Justice: *Slumdog Millionaire*'s dehumanizing view of India's poor," *Counterpunch*, February 20, 2009. Online: http://www.counterpunch.org/sengupta02202009.html (accessed 7 May 2010). See also Sengupta's essay in this volume.)

20 Swarup, *Q & A* (New York: Scribner, 2005), 133–4.

21 Lim, "What, Exactly, Is *Slumdog Millionaire*?"

22 In a similar vein, Fredric Jameson elucidates a counterintuitive relationship between fantasy and realism in his reading of the "utopic realism" of David Simon's *The Wire* (see also Gehlawat, *Reframing Bollywood: Theories of Popular Hindi Cinema* (New Delhi: Sage, 2010), 138n26). Jameson points to specific moments in the show in which "*The Wire* can be observed to be ceasing to replicate a static reality or to be 'realist' in the traditional mimetic and replicative sense. Here [i.e., in these moments] society, on microlevels of various dimensions, is finding itself subject to deliberate processes of transformation, to human projects, to the working out of Utopian intentions that are not simply the forces of gravity of habit and tradition" ("Realism and Utopia in *The Wire*," *Criticism* 52.3–4 (2010): 365). It is precisely these moments of possibility that inflect the series' realism with a utopic political vision, even when the surface text is so bleak.

23 Amir Hetsroni, "The Millionaire Project: A Cross-Cultural Analysis of Quiz Shows From the United States, Russia, Poland, Norway, Finland, Israel, and Saudi Arabia," *Mass Communication and Society* 7.2 (2004): 140.

24 Ibid., 140–41.

25 Elizabeth A. Maylor, "Ageing and the Retrieval of Specialized and General Knowledge: Performance of *Masterminds*," *British Journal of Psychology* 85 (1994): 106.

26 Ibid.

27 Colin McFarlane, *Learning the City: Knowledge and Translocal Assemblage* (Oxford: Wiley-Blackwell, 2011), 175.

28 Smile Pinki website. Online: http://www.smilepinki.com (accessed 27 January 2012).

29 For a critique of the redemptive assumptions of *Born Into Brothels*, see Partha Banerjee's letter to the Academy of Motion Picture Arts and Sciences, "Documentary 'Born Into Brothels' and the Oscars: an insider's point of view," Mukto-Mona. Online: http://www.mukto-mona.com/Articles/partha_ban/born_into_brothels.htm (accessed 27 January 2012).

Chapter 6

A MILLION DOLLAR EXIT FROM THE SLUM-WORLD: *SLUMDOG MILLIONAIRE*'S TROUBLING FORMULA FOR SOCIAL JUSTICE

Mitu Sengupta

Soon upon its release in December 2008, *Slumdog Millionaire* (hereafter *Slumdog*), a rags-to-riches story about a fictional Mumbai slum dweller, Jamal Malik, took its place among the most celebrated films of our times. Riding on a wave of rave reviews, the film won Hollywood's highest tribute in February 2009, the Academy Award for Best Picture, along with seven more Oscars, including one for British filmmaker Danny Boyle as Best Director. The film earned effusive praise not only for being an enjoyable work of fiction, which it arguably is, but for its potential to give voice to poor and marginalized children such as Jamal, the slumdogs born and raised in India's slums. This essay takes issue with the latter expectation, arguing that, given *Slumdog*'s reductive and demeaning depictions of slums and slum dwellers, there is a much stronger likelihood that the film will work against the interests of those who live and work in India's slums, lending justification to policies that only deepen their distress.[1]

Slumdog depicts the slum as a feral wasteland, a place of evil and decay that is devoid of order, productivity and compassion.[2] Glossing over many indicators of community solidarity and organized political resistance among slum dwellers, it privileges only haphazard and individualistic forms of agency. The film's explanation of poverty and violence is also purely localized and individualized. Indeed, by dividing humanity into the good and evil, lucky and unlucky, *Slumdog* does little to question the structures of material inequality that define Northern development and empire, and, in the bargain, also reinforces the representational inequality of an Orientalist and commodified view of extant cultures and spaces of struggle. The conceptualization of slums as worthless, self-contained spaces by a film of *Slumdog*'s popularity and stature is worrying, in that it extends legitimacy to the sorts of interventions – undemocratically-conceived and environmentally destructive land-grab schemes – that enable what David Harvey terms "accumulation by dispossession," a process that has undergirded "the new imperialism."[3]

Slumdog, as a film, makes little attempt to draw on the lived experiences of local residents in a meaningful way, and thus appears designed to validate the values, ideologies and ways of life associated with Northern "development" and the West. Surprisingly, however, its colonialist assumptions have largely escaped questioning by India's vociferous mass media, which have celebrated the film's staggering success as India's own.[4] In the penultimate section of this paper, I explore the intriguing question of why criticism of *Slumdog* in India has not moved beyond a few snarling commentaries inspired by feelings of wounded national pride that have objected not to the film's debasing portrayal of slum spaces and slum inhabitants, but to the notion that a foreigner has relayed an unflattering tale of Indian poverty to a large, global audience.[5] I also compare *Slumdog* with Roland Joffe's *City of Joy* (1992), arguing that unlike the easily palpable and arrogant Orientalism of such older films, *Slumdog*'s culturalization of poverty is harder to detect, given the absence of white bodies and an obvious narrative of superior Western culture. *Slumdog*'s culturalization of poverty is new also in that the film utterly disregards the labor struggles of the poor and unabashedly celebrates consumer capitalism. In these and other ways, as I suggest below, *Slumdog* represents a thoroughly neoliberal moment.

Why Film? Why *Slumdog*?

The movie camera has arguably had a tremendous impact on international public perceptions of places beyond their own. Films offer potential visitors a set of images about a country even before they arrive and, at times, compensate for visits altogether, leaving viewers with a sense of familiarity, even memories, about places they may never actually encounter. Yet "roaming about with the camera is not value-free."[6] Film and photography call to mind important questions of who is looking at whom; of the relationship between the object/culture of the camera's gaze, and the subject/culture involved in the gazing. The relationship is often one of unequal power, with the subject/culture producing images of an object/culture that lacks the power to produce its own images. This is nowhere more evident than when filmmakers in the affluent North create films about the South primarily for affluent Northern audiences. "The magic carpet provided by [film] flies us around the globe and makes us, by virtue of our subject position, its audio-visual masters," producing us as subjects, and "affirming our sense of power while making the inhabitants of the Third World objects of spectacle for the First World's voyeuristic gaze."[7]

Many popular and critically acclaimed films produced in the North, such as *Gandhi* (1982), *The Constant Gardner* (2005) and *Blood Diamond* (2006), are based on Third World struggles against imperialism, poverty, corruption and so on. Over time, they have created an extensive repertoire of images about the South that has considerable bearing on how Northern audiences view the South and, arguably, on how Southern elites see their own subalterns. These films' claims to realism and giving voice to the South's downtrodden, however, are premised on the flawed idea that the camera is but "a simple extension of sight."[8] The failure to acknowledge the interpretive choices and moralities of the producers, directors, actors and audiences involved in the making and consumption of such films has led to the normalization and growing hegemony of various disingenuous narratives about struggles for social justice in the South, which tend to reflect what the North expects or needs from the South rather than how Southern subalterns might articulate their own problems.

As I argue in this paper, *Slumdog* is one film that will accelerate the dissemination of such problematic narratives, as it represents a specific commercial genre of Hollywood movies that carries colossal appeal. Its triumphs at the box office, critics' corner and awards circuit will secure its place in thousands of audiovisual outlets, from the Ivy League university to the local strip mall.[9] Within a year or two, it will probably feature routinely on television, its feel good story being perfect for the holiday season. In fact, UK's Channel Four commissioned and funded a documentary by Nick Read, *The Slumdog Children of Mumbai* (see slumdogchildren.org), whose release was to coincide with the UK television premiere of *Slumdog* in January 2010. Indeed, for tens of thousands of moviegoers in the North, *Slumdog* – and its various spin-offs – will possibly be their one and only visual of the Indian slum, shaping public perceptions to an extent that less mainstream though more complex films on the subject cannot hope to do, even those, like *Slumdog*, that are produced outside India and packaged primarily for Western consumption, such as Mira Nair's *Salaam Bombay!* (1988) and Chris Smith's *The Pool* (2007).

Based loosely on Vikas Swarup's novel, *Q & A*, *Slumdog* chronicles the journey of Jamal, a young slum dweller, as he navigates through a wretched childhood spent amid desperate poverty to become a star contestant on the Indian version of the American game show, *Who Wants to Be a Millionaire?* (hereafter *Millionaire*).[10] The film cleverly shuttles between scenes of Jamal in the *Millionaire* hot seat and flashbacks from his earlier life. He knows the answer to eight of *Millionaire*'s nine questions because they resonate with one harrowing event or another he has personally experienced, such as the murder of his young mother by marauding Hindu extremists, an incident that leaves him and his brother, Salim, destitute and orphaned.[11] Jamal is apparently destined to win the show's jackpot of 20 million rupees. Although he does not know the answer to the final question, he guesses it correctly, following a joyful reunion with Latika, a lost childhood companion, for whom he has spent much of his life yearning. Though obviously far-fetched, *Slumdog*'s fast-paced love story makes for an entertaining movie that has the feel of a slickly produced music video. Yet praise for *Slumdog* has stretched far beyond an understandable appreciation of its ability to regale.

Slumdog's cast and crew have helped propagate the idea that the film accurately conveys the harsh realities of Mumbai's slum life and, moreover, that it was inspired by a noble aim, and can thus be put to good use. Several of the Oscars won by *Slumdog* were accepted in the name of the children, and the child actors who played Jamal, Salim and Latika in the first third of the film – and who actually live in Dharavi, a slum in Mumbai – were paraded about the awards ceremony in tuxedos and colorful frocks.[12] Critics, too, have followed suit. "The film's universal appeal will present the real India to millions of moviegoers for the first time," gushed Roger Ebert even before *Slumdog*'s commercial release.[13] *Rolling Stone* applauded the film for its "no-bull honesty,"[14] and the *Washington Post* for its "unflinching portrait of India's abject poverty, crime, corruption and communal tensions."[15] A columnist with the *Huffington Post* – a popular webzine – waved aside criticism of *Slumdog*'s plot absurdities, and asserted: "what really matters is that this film has focused attention on the poverty that's so prevalent in this part of the world. This creates a unique opportunity to leverage the success of this Best Picture winner into action [...] Popular culture has proved an awesome agent of change throughout history [...] [It] can shock, educate and, yes, even entertain people into taking action for a compelling cause."[16]

While this paper does not dispute the connection between popular culture and taking action, it asks why this connection must be drawn so flatly, without any consideration of who produces cultural texts like film, why, and for whose consumption? The call to action on behalf of the downtrodden inspired by a film may have little or no relation to how the downtrodden in question might explain their own condition or articulate their needs. All films about Southern struggles are not equal, as it is often assumed. Indeed, my objection to *Slumdog* is not that it exposes the ugly underside of Indian poverty to a global audience – such poverty does exist and its story should be told – but that it tells a misleading story of this poverty, and of resistance to this poverty, that does little service to the poor but, rather, lends legitimacy to policies, practices and attitudes that further undermine their dignity and agency. "The cinema," as Gilles Deleuze has noted, "does not just present images. It surrounds them with a world."[17] In *Slumdog*'s case, it is the representation of this world that is problematic.

The Anarchic Slum-World

Boyle delivers the most crucial aspects of his story through a kaleidoscope of rapidly shuffling images of Mumbai's slum-life. In a series of long-distance and overhead shots, the camera glides above tattered tarpaulin-covered roofs of flimsy shacks, dingy alleyways, open drains, pools of excrement, and mounds and mounds of garbage. Jamal and other slum children are seen playing, working and even sleeping in the all-encompassing filth. *Slumdog*'s shifting panoramas of grimness call to mind Edward Said's observation, that one of the enduring techniques through which the "inscrutable" Orient is delivered to the Occident is surveillance from a distance, with "the aim of getting hold of the whole sprawling panorama before him [...] every detail [is seen] through the device of a set of reductive categories."[18] Differences are diminished, and the Orient is reduced to a homogeneous space, defined only by markers that convey a sense of a malfunctioning social and political system. The camera's close-up shots only add to an all-pervading feeling of chaos and evil. The audience witnesses the brutal blinding of one of Jamal's childhood friends by Maman, a fiendish criminal who runs a gang of child-beggars (Maman believes that disfiguring the child will improve his income potential as a singing beggar), and also Jamal's merciless torture in a grimy backroom of a Mumbai police station (in an effort to make Jamal confess to cheating on *Millionaire*, the police, apparently in the pay of the show's detestable host, hang him upside down, and pump electric shock into his bruised and bloodied body).

Having said this, however, it is not my intention to contest the verity of *Slumdog*'s distressing visualization of slum poverty. Though at times embarrassingly contrived, most of the film's upsetting scenes are inspired by a sad but well-documented reality. Corruption is rampant among the police, and many will gladly use torture, though none is probably dim enough to target an articulate, English-speaking young man whose only crime is having cheated on a game show and that, too, on the eve of his becoming a nationwide celebrity. Beggar-makers do round up abandoned children and mutilate them in order to render them more sympathetic, though it is doubtful that any such child will ever chance upon a US$100 bill, much less know which American president's portrait adorns it.[19] If anything, Boyle's magical tale, with its unconvincing characters and absurd plot devices, greatly understates the depth and suffering of India's poor. It is quite impossible, for instance, that Jamal would emerge from his ravaged life with a dewy complexion and polished, upper-class accent. But my quarrel with *Slumdog* is not its shallow, impressionistic portrayal of poverty. What I dispute about the film is the *use* to which the snapshots collected by Boyle's cameras are put; the troubling *narrative* they are deployed to create. These cameras skillfully create an intense sense of difference between the viewer's (affluent, comfortable, developed) world and Jamal's impoverished one. The interesting question, however, is how this "difference is transformed into Otherness or exploited by and for power."[20]

Perhaps the most salient aspect of *Slumdog* is that it frames Mumbai's slums as anarchic wastelands, overrun by petty warlords and devoid of any constructive relationship with formal political authority. No state officials are in sight, other than the police, who are portrayed, without exception, as corrupt and sadistic. Everything, it seems, is owned by mobsters and racketeers. In one scene (the opening sequence of the first flashback), Jamal and Salim are chased away ferociously from a makeshift playground near an airport runway by truncheon-wielding security guards on motorbikes (or are they policemen?). While in hot pursuit of the brothers, one guard, wearing a khaki uniform, accidentally slams into a chauffeur-driven Mercedes carrying Javed, a gangster who, it is later revealed, is caught in a turf war with Maman, the beggar-maker. The guard/policeman nervously removes his beret at the sight of Javed and salutes him, leaving it amply clear that it is Javed who is in charge. In a scene towards the end of the film, meant to reflect a more contemporary Mumbai, Salim sits atop an unfinished building that has sprouted up amid the slums and tells Jamal: "Everything you see around you belongs to Javed."

Certainly one of the more disquieting aspects of the film is that virtually all the labor performed by the poor is linked to either petty hustling or out-and-out criminality. During their stay in Agra, Jamal, Salim and the other street children survive by cheating and stealing (decamping with tourists' shoes is a favorite pastime). When they return to Mumbai in search of Latika, Jamal and Salim work in a restaurant's kitchen, where Salim is seen filling empty mineral water bottles with tap water, and then resealing them to appear new. In the slum of Jamal's childhood, no one seems engaged in any meaningful, productive work, other than a handful of scrawny rag-pickers, who drift through a few, fleeting frames towards the start of the film.

There is no associational life whatsoever: no self-help group, no community organization, no recreational club, and no charitable society. This barren world is also without familial bonds of any depth, or even specific individuals capable of empathy and compassion. When Jamal's mother is butchered by religious fanatics, he and Salim are instantly transformed into street urchins, ripe for the plucking by Maman. Why no one tries to help the brothers (perhaps a neighbor or a relative or their local mosque?) is a question left unanswered. In fact, as far as filmic renditions of the Indian slum-world go, *Slumdog*'s is possibly the darkest; far more so than of films such as Nair's sentimental *Salaam Bombay!*, Smith's low-budget masterpiece, *The Pool*, or even Joffe's sanctimonious saga, *City of Joy* (which I discuss at greater length in the closing sections of this paper). Though wanting in other ways, these films do more justice to the routine aspects of the arduous labor performed by slum dwellers – particularly slum children – and to the supportive relationships they experience despite their punishing circumstances.

In *Slumdog*, however, virtually every adult the children encounter is utterly heartless. A bespectacled schoolteacher, who reads to his class from *The Three Musketeers*, seethes with rage when the brothers arrive late to his class, and pounds them on their heads with the book.[21] Indian adults outside the slum are no better. The host of *Millionaire* ridicules Jamal mercilessly, and is egged on by an equally cruel audience. "What the hell can a slumdog possibly know," he jeers, eliciting peels of spiteful laughter. In another scene, when Salim dangles perilously from the roof of a moving train in order to pinch a piece of bread through an open window, an otherwise sedate-looking Sikh family seated inside the compartment reacts with inexplicable callousness. A man lurches towards the window and viciously tugs at Salim, hauling him off the train, along with a bewildered Jamal.

Conspicuously, the only adults who are kind to the boys are white tourists. They are depicted as naïve and at times worthy of ridicule but nonetheless even-tempered, polite and humane. When Jamal takes a sleek American couple on a deliberately meandering sightsee while his friends dismantle their car and steal its parts, he is beaten by their cagey Indian chauffeur, who sees through the boy's trickery. The Americans hurry to Jamal's rescue, shielding him from their driver's blows, and hand him a US$100 bill in the name of "American justice" (while the well-meaning charity of the innocent American tourist is mocked, the bill becomes central to *Slumdog*'s storyline, appearing in several scenes of the film). When a European budget traveler mistakes Jamal for a tour guide at the Taj Mahal, she treats him with patience, even though she senses that something is awry. Boyle's cameras linger over the particularities of these white bodies for far longer – exploring their expressions, moods and markers of class position – than they do on the torrent of blurry-faced Indians that rushes through the film, kicking, slapping, beating, taunting and cursing Jamal and other small children.

Misrepresenting Dharavi

It is no secret that *Slumdog* is meant to reflect life in Dharavi, the 550-acres spread of slums in the heart of Mumbai. Many of the film's sequences were filmed in the back alleys of this legendary slum, which is home to some one million people of enormous ethnic and religious diversity.[22] But Dharavi is not only a residential space: it is a hub of entrepreneurial activity. In it are located thousands of highly profitable small businesses, in areas such as embroidery, pottery, jewelry-making, woodwork, soap manufacturing, leather tanning and food processing. Waste recycling is an especially prosperous industry.[23] In one conservative estimate, the annual value of goods produced in Dharavi is placed at US$ 500 million.[24]

While Dharavi no doubt has its share of underworld bosses and simmering communal tensions (the latter fueled continually by Mumbai's Shiv Sena movement), its residents have nurtured many collaborative networks, often across potentially volatile lines of religion and caste, to set up community organizations that address a range of needs, such as affordable childcare, waste disposal and clean water.[25] Arjun Appadurai has documented the work of a pro-poor coalition of housing activists based primarily in Dharavi that lies "at the heart of a global network of community-based housing activists called the Slum/Shackdwellers International." Comprising three powerful community organizations, including the Mahila Milan (a women's saving group), this coalition, which refers to itself as the "Alliance," has worked towards "gaining secure tenure in land, adequate and durable housing, and access to urban infrastructure, notably to electricity, transport, sanitation and allied services."[26]

While it is true that Dharavi's perennially under-resourced community groups have touched only the tip of the proverbial iceberg, it is important to acknowledge their efforts and agency, along with the simple fact that the slum's residents, despite their grinding poverty, have valuable lives, generous spirits and a resourcefulness that stretches far beyond the random, Darwinian sort depicted in the film. In fact, the extraordinary perseverance, ingenuity and agency of slum dwellers in the Global South have been the subject of a great deal of academic research in recent years. Mercedes de la Rocha, for example, has highlighted the intricate social networks that have helped poor urbanites in Mexico build up a system of informal social security at the household and community levels, while Jo Beall has illuminated the dense rural-urban linkages that have allowed slum dwellers in Pakistan to rely on relatives in the countryside during particularly hard times.[27] In relation to India, Kaveri Gill's volume on Delhi's low caste "scavengers" (garbage collectors) and "scrap traders" deserves mentioning, as it draws attention to the remarkable entrepreneurial abilities and political savvy of these severely marginalised communities.[28] Also worthy of notice is Zainab Bawa and Parth Shah's recent study of how migrant groups, squatters and slum dwellers across the country have played a crucial role in developing low-income housing, and have thus contributed to the wider urban economy.[29]

It is not surprising, in this context, that many Dharaviites were puzzled by *Slumdog*'s desolate sequences. When asked about the film, one said: "Here we know what everyone is doing. We live so close to each other that if someone gets in trouble we come to help them because we can hear them. We look after each other because we live with each other." Another offered: "We have families, we have jobs, and we actually raise kids. I don't have time to watch films anyways – I wake up at 4:30 each morning and go to work."[30] The state's interventions in Dharavi are also of a more complex and contradictory nature than that depicted in the film. Rather than being wholly absent or uniformly malevolent, they reflect what Partha Chatterjee views as an ongoing tension between the Indian state's defense of private property rights and its mandate of welfare of all citizens.[31] Thus, while the state and municipal governments have insisted that most Dharaviites occupy land illegally, they have provided the slum with a few basic amenities such as water taps, toilets, drains and electricity.[32] Appadurai points out that the "Alliance" has developed a "complex political affiliation" with various levels and forms of the state bureaucracy, ranging from national civil servants at the highest levels in the Maharashtra state government and "quasi autonomous arms of the federal government" (such as the Bombay Electric Supply and Transport Corporation), to municipal authorities and the Mumbai police.[33] But how sanguine should one be about such relationships?

Chatterjee points out that state agencies "deal with these associations not as bodies of citizens but as convenient instruments for the administration of welfare," and are driven by "calculations of political expediency" (the interactions between the state and subaltern groups are shaped by the exigencies of political management rather than of citizenship rights). Nevertheless, some constructive relationships do arise, allowing marginalized groups to interrelate with the state outside of the more recognizable channels of "parties, movements, and non-party political formations," and create what Chatterjee calls "political society."[34] By urging the recognition of political society as an arena of democratic political engagement, Chatterjee challenges the binary and Eurocentric formulations of state-society relations that have pervaded the discipline of political science, narrowing our grasp of the full ambit of possible political action. Chatterjee's intervention is an important one that enables us to see what *Slumdog* does not; to venture beyond Boyle's stock narrative of the "illegal" slum that lies outside of politics, cut off from the state, as well as of the eternally victimized or "criminal" slum dweller, who stumbles upon the state's officials in only the most random and sinister ways.[35]

It is possible to argue, of course, that *Slumdog* is a movie, not a documentary, and that it is ultimately futile to chastise a work of fiction for not being faithful to reality, even when it *is* admired in some circles for its gritty realism. Besides, Boyle could easily claim that his film portrays one sliver of slum-life, not the whole thing, and that boys like Jamal and Salim, who live in permanent exile from society and fail to experience even one moment of affirmation or achievement, may very well exist. Yet one wonders why none of the other, more heartening dimensions of Dharavi life is put before the audience. Why does Boyle select to focus on this exceptionally bleak sliver, and not others? The choice is intended, no doubt, to heighten the appeal of the film's outlandish plot. By depicting Dharavi as a wild, anarchic space, consumed by criminals and bereft of all forms of human solidarity, Boyle creates the perfect setting for Jamal's rescue by destiny, which manifests itself in the form of an imported quiz show. Since there are no internal resources, the solution must arrive externally. This thesis bears troubling implications.

Although Boyle's cameras appear to neither seek nor offer an explanation for the miseries they survey in Dharavi, they *do* tell a story about poverty, one in which the problems of the poor are explained away as arising from passivity and purely localized exploitation. No attempt is made to analyze Mumbai's grueling poverty and communal strife in relation to broader economic, social and political developments, either in India or globally. Given that *Slumdog*'s most poignant scenes (of Jamal's childhood) are situated in the early 1990s, when India was in the first stages of an ambitious program of market-oriented reform, these silences are especially significant. Detached as it is from any analysis of underlying economic relationships, and engrossed as it is by criminals and criminality, the film's simplistic "good versus evil" narrative resonates with the culture of poverty arguments of the 1950s and 1960s, which construed poverty as created by the poor themselves; by their distinctive value system, a set of repugnant cultural traits – such as dysfunctional patterns of family life and apathetic, resigned attitudes – that supposedly stymied their progress in the modern world. With children socialized at an early age into the values of their parents, the intergenerational transmission of these disagreeable traits was thought inevitable, rendering it difficult, if not impossible, to escape poverty.[36] The "culture of poverty" thesis typically worked in tandem with purported distinctions between the "deserving" and "undeserving poor" to produce a thoroughly unsympathetic portrayal of the urban poor – and of slum dwellers in particular – as people who had rejected the dominant norms of their society, and were therefore "disreputable," even "dangerous."[37] The solution was obvious: the poor had to be removed from the slum or, better yet, the slum removed altogether.

Such shrill arguments were rooted in none other than modernization theory, the intellectual poster child of the post-World War II development project, which roundly located the causes of poverty within the poor themselves, in their bad or backward cultural habits, rather than in the inequalities of class and global economic relations. Although many of the cruder aspects of the modernization literature were gradually discredited, its core assumptions lingered on, especially the notion that the sources of poverty and other problems in developing countries are internal/domestic, such as bad governance, and could therefore be erased with the adoption of good policies by national governments, with the benign assistance, whenever needed, of First World donors. No adjustment to the structures of the global economy was thought necessary: such was, indeed, the foundational assumption of the Washington Consensus model of market reform, and later, of its renovated "human face."[38] To be sure, *Slumdog*'s localized understanding of slum poverty follows a venerable (cultural) tradition.

"Accumulation by Dispossession"

The thesis that the roots of the slum's problems are internal to the slum has not escaped challenge. In a classic text that appeared in 1973, David Harvey placed the growth of slums in the context of the advancement of capitalist development, arguing for cities to be viewed not as neutral spaces but as concrete manifestations of hierarchical social relations based on power, especially economic power.[39] In an influential piece published in the Indian periodical, *Seminar,* in 1976, social activist Jai Sen echoed this perspective, arguing that the city's affluence and poverty are fundamentally intertwined, with the slum supplying the labor that the rich cannot do without, and that is essential for the creation of their wealth.[40] In the 1980s and 1990s, moreover, a host of studies revealed that the "structural adjustment" policies that had spurred the growth of Third World cities had also deepened their poverty.[41] More recently, Mike Davis has associated "the mass production of slums" and increasing urban poverty in the South with the economic liberalization programs enforced by the International Monetary Fund (IMF), World Bank and the World Trade Organization (WTO), arguing that the elimination of agricultural subsidies, agricultural deregulation, privatization and other policies of state retrenchment have accelerated the exodus of surplus rural labor to urban slums "even as cities [have] ceased to be job machines."[42] Despite the disruptions achieved by such questioning, however, the idea that slums *cause* the city's problems retains hegemony, guiding the policy decisions of national governments and framing their ham-handed, top-down plans to dismantle slums and assimilate slum populations.

In India, the most recent of these is the Dharavi Redevelopment Project (DRP), which proposes to convert Dharavi's neighborhoods into blocks of residential and commercial high rises. Approved by the state government of Maharashtra in 2004, the DRP requires private developers to provide small flats (of about 250 square feet each) to families that can prove they settled in Dharavi before the year 2000. In return for re-housing residents, the developers obtain construction rights in the area. Though perhaps marginally more humane than razing slums by bulldozers, the DRP will potentially evict some 500,000 people who cannot legally prove that they settled in Dharavi before the year 2000. It may decimate myriad livelihoods by rendering unviable countless household-centered businesses. The slum's rambling recycling centers, artisans' workshops and cottage industries can hardly be repackaged into vertically stacked, warren-like flats. Not surprisingly, critics see the DRP as little more than an ecologically harmful land-grab scheme that was initiated without consultation with residents.[43] Mumbai's real estate prices are comparable to Manhattan's, and by one estimate, Dharavi's land is worth approximately US$ 10 billion.[44]

One may see the relentless push for the DRP as a clear indication that the government's policy on Dharavi has become disproportionately influenced by the interests and prejudices of Mumbai's more affluent residents, who would prefer to see the "eyesore" erased, and its "problem population" absorbed into the creeping sprawl of the "modern city." As Leela Fernandes suggests, the city's middle and upper classes appear to have gained access to state power not through electoral politics (which they see as captured by the poor, religious minorities and low castes), but through a "wide range of associational activities within civil society including conventional organizational practices through civic organizations, public narratives and discursive practices within the media and public sphere."[45] They have organized as "citizens groups" to launch "campaigns in the press to oppose government policy to recognize the residential rights of slum-dwellers and the right to rehabilitation of those who are evicted by the development programs of the state,"[46] along with "beautification" drives aimed at "cleaning up" public spaces and land, such as beaches, promenades and *maidans* (public squares and gardens) of hawkers, beggars and "illegal slums." [47]

Public officials in Mumbai and other cities have proven tremendously receptive to such aggressive middle-class mobilizations against slum dwellers, though they have tried to embed ensuing policies in the language of a public need for sanitation, security and environmental protection (Amita Baviskar refers to the latter phenomenon as "bourgeois environmentalism").[48] Fernandes points out that a "central dimension of the model of urban development that caters to the new middle class is the emergence of new forms of collaboration between the state and private sector." In fact, as D. Asher Ghertner reveals in a recent study of Delhi's *Bhagidari* system – a governance experiment launched in 2000 –urban middle-class power did not emerge from internal changes within this class, as is commonly thought, but was "rather produced by the machinations of the local state." In particular, Ghertner shows how *Bhagidari* has "realigned the channels by which citizens can access the state on the basis of property ownership. In so doing, it has undermined the electoral process dominated by the poor and privileged property owners' demands for a world-class urban future."[49]

There have been tangible shifts on the ground. State-led beautification projects, such as in Mumbai's Chowpatty (one of the city's best-known beaches), have been undertaken with financial support from the corporate sector, with private security firms awarded contracts for the surveillance of freshly cleaned up public spaces.[50] Other Indian cities have endured similar transformations. In a recent article that explores the process of converting Bangalore into a "world city," Michael Goldman examines how new forms of "speculative government" engage in land speculation and actively dispossess those working in the rural periphery, on land upon which the new world city is being built.[51] Delhi, too, has gone through similar changes, particularly in the wake of the 2010 Commonwealth Games, an international sporting event that was designed to affirm the national capital's stature as a global city.[52]

Indeed, such gentrification, and its associated dynamics, can be thought of as a form of enclosure, or what Harvey terms "dispossession by accumulation," a process through which assets belonging to the state or community are discharged into the market, prying open new vistas for capitalist development. Yet Harvey also challenges the dogged conviction – prevalent even within the Left – that the poor cannot produce viable solutions to their own problems or resist the inexorable logic of capital. He suggests that practices of enclosure, though strengthened by the rise of neoliberalism, have almost always been met by vigorous resistance. Slums, in this sense, are also spaces of hope where people refuse their stereotyping as marginal or dysfunctional by enjoining in struggles that evoke community, permanence and strength.[53] The intense opposition to the DRP is illustrative of Harvey's point. The myriad human rights and slum dwellers' associations struggling against the project achieved an important victory in July 2009, when a committee of experts established by the state government to inquire into the project's viability deemed it a "sophisticated land grab driven by personal greed," and urged the recognition of Dharavi as "a thriving place, with residents who cooperate with each other and have learned to live harmoniously in very trying physical circumstances" (the panel, appointed in response to the DRP's critics, included the president of the National Slum Dwellers' Association, Jockin Arputham, who is also a leading figure in the "Alliance" described by Appadurai).[54] *Slumdog*, predictably, shines no light on such counter-narratives of resistance and refusal.

It is certainly ironic that the film, for all its righteousness of tone, shares with many government officials and middle classes in India – whom it vilifies so tirelessly through its racist depictions – a profoundly dehumanizing view of those who live and work in India's slums. Grounded in the ever-resilient "culture of poverty" narrative, this view will now obtain a powerful boost from *Slumdog*, a heavily fêted film that millions will watch eagerly. But if *Slumdog* will widen the reach of this problematic outlook, this problematic outlook is precisely what lies at the core of the film's appeal. Perhaps the crucial ingredient of *Slumdog*'s success among Western audiences and Indian middle classes is not its "feel good" tenor, but its understanding of poverty as the product of aberrant local cultures that must be shaken off and replaced by liberal modernity. Despite appearances to the contrary, *Slumdog*'s stunning sweep of the box office and awards' circuit signals the West's celebration of itself, of its longstanding ideals and cherished myths, along with some newer ideals and myths that reflect the West's neoliberal present. The largely uncritical acceptance of *Slumdog*'s triumphalism in India, on the other hand, indicates the acquiescence to such ideals and myths by the country's upwardly mobile middle classes.

Celebrating Liberal Modernity

At its core, *Slumdog* is a celebration of Jamal's undeterred individualism and autonomy. Jamal rises above the moral decay that surrounds him and persists in his search for Latika. Though not conniving or greedy, Jamal is nobody's fool (he rejects the incorrect answer handed to him by *Millionaire*'s odious host) and knows how to stand up for himself (he quips at the police despite being tortured). The film also celebrates the tourist dollar and the call center – unmistakable markers of globalization in India – as conduits of material advancement and self-reliance for the absolute poor. The *Millionaire* show, in its turn, injects the values of merit and neutrality into a society evidently beleaguered by corruption, communal strife and class segregation. It is blind to Jamal's lowly socioeconomic status (while the local quiz master and audience clearly are not) and rewards him, as a matter of routine, when his answers are correct. The audience is reminded, at a time of a severe global recession, that market competition, as a process and logic, is not the problem but rather the avarice of a few degenerate people, such as *Millionaire*'s loathsome host. *Slumdog* denies not only the West's complicity in the making of the Third World, but also the role of poorly fettered markets in the creation of material inequalities and vulnerabilities within the West. Perhaps *Slumdog*'s message of hope is so powerful because it demands nothing of its viewers, no change in perspective or way of life.

But what specific issues are raised by *Slumdog*'s almost uniformly warm reception in India?[55] "Hats, caps and wigs off," burbled the influential *Hindustan Times*, upon the film's Mumbai release.[56] Following the film's adulation at the Oscars a month later, the storm of applause grew stronger, with its most recognizable song, "Jai Ho," adapted by India's Congress party as its campaign anthem for the May 2009 national elections. One may contrast this with the unfavorable reaction in India to *City of Joy* (hereafter *City*), a film by another British director (Joffe) on the theme of slum poverty in Kolkata. The film, and the novel on which it is based (by Dominique Lapierre), was summarily condemned by West Bengal's Minister of Information, Buddhadeb Bhattacharya, who thundered that it "smack[ed] of apartheid" and was "an insult to every self-respecting Indian."[57] *City*, released in 1992, was apparently filmed under extraordinarily trying circumstances, with "riots outside, invasions of the set, hijacking of the cast's food truck, union bans [...] stone throwing."[58] What explains the difference in the Indian reaction to these two films?

City is about a young American doctor, Max Lowe (played by Hollywood superstar Patrick Swayze), who arrives in Kolkata seeking spiritual healing after losing a patient in the United States. He inadvertently gets involved with the city's slum dwellers, whose lives he tries to improve through his moral support and medical expertise (he runs a clinic with an Irish nun, Joan). There are many similarities between *City* and *Slumdog*. The former, like the latter, was commended widely in the media for its "noble goal."[59] Swayze reportedly swallowed a steep pay cut "for the people of Calcutta."[60] It was also praised for capturing Kolkata's slums in "vivid and astonishing detail," the evidence of which is its barrage of unsettling Orientalist images: heaving crowds, pitiful squalor, disfigured beggars, stumps of leprosy and exhausted rickshaw pullers.[61] Indeed, the slum of Max's visitation is much like that of Jamal's childhood: an anarchic wasteland untouched by formal authority, devoid of functional governing structures, and bereft of expressions of political agency and community power. It is up to Max to kindle a spirit of cooperation among the slum dwellers ("I am just here to get you organized"), and to teach the locals to "stand up" for themselves (he scolds the rickshaw puller Hasari for being a "little brown illiterate gutless victim" when Hasari buckles under pressure from the slum's gangsters). Towards the end of the film, Hasari tells Max, "I'm glad you came to my country [...] you made me feel things I have never felt before."

City's explanation of all the wretchedness it surveys, like *Slumdog*'s, is both localized and individualized, boiling down to nothing more than exploitation by the petty bully boy and bad cultural traits, such as passivity (in one frame, Joan tells Max: "In the beginning it was really frustrating trying to convince them to not be so bloody passive [...] then I realized I was fighting a thousand years of passive acceptance").[62] The solution is Max, a white American, who shakes Hasari out of his complacency, awakening him to the spirit of enterprise (by the end of the film, the hardworking and ferociously perspiring Hasari has earned enough to pay for an extravagant wedding for his daughter). With its blunt dialogue and caricatured vision of the native, *City* is reminiscent of dated "white savior" films such as David Lean's epic, *Lawrence of Arabia* (1962).[63] Herein is one of its main fault lines of contrast with *Slumdog*.

While *Slumdog* shares with *City* a strikingly similar view of the slum-world in terms of visual depiction, internal explanation and external solution, *Slumdog* deftly avoids the use of white bodies to propel its central storyline. All its major characters are local, as is the author on whose novel it is based. This is possibly why *Slumdog* evades the labels of colonialist or racist, which still bear considerable sting in India. Middle and upper class moviegoers who are otherwise ardent modernizers and hold the same ahistorical and depoliticized view of slums and slum dwellers as conveyed by *City* and *Slumdog*, will nonetheless balk at the thought of receiving instruction from an American or European. *Slumdog*, like *City*, easily fits into "the grammar of imperialism," only it successfully dodges the charge.[64]

It helps, of course, that *Slumdog*'s local hero (Jamal) more faithfully reflects contemporary middle-class aspirations in India, by *exiting* the slum and claiming success within the domains of the modern, globalizing city (the toiling Hasari never leaves the slum). *City* was made at a time when the ideals of state-led development and "citizen-worker" were arguably still in sight, especially in Kolkata, the heart of communist-ruled West Bengal.[65] *Slumdog*, in contrast, arrives in the heyday of the assertive "consumer-citizen" of post-liberalization India, who extols the ideal of personal responsibility, is contemptuous of corrupt and bungling government officials, and advocates for his right, as a consumer, to a suitable lifestyle.[66] With polished accents, starched appearances and luck on their side, the brazenly individualistic Jamal and Latika of the film's last third (played by British-born Dev Patel and L'Oréal model, Freida Pinto) are personifications of this new, neoliberal archetype.

Boyle's lionizing of a local hero that embodies the virtues associated with Western culture and Northern development is strategically brilliant. The tactic resonates with the work of a new breed of developmentalists, who indignantly reject colonialism and modernization theory's overtly paternalistic distinctions between a modern/ civilized West and a traditional/ backward Third World – who argue for a robust appreciation of culture and intercultural learning in the making of human development indices, good governance models and so on – but who nevertheless read cultures beyond their own as having both good and bad elements, with the former consistently mirroring the West's prized values, and the latter, in need of speedy obliteration. Development is no longer legitimated by reference to the West's civilizing mission, but by invoking the urgency of rescuing good locals, such as Jamal, from the bad that surrounds them.

Indeed, the culturalisms of the colonial past and modernization theory resurface in development's new, cultural turn through denials of history, and by denying agency at selective moments when voice might count. The ideas and idioms of the new culturalism that proliferate in *Slumdog* also prevail among Indian middle classes, who mobilize to translate into legislation and policy their sense of cultural difference in relation to the "dirty," "chaotic" and "criminal" poor, but nevertheless frame these interventions as serving the long-term interests of the poor.[67] The popularity of *Slumdog* among Indian middle classes is thus no more surprising than the popularity of *Three Cups of Tea* among educated urban elites in Pakistan, who, as Nosheen Ali has suggested, have eagerly embraced the book's thesis, perhaps to make better sense of their own context post-9/11: that the religious extremism in their country has nothing to do with their own choices, including their alliance with the United States in the "war on terror," but with the poverty and backwardness of the untamed rural north.[68] If the answer to Indian urban poverty from this perspective is the repackaging of slums into privately developed high-rises, the marketed solution to Pakistani "terrorism" is education, delivered through international NGOs, American corporate contractors via USAID and even the military.

Conclusion: In the "Master's Image"?

In the year that *Slumdog* was released, more people watched the movie than visited India (easily accessible data from India's Ministry of Tourism suggest that the country receives about three million tourists annually). Such is the power of the "magic carpet of film," a point that is surely recognized by those who see, in *Slumdog*, a potential for advocacy and humanism. But by framing slums as worthless spaces that are worlds unto themselves, *Slumdog* betrays this promise, not only reinforcing Orientalist stereotypes about slum dwellers, but also legitimating accumulation by dispossession. Furthermore, by celebrating a brown, local hero who embodies the virtues regarded as the wellsprings of the West's advancement, it also depoliticizes and universalizes values associated with a highly specific and power-laden history of Northern development. This is, in fact, the sleight of hand that undergirds the new culturalism. Although the audience is treated to panoramic vistas of Mumbai's cityscape, Indian actors and situations and – as the film's credits roll in towards the end – a pulsating dance sequence choreographed to the melodies of A. R. Rahman, one of India's most distinguished musicians, *Slumdog* never departs from "the Master's image of progress."[69]

Notes

1 This essay builds on an earlier review of *Slumdog Millionaire* published by the author: Mitu Sengupta, "Hollow Message," *Frontline*, 26.6 (March 2009): 14–27.

2 The UN has defined the slum as "an area that combines, to various extents, the following characteristics: inadequate access to safe water; inadequate access to sanitation and other infrastructure; poor structural quality of housing; overcrowding;

insecure residential status." This definition, as the authors readily concede, is restricted to the physical and legal characteristics of the settlement, and excludes "some of the more difficult social dimensions." See UN-Habitat, *Challenge of the Slums: Global Report on Human Settlements 2003* (London: UN-Habitat, 2003), 12.

3 David Harvey, *The New Imperialism* (Oxford: Oxford University Press, 2003), 137–182.

4 See Somini Sengupta, "Indians Embrace the Triumph of "Slumdog" as a Victory for Their Country," *New York Times*, 24 February 2009. Online: http://query.nytimes.com/gst/fullpage.html?res=9401E3DA1331F937A15751C0A96F9C8B63 (accessed 24 February 2009).

5 Such was the basis of much of the criticism of the film in India. See Madhur Singh, "Slumdog Millionaire is No Hit in India," *Time*, 26 January 2009. Online: http://www.time.com/time/arts/article/0,8599,1873926,00.html (accessed 26 January 2009).

6 Trinh T. Minh-ha, *Framer Framed* (New York: Routledge, 1992), 117.

7 Robert Stam and Louise Spence, "Colonialism, Racism and Representation," *Screen* 24.2 (March–April 1983): 4.

8 John Hutnyk, *The Rumor of Calcutta* (London: Zed Books, 1996), 196..

9 According to Box Office Mojo, *Slumdog*'s total worldwide gross for 28.3 weeks in release is US$ 361,273,610. Its production budget was US$ 15 million. "Slumdog Millionaire," Box Office Mojo. Online: http://www.boxofficemojo.com/?id=slumdogmillionaire.htm (accessed 10 July 2012).

10 Vikas Swarup, *Q & A* (New Delhi: Black Swan Books, 2005).

11 As the third question of *Millionaire*, Jamal is asked: "What weapon does Lord Rama hold in his right hand?" He answers correctly ("bow and arrow") because he recalls running into a child dressed as the Hindu deity while fleeing from the site of his mother's murder.

12 The film's central characters, Jamal, Salim and Latika, are played by three sets of actors to correspond with three different stages in their lives (childhood, early teens and young adulthood). The child actors are Ayush Khedekar (Jamal), Azharuddin Ismail (Salim) and Rubena Ali (Latika).

13 Roger Ebert, "Slumdog Millionaire," *Chicago Sun Times*, 11 November 2008. Online: http://rogerebert.suntimes.com/apps/pbcs.dll/article?AID=/20081111/REVIEWS/811110297 (accessed 11 November 2008).

14 Peter Travers, "Slumdog Millionaire," *Rolling Stone*, 13 November 2008. Online: http://www.rollingstone.com/reviews/movie/20192670/review/24013911/slumdog_millionaire (accessed 13 November 2008).

15 Emily Wax, "Protests and Praise: 'Slumdog's' Mumbai Realism is Divisive," *Washington Post*, 23 January 2009. Online: http://www.washingtonpost.com/wp-dyn/content/article/2009/01/22/AR2009012204082.html (accessed 23 January 2009).

16 Richard Chin, "Slumdog Millionaire: Debate Poverty not 'Poverty Porn,'" *Huffington Post*, 6 March 2009. Online: http://www.huffingtonpost.com/richard-chin/slumdog-millionaire-debat_b_172646.html (accessed 6 March 2009).

17 Gilles Deleuze, *Cinema 2, The Time – Image*, translated by Hugh Tomlinson and Robert Galeta (Minneapolis: University of Minnesota Press, 1985,1989), 68. As quoted in Hutnyk, *The Rumor*, 194.

18 Edward Said, *Orientalism* (New York: Random House, 1978), 239. As quoted in Raka Shome, "Race and Popular Cinema: the Rhetorical Strategies of Whiteness in City of Joy," *Communication Quarterly* 44.4 (1996): 507.

19 The fifth question asked of Jamal is: "Whose picture appears on a US$100 bill?" He is able to answer this question correctly because he recalls chancing upon the childhood friend blinded by Maman's gang of beggar-makers in a dirty Mumbai underpass. When Jamal gave his friend a US$100 bill (which he'd extracted from an American tourist couple), the latter impressed him by pointing out that Benjamin Franklin's image is on the note.

20 Stam and Spence, "Colonialism," 3.

21 This novel is central to the film's plot. As a child, Jamal refers to Salim and himself as the musketeers Athos and Porthos, and to Latika as the third musketeer, whose name he does not know. For *Millionaire*'s final question, Jamal is asked to name the third musketeer.

22 My description of Dharavi draws, among other sources, on an untitled essay posted on www.dharavi.org by Katia Savchuk, Matias Echavone and Rahul Srivastava, academics affiliated with the research collective Partners for Urban Knowledge Action and Research (PUKAR). See http://www.dharavi.org/B._Introduction (accessed 10 July 2012).

23 Dan McDougall, "Waste not, Want not in the £700m Slum," *Guardian (The Observer)*, 4 March 2007. Online: http://www.guardian.co.uk/environment/2007/mar/04/india.recycling (accessed 10 July 2012).

24 "Inside the Slums," *Economist*, 27 January 2005. Online: http://www.economist.com/world/asia/displaystory.cfm?story_id=3599622 (accessed 27 January 2005).

25 Thomas Blom Hansen, *Wages of Violence: Naming and Identity in Postcolonial Bombay* (Princeton: Princeton University Press, 2001), 70–100.

26 Arjun Appadurai, "The Capacity to Aspire," in *Culture and Public Action*, edited by Vijayendra Rao and Michael Walton (New Delhi: Permanent Black, 2004), 70–71.

27 Mercedes Gonzalez de la Rocha, *The Resources of Poverty: Women and Survival in a Mexican City* (Oxford: Blackwell, 1994), and J. Beall, "Social Security and Social Networks Among the Urban Poor in Pakistan," *Habitat International* 19.4 (1995): 427–45.

28 Kaveri Gill, *Of Poverty and Plastic* (New Delhi: Oxford University Press, 2010).

29 Zainab Bawa and Parth J. Shah, "Low-Income Housing in Indian Cities: Some Considerations for Policy," *Development Policy Review* 28.3 (2010): 259–293.

30 Jarrett Wrisley, "Real People, Not Slumdogs," *Atlantic*, 23 February 2009. Online: http://www.theatlantic.com/magazine/archive/2009/02/real-people-not-slumdogs/307312/

31 Partha Chatterjee, *Politics of the Governed* (New York: Columbia University Press), 2004.

32 Savchuk, Echavone and Srivastava. Also see Sundar Burra, Sheela Patel and Thomas Kerr, "Community-Designed, Built and Managed Toilet Blocks in Indian Cities," *Environment and Urbanization* 15.11 (2003).

33 Appadurai, "The Capacity to Aspire," 72–3.

34 Chatterjee, *Politics*, 40, 46.

35 See also Marcus Taylor, "Conscripts of Competitiveness: Culture, Capital and Institutions in Contemporary Development," *Third World Quarterly* 31.4 (2010): 561–79, for a discussion of spaces of informal economy and non-capital as constituted by capital accumulation itself.

36 The expression "culture of poverty" is associated with anthropologist Oscar Lewis's 1965 study on peasants in urban contexts, who experience acute dislocation and rapid social change as they move from the countryside to the city. See O. Lewis, "Further observations on the folk-urban continuum and urbanization with special reference to

Mexico City," in *The Study of Urbanization*, edited by P. M. Hauser and L. F. Schnore (New York: Wiley, 1965).

37 D. Matza, "The Disreputable Poor," in *Class, Status and Power: Social Stratification in Comparative Perspective*, edited by Reinhard Bendix and Seymour M. Lipset (New York: Free Press, 1966); Louis Chevalier, *Laboring Classes and Dangerous Classes* (London: Routledge and Kegan Paul), 1973.

38 On this, see Charles Gore, "The Rise and Fall of the Washington Consensus as a Paradigm for Developing Countries," *World Development* 28.5 (2000): 789–804.

39 David Harvey, *Social Justice and the City* (Oxford: Blackwell Publishers, 1973).

40 Jai Sen, "The Unintended City," *Seminar* 200 (April 1976): 33–40.

41 See, for example, Nazneen Kanji, "Gender, Poverty and Economic Adjustment in Harare, Zimbabwe," *Environment and Urbanization* 7.1 (1995): 37–56.

42 Mike Davis, "Planet of Slums," *New Left Review* 26 (March–April 2004): 10–11. Davis's stinging indictment of neoliberal reform draws heavily upon UN-Habitat's groundbreaking report, *Challenge of the Slums*, which grimly states that "the main single cause of increases in poverty and inequality during the 1980s and 1990s was the retreat of the state" (48).

43 These concerns are articulated in some detail in S. Patel and J. Arputham, "An Offer of Partnership or a Promise of Conflict in Dharavi, Mumbai?" *Environment and Urbanization* 19.2 (October 2007): 501–8.

44 "Urban Poverty in India," *Economist*, 19 December 2007. Online: http://www.economist.com/world/asia/displaystory.cfm?story_id=10311293 (accessed 19 December 2007).

45 Leela Fernandes, *India's New Middle Class* (Minneapolis: University of Minnesota Press, 2006), 195.

46 P. K. Das, "Slums: The Continuing Struggle for Housing," in *Bombay and Mumbai*, edited by S. Patel and J. Maselos (New Delhi: Oxford University Press, 2003), 208. Also see John Harriss, "Middle Class Activism and the Politics of the Informal Working Class: A Perspective on Class Relations and Civil Society in Indian Cities," *Critical Asian Studies* 38.4 (2006): 445–65.

47 Fernandes, *India's New Middle Class*, 147.

48 See Amita Baviskar, "The Politics of the City," *Seminar* 516 (2002): 40–42, for a critique of judicial orders in Delhi calling for slum demolition or industrial relocation in the name of the environment.

49 D. Asher Ghertner, "Gentrifying the State, Gentrifying Participation: Elite Governance Programs in Delhi," *International Journal of Urban and Regional Research* 35.3 (May 2011): 504.

50 Fernandes, *India's New Middle Class*, 156.

51 Michael Goldman, "Speculative Urbanism and the Making of the Next World City," *International Journal of Urban and Regional Research* 35.3 (May 2011): 555–81.

52 See Veronique Dupont, "The Dream of Delhi as a Global City," *International Journal of Urban and Regional Research*, 35.3 (May 2011): 533–54. Also see Mitu Sengupta, "World Class Dreams and Urban Change: A Critique of the 2010 Commonwealth Games," *Indian Journal of Human Development* 4.2 (2010): 433–43.

53 David Harvey, *Spaces of Hope* (Berkeley: University of California Press, 2000).

54 See N. Barucha, "Dharavi Remake a Land Grab, Says Panel," *Times of India*, 8 July 2009. Online: http://articles.timesofindia.indiatimes.com/2009-07-08/mumbai/28167091_1_dharavi-redevelopment-project-consultant-mukesh-mehta-sophisticated-land

55 One notable exception to this rule is Nivedita Menon, "Reading Swarup, Watching Boyle," *Outlook*, 28 January 2009. Online: http://www.outlookindia.com/article.aspx?239578 (accessed 28 January 2009).

56 Khalid Mohammed, "Cuts straight to the heart," *Hindustan Times* (Mumbai), 23 January 2009.

57 Laetitia Zecchini, "Filming Poverty in the *City of Joy*," *World Press Review* (May 1991): 59. As cited in Shome, "Race and Popular Cinema," 505.

58 Hutnyk, *The Rumor*, 193.

59 Shome, "Race and Popular Cinema," 505.

60 Hutnyk, *The Rumor*, 209. Swayze apparently stated at the film's Melbourne premier that while he would normally command seven million dollars for a film, he accepted just one million for *City of Joy*.

61 B. D. Johnson, "Misery's Happy Face," *Maclean's*, 20 April 1992, 48.

62 Hutnyk, *The Rumor*, 180.

63 See Pierre Boulanger, *Le Cinéma Colonial* (Paris: Seghers, 1974).

64 Shome, "Race and Popular Cinema," 508.

65 Many Hindi films in the 1950s depicted these ideals, though by the 1980s, they conveyed more cynicism towards the state. See Rajni Bakshi, "Raj Kapoor: From *Jis Desh Mein Ganga Behti Hai* to *Ram Teri Ganga Maili*," in *The Secret Politics of Our Desires*, edited by A. Nandy (Delhi: Oxford University Press, 1998), 92–133.

66 The contrast between "citizen-worker" and "consumer-citizen" is formulated, most insightfully, by Fernandes, who argues that the "identity of a consuming-liberalizing middle class is transformed into a generalized form of consumer citizenship, one that is marked by a shift from workers' rights to the rights of the consumer" (*India's New Middle Class*, 182).

67 One must be careful, however, to not treat middle class as a homogenous category that is synonymous with elite. Fernandes, for example, provides a more complex account of such middle class discourses than is possible in this paper. She points out that middle class anger has also been directed at "perceived cultural and political elites" (*India's New Middle Class*, 184).

68 Nosheen Ali, "Books vs. Bombs? Humanitarian Development and the Narrative of Terror in Northern Pakistan," *Third World Quarterly* 31.4 (2010): 541–59.

69 Trinh T. Minh-ha, *When the Moon Waxes Red* (London: Routledge, 1991), 97.

Chapter 7

SLUMDOGS AND MILLIONAIRES: FACTS AND FICTIONS OF INDIAN (UNDER)DEVELOPMENT

Snehal Shingavi

Much ink has been spilled on the differences between Vikas Swarup's *Q & A* (2005) and the movie that was based on it, Danny Boyle's *Slumdog Millionaire* (2008). The differences are important and substantial enough that repeatedly, when interviewed, Swarup was asked to explain whether or not he was jarred (as presumably were the interviewers) by the thinness of the relationship between the novel and its cinematic offspring. One such conversation was recorded in the *Guardian*, for instance:

> They changed the title from *Q & A* to *Slumdog Millionaire*. ("That made a lot of sense," says Swarup.) They changed the ending. ("Danny thought the hero should be arrested on suspicion of cheating on the penultimate question, not after he wins as I had it. That was a successful idea.") They made friends into brothers, axed Bollywood stars and Mumbai hoodlums and left thrilling subplots on the cutting-room floor. Crucially, they changed the lead character's name from Ram Mohammad Thomas to Jamal Malik, thereby losing Swarup's notion that his hero would be an Indian everyman, one who sounded as though he was Hindu, Muslim and Christian. Instead, they made Jamal a Muslim whose mother is killed by a Hindu mob. ("It's more dramatically focused as a result, perhaps more politically correct.")[1]

These differences in plot came to stand in for the flexibility and malleability of the story whose fundamental message was impervious to change despite the translation from one medium to another, from one social and geographic context to another, suggesting perhaps dangerously, as Swarup's nod to a lingering critique of liberalism suggests, that the stories of the poor are, at their core, unproblematically and untroublingly similar.

The breezy, generous way that Swarup embraces the cinematic version of his story reveals and occludes the central tension in both the novel and the film: the heroism of the main character is supposed to be specific to his life, to the "facts" generated by his past, to the necessary outcome of his virtuously lived, faithful devotion, certainly not to be copied without immense personal risk and definitely not reproducible as a series of trivial and interchangeable details. Facts are important because they cannot be traded for one another so easily; otherwise the feel of the fictive and cinematic exposé of the travails of poverty collapses back into the con game with which it shares so many features. Ram Mohammad Thomas and Jamal Malik are only attractive as heroes in their respective stories because of their exceptional, rare and rarefied personalities, their ability not to sink into the worlds around them, their seemingly endless ability to adapt to their ever-changing circumstances; in the worlds of each, the other is not supposed to be possible, especially since both the novel and the film are filled with examples of poor children who do not, at the end of the day, make it out of poverty. In fact, our ability to believe in the narrative depends ironically on its impossibility, on its reliance on those bulky, impossible terms, "fate" and "luck," which have come to mean more or less the same kind of secular providence that is smuggled into the narrative as *deus ex machina*. These terms, however, mask the fact that the selection of this particular hero from the tens of millions who now live in the sprawling slums of every major conurbation in India is itself a kind of rigged literary-cum-cinematic lottery that is an alibi for an ideology of aggressive meritocracy. Ram and Jamal not only win the game show (itself a test of middle-class education) but they do so because they are defined as exceptionally virtuous characters (Jamal with his enduring love; Ram with his fierce commitment to justice).

This, however, is normally the provenance of Romance, and the success of the Romantic hero is predicated on his ability to survive the tests that are placed before him to prove his fitness for the unimaginable erotic and material rewards which await him.[2] In both the film and the novel, however, the transposition of the real – the very fact of poverty, the almost anthropological curiosity about how the poor actually live, the need to use real slums and real slum children – onto the fantastic narrative structure of Romance produces an important contradiction which structures both of the works and explains the contradictory reactions that both have produced amongst their audiences. If, on the one hand, both the novel and the film need to explain why a slum dweller can succeed where the middle-class reader/viewer presumably could not, the only answer that can reasonably be provided are themselves tropes of illegibility: in the novel, luck is figured as a two-headed coin that Ram has used throughout the narrative to make important decisions; in the film, the fate of the romance plot is merely "written" (which, perhaps to complete the *mise en scene* of the quiz show trope, also refers to the skimpiness of its origins in Swarup's novel). In each of the episodes of the novel and the film, the origin of the answer to a supremely difficult question on a quiz show must always be tied to another supremely difficult situation from which the slum dweller must escape by demonstrating his supremely unique generosity, creativity, and wit. This creates the effect that the rhetorical construction of verisimilitude folds in on itself: impossibility becomes the explanation for implausibility and fate and chance become surrogates for utopian fantasies. Winning the game show is so tied to the characters in both fiction and film, the audience so compelled by the ethical fitness of both Ram and Jamal, that the impossibility of the outcome is directly related to the extraordinariness of their personalities; real slum children in the novel and in the movie are ignored or scorned while sympathy can be generated only for the exceptional. Serendipity and fate double in this instance as a kind of protective halo in which disbelief can and should be suspended in order to enjoy the plot. Serendipity and fate also ensure that the liberal sympathy generated for individual slum dwellers does not seep into concern for the millions.

At the same time the barest of genealogical relationships between the novel and the film and Swarup's defense of the later as a success suggests, in fact, the opposite. If every detail of the plot and the character can be exchanged for another, then the road from poverty to wealth is in fact much more traversable and accessible: all slum life is impossible, and so an implausible millionaire should then be lurking within every slumdog. One of the other conceits of both the novel and the film is that slum dwellers are capable, in general, of incredibly intelligent, creative and generous acts, and the only thing which prevents torturing police officers, human rights attorneys, quiz show celebrities and landlords from realizing this is their own chauvinism. As Ram Mohammad Thomas angrily responds when his explanation for knowing the answers on *Kaun Banega Crorepati* is seen as too outlandish: "Like Godbole, you believe that I am good only for serving chicken fry and whisky in a restaurant. That I am meant to live life like a dog, and die like an insect. Don't you? […] Well, madam, we poor can also ask questions and demand answers. And I bet you, if the poor conducted a quiz, the rich wouldn't be able to answer a single question."[3] Here, not only is a the epistemology of the poor shown to be the limits of the knowledge of the rich, but the very fact of poverty – what life in a state of abjection is like – is so outside the ken of the middle-class interlocutor that it also serves as an indictment of middle-class monopolies on fact. The imperiousness of middle-class empiricism is not only hollow but dangerously so, as it leaves the interlocutor vulnerable to critique on terms that she implicitly concedes: facts are after all facts, and Ram Mohammad Thomas can prove that he knew enough to pass a single test of his intellect. The fact of Ram Mohammad Thomas and Jamal Malik is also supposed to serve as a critique of an ideology which deems them impossible, insofar as the impossibility of slumdog success is a product of middle-class chauvinisms and stereotypes of what the poor are actually capable of. As both Ram and Jamal prove how they knew the answers, they also reveal the exceptional nature of all ordinary slum life; after all, the more the middle class believes that a Ram or Thomas is possible, the less it should be able to believe that smart slum dwellers are rare. This is perhaps the sense in which Swarup defends his character as a kind of "Indian everyman," a democratic ideal to encounter the problems faced by the everyday poor.

The aristocratic and the democratic exist side-by-side in both the novel and the film, and, in fact, only become clear when the two are counterposed to one another, as necessary correlatives to the ideology of a certain set of representational norms about the very poor which both the novel and the film believe they are undermining but ultimately only shore up differently. This is not merely to argue that there is a deterioration of form and ideology when the narrative shifts from print to digital media, but it is rather to suggest that when it comes to an understanding of poverty, abjection, opportunity, and providence, the ideological frame through which people like Danny Boyle and Vikas Swarup view the very poor in India is itself cleft between an ideology of hope and hopelessness, between ideas of philanthropy and nihilism, whose contradictions produce the dizzying shuttling between realism and romance that characterizes both narratives. Both the film and the novel are structured simultaneously as exposé and as fantasy, as realist and romantic generically, not because they are wedded to narrative forms which compel certain conclusions, but because of the features of neoliberal capitalist development globally which have preserved, intact, critiques of uneven development patterns at the same time as they have led to the conclusion that little can be done to alter those patterns. All of this, this essay contends, happens under the sign of the fact and the competition over its accuracy.

Despite the factual differences between the novel and the film that continue to trouble readers and viewers of both, one important thematic difference between the novel and the film seems to have escaped most critics: Swarup's *Q & A* is dispositionally an *anti-cinematic* novel. In one of the more dramatic scenes of the novel, Ram Mohammad Thomas attempts to avenge his neighbor, Gudiya, who has been molested by her father, Shantaram, an unemployed astronomer. After he pushes Shantaram over the railing, Ram describes what he sees: "*In films*, they show a villain falling from the roof of a skyscraper and it seems as if he is floating in the air; he twists his legs and flaps his arms and screams, 'Aaaaaaaaaaaaaah!' *In real life*, it doesn't happen like that at all. Shantaram drops down like a rock. There is no flapping of hands or legs. He hits the ground facedown and lies spread-eagled, hands and legs outstretched."[4] This particular scene is only one of many in which fiction's attention to "truth" is highlighted at the expense of film's desire for sensationalism and set pieces, including the one murder that Ram actually commits in the novel when he shoots a dacoit who is about to molest Meenakhsi, a fellow train passenger: "It is not like they show you *in the movies*, where a bullet produces an instant little red patch and it remains like that till they cart away the body in an ambulance. No. The blood begins to seep out very gradually. First there is a tiny red dot, no bigger than a thumbtack, then it becomes a circular patch the size of a coin, then it grows as large as a saucer, then it expands to the size of a dinner plate, and it just keeps growing and growing till the flow becomes a torrent."[5] In both instances, the critique of cinematic verisimilitude does not produce important details or meaningful differences (the range of sizes of blood stains is hardly an improvement over the "instant little red patch"); it functions instead as an index for the accuracy of the novelistic description that it negatively endorses. For Ram and for the novel, authenticity in description, the structure of the novel's carefully (though flimsily) constructed verisimilitude, is always bought at the expense of overly dramatized and chintzy analogs in cinema and film, popularly understood as *masala*; novelistic and narrative truths are set against a deep suspicion of the cinematic frame.

Real tragedy, real violence and real poverty are repeatedly invoked in the novel against their falsified cinematic counterparts which, because they obscure reality, leave one hopelessly confused about the real world, "unable to figure out whether this was a comedy, a drama, or a tragedy."[6] And even though the novel invokes cinematic tropes, using them repeatedly (especially for Ram's fantasies about the mother who abandoned him and his future family), the novel sticks throughout to the idea that there is something dangerous about the necessary conflation between fantasy and film. Novels recreate reality in a more substantial and meaningful way (at least certain aspects of it) than films, the argument in *Q & A* goes, and one would do well to trust fiction over film as there are substantial costs to being seduced by cinematic fantasies. In the novel, films leave one vulnerable to molestation by either deviant priests or closeted Bollywood actors; they dupe one into being fooled by con artists and believing that one can be brave in the middle of a communal riot; they can make you believe that it is easy to commit murders; they can turn you into a self-centered has-been unable to adapt to the world; but, most of all, they can set up a pattern of expectations about life that are betrayed by real experiences.

The reality created by this procedure of rivaled accuracy is rhetorical and provisional, depending as it does on a verifiably inaccurate deployment of a fact that it stands next to (e.g., on screen, Armaan Ali is a heterosexual hero; in real life, he is the molester trying to take advantage of Ram's friend in the theater). The way that *Q & A* mobilizes verisimilitude depends on the aesthetics and pleasures of a kind of competitive empiricism, of a confident belief generated from the slightest of improvements in degrees of accuracy and truth, on a perpetually reflexive and situational strategy of shoring up one's own claim to a superior description of reality by bursting the closest competitor's. So the facts of *Q & A* are measured in their distance first from film and then from middle-class ideologies of the poor; one doesn't really learn all that much more, but the little one does learn is designed to give one certainty that the world need not be mastered completely, simply mastered better than one's neighbors have. Indeed, the facts about poverty and urban life which are revealed in the fiction amount, ultimately, to little more than a series of sentimental clichés, providing little insight into how the poor actually live. What they do provide is the fantasy that slum life, too, can be understood though a series of trivia, of facts, which have the ability to both secure one's position in the ranks of the philanthropic (because knowledge and sympathy are made cousins, here) but also to inure one to the dangers produced by trusting film. Abandoning film for fiction, with its marginally more nuanced details, it is the slightest of shifts in popular cultural tastes but it provides one with two important kinds of social capital: possessing better knowledge about the poor proves one cares more about poverty than others and knowing certain facts means that urban spaces are easier to navigate without the dangers of fraud, deception and crime. The same knowledge marks the possessor simultaneously as a concerned, worldly liberal and a vigilant, reclusive neoliberal.

This anti-cinematic disposition should have made the transition from fiction to film more difficult for *Q & A*, except for the fact that the same feeling of competitive empiricism manages to attach itself to the structure of *Slumdog Millionaire*. It is not incidental that the climactic moment in the film is a critique of the relevance of certain kinds of knowledge of fiction: winning the quiz show is absolutely disconnected from knowing the names of the characters of Alexander Dumas's *Three Musketeers*, which despite being central to the romance plot must here be returned to the narrative as pure chance. Marshalling the facts provided in fiction is made useless in the "real" world of the film. But the film and novel agree, ultimately, that fact and truth are important defenses against the ravages of poverty and urban spaces in India (European novels, then, are hardly practical). In the film, competitive empiricism is almost always troped as the duping of the non-Indian by the Indian (a sign, too, that we have moved from national to international audiences, where the problems of poverty are also problems of touristy naïveté). Not being able to know what you are looking at or listening to means that the Indian, Jamal Malik, who uses the dependence of the non-Indian on the native informant to his advantage, is able to swindle the unsuspecting tourists out of their money. While taking an American couple out to see "the largest *dhobi ghat* in all of India," Jamal's friends dismantle the tourists' car; when he is beaten by the Indian driver who correctly understands Jamal's complicity in the theft, he remarks to the American couple, "this is the *real* India." The wife then prods her husband to give the boy some money, with the concession, "well, this is the real America." All of this, though, happens before a cosmopolitan audience who knows that the couple has been duped yet again. The same skill is later used to swindle unsuspecting tourists of their cash as irrelevant and incorrect information about the Taj Mahal is passed off as genuine history. In both instances, nothing new is learned about either the *dhobi ghat* or the Taj Mahal, but spectators are given access to one more fact than is available to the duped foreigners: they are given one of the codes through which they can feel secure from the threats of similar scams. The ethic of competitive empiricism in the film is a residue of its novelistic counterpart, producing a safe comedic distance for the audience, who are never at risk of being cheated and can instead enjoy the view safely from the perspective of the street-wise Indian. Verisimilitude in the film is bought at the expense of (primarily) Western ignorance, which the spectator must recognize as her own so that it can be evacuated of any real danger. But it is also bought at the expense of another, more dangerous truth, which risks piercing the bubble of liberalism that it is designed to preserve: all interactions between the rich and the poor are performances which the rich decodes incorrectly at its own peril.

The way that fact and truth are deployed in both the novel and the film (whose dominant structure is the quiz show with its hard and fast answers) makes them sites of a series of expectations and aesthetic and ethical judgments, in which the right is also the good and the just. Not only are Ram and Jamal rewarded for their right answers, but their access to the right answers is supposed to be compensation for the unfairness which they have had to endure. In a scene omitted from the film, Ram's desire to help Shankar when he contracts rabies or Nita when she is beaten by Prem Kumar puts him inevitably into contact with his lifeboat and English professor Mr. Chatterjee, who returns the favor of Ram's generous gift of 400,000 rupees with the answer to the 100,000,000-rupee question: "Then go for *Love's Labour's Lost.* But as I said, I am not very sure. Sorry I cannot be more helpf—"[7] Here, facts are also rewards in an economy of virtue which has a long circuit before good deeds can bear their appropriate monetary rewards (with interest). There are distinct privileges that go with being able to recollect and retrieve facts, when facts are now understood as a kind of karma, accruing to the virtuous like so much test preparation and hard work. But there is also a way that this specific kind of fact-based reward is a metonymy for a larger culture of English language education and the cultural assimilation of western trivia that is the purview of the urban middle class in India. As Chaise LaDousa has argued in another context, upward class mobility in India depends on examination preparation and specific knowledge of English, since entry to "only some schools" can provide "a vehicle for middle class aspirations in India's liberalizing economy."[8] Knowledge of Shakespeare, irrelevant television programs, archaic Scottish geography, and Indian medals of valor double the meaning of fact in Swarup's novel: Ram Mohammad Thomas is not merely good but also qualified to enter into the ranks of the middle class. He takes, on the quiz show, one variant of the board exams that open up the pathways into middle-class life. He also offers, through his life, an adventurous compensation for those whose educations were paid for with endless hours in dull history classes; Ram necessarily reflects the fantasy of meritocracy back to the class which only anxiously sees itself as the subject of that fantasy.[9]

But the relationship between the quiz show and entry into middle-class life is not merely structured through a homology with middle-class struggles for social and economic advancement; it is also mirrored in a certain habituated relationship to social facts, in which the marshaling of trivia stands in for certain kinds of knowledge of the real, in which the barest of knowledge induces the broadest of social judgments. For instance, the aesthetic obsession with the fact and reality of poverty, the need to place on screen all of the gritty detail of urban underdevelopment, is also shrouded with the deep ambivalence that both works have to their own facticity, the extended trope which is the anxiety about their own verisimilitude. In the novel anxiety about the accuracy of representation happens in the form of "info-dumping," a term I borrow from critics of science fiction to describe the process where a narrator must unload a large amount of alien facts because the life-world in question is outside the ken of the reader. Info-dumping in *Q & A* is the style in which poverty is generally described:

> There are a million people like me, packed in a two-hundred-hectare triangle of swampy urban wasteland, where we live like animals and die like insects. Destitute migrants from all over the country jostle with each other for their own handful of sky in Asia's biggest slum. There are daily squabbles – over inches of space, over a bucket of water – which at times turn deadly. Dharavi's residents came from the dusty backwaters of Bihar and UP and Tamil Nadu and Gujarat. They came to Mumbai, the city of gold, with dreams in their hearts of striking it rich and living upper-middle-class lives.[10]

Tourist guide, journalistic reportage, Wikipedia entry – there are several different registers through which we can understand the style of this description, but info-dumping gets one closest to the notion that the actual space being described does not become more real by virtue of more facts being aggregated, even as it mimics the breathless syntax of memorized answers to board examinations. There are details, here, but no depth, with specific lists ("Bihar and UP and Tamil Nadu and Gujarat") standing in for thick description, while other claims ("dreams in their hearts of striking it rich") are pure, petit bourgeois projection. In fact, Swarup's need to get close to Dharavi is supposed to compensate for readerly disgust at the object under review ("Dharavi is not a place for the squeamish"), but it only ends up reproducing language that had already been discarded as inaccurate and chauvinist: "live like animals and die like insects" is too close to the language that Ram had previously critiqued as the hallmark of class-based chauvinism to be taken seriously now as an idiom of sympathy.[11] The language of fact becomes a sort of veil for the uneasy compromise with liberal attitudes towards the poor under which the plot of the novel moves, so that the very move which is designed to produce sympathy with the abject also reproduces the disdain of the privileged.

In the "100,000 Rupees" chapter, for example, Ram Mohammad Thomas serves drinks to Prakash Rao, managing director of Surya Industries, who is now involved with a Haitian woman who cursed his brother into madness with voodoo. When Rao has to explain how this happens to a confused Ram, this is the conversation that occurs:

> "Voodoo? What's that?"
>
> "You don't want to know, my friend. Voodoo is a religion in Haiti. Its practitioners worship spirits called *loas* and believe that the universe is all interconnected. Everything affects something else. Nothing is an accident, and everything is possible. That is why people who know voodoo can do all kinds of amazing things. Like bringing a dead man to life."
>
> "You must be joking."
>
> "No, not at all. These dead people are called zombies. I told you I am drunk. And a drunk man always tells the truth, right?"[12]

The melding of fact with fantasy, of plausibility with impossibility happens through the combination of three different rhetorical structures. First, the representation of fact through a series of definitions ("Voodoo is a religion," "spirits called loas" and "dead people called zombies") functions both as a kind of amateur anthropology (dare we call it a quiz show factoid?) and as a sort of science fictionalized info-dumping: even if we were to disbelieve in magic, here the reader is offered the opportunity to believe in the details of the conversation as a specific rule of the game internal to the unfolding of the narrative, and thus the fact exists in the uneasy zone between social reality and rhetorical performance. Secondly, we are offered the specific narrative conditions of fact creation under a commonsensical view of intoxication as truth inducement; if the fact is not itself a fact, it can be made factual through a certain kind of easily understood social relation. And finally, we are offered one set of impossible propositions about voodoo (largely for an Indian audience who knows little about voodoo but already has access to certain ideas about well-developed superstitions and magic that it holds to be commonsensical which can serve as an analog) in order to smuggle in a social truism, now turned into fact: "Nothing is an accident, and everything is possible." In overdetermining its own ability to speak truthfully, the novel also manages to speak ideologically.

This combination, though, of the fatedness of pure possibility, of the shared factual codes of compassion and bigotry, is simultaneously the worldview in which it is possible for a particular slumdog to become a millionaire and the conditions in which the mere mastery of fact has been turned into the advantage of an immensely powerful and consumptive middle class in India in the era of liberalization. The language of fact is actually the intersection between the ideology of meritocracy and the ideology of concern, which the middle class contradictorily mobilizes in order to justify its own position with respect to the poor (whom it exploits and fears) and the rich (whom it emulates and mistrusts). And when the novel then needs to interrogate its own relationship to the seduction of fact, the ideology which hides behind "fact," it learns that facts are more or less irrelevant to ideology. In the "500,000 Rupees" chapter, "A Soldier's Tale," Ram Mohammad Thomas encounters a con artist, a soldier who lies about his heroic participation in the 1971 war with Pakistan. Most probably set in 1999 during the conflict over the Siachen glacier in the Kargil district in Kashmir, the chapter begins with the residents of the chawl being forced into a bunker beneath a local school in response to air-raid sirens. In the bunker, where the residents have now constructed new, makeshift homes, they watch TV reports of the war, while the children play War and Peace and thank the war for getting them out of school. Infuriated by the lightness with which war is being discussed, Lance Naik (retired) Balwant Singh launches into a tirade about the realities of war, realities which neither cinema nor television can convey, but which his body demonstrates, since he has lost one of his legs. But his narrative can also invoke realities, so over a series of nights, Balwant Singh recounts to the residents of the bunker the story of his valiant participation in the important Chhamb sector of the western front, and, over the course of his telling, he wins the admiration and love of the residents. It is through the details, the carefully recounted stories, dates, religious rivalries, and patriotic conclusions, that Balwant Singh convinces his listeners that he really did participate in the war, and that he has been cheated out of justice: "Three of my colleagues got Sena medals, and a memorial was constructed for Jaurian. But they didn't give me anything, not even a mention in the dispatch."[13] Singh's lies are quickly exposed when new soldiers arrive to ask for collections for the current war effort and the colonel recognizes Balwant Singh as a deserter. This is how the colonel recollects Balwant Singh's role:

> Balwant Singh was not in a good frame of mind when war broke out, because his wife had just given birth to his first child in Pathankot. He was desperate to be with his family. So great was his longing that at the first sign of trouble in Jaurian, when Pakistan attacked with artillery in full strength, he deserted his post and ran away. He managed to reach Pathankot and hid in his ancestral house. He must have thought he had left the war far behind, but the war did not leave him. Two days after his arrival, the Pakistani Air Force strafed Pathankot air base. They didn't hit any of our planes, but two thousand-pound bombs fell on a house close to the airfield. Turned out that the house was Balwant's. His wife and infant son perished instantly in the attack, and he lost a leg to shrapnel.[14]

When asked by one of the residents how Singh could have fabricated his marvelously detailed stories if he hadn't actually lived them, the colonel replies that twenty eight years is time long enough to read newspapers and histories, enough time to "fool you people and earn some cheap thrills through his fake tales of valor."[15] The following day, Balwant Singh kills himself. The reaction of the residents is not like the colonel's, though, because the real story actually reveals the truth of the fake story. Our narrator tells us on the following page: "Those of us for whom this was the first war, we knew then. That war was a very serious business. It took lives."[16]

At the very moment when fact no longer stands on stable ground, ideology demonstrates its coherence, its absolute disconnectedness from the details, the specifics, the local. Even as Balwant Singh's lies are exposed, the ideology of patriotism, merit, justice, and even, ironically, the reality that "war was a very serious business," all manage to emerge from a false narrative unscathed. But the novel does not linger on the awkwardness of the moment even a little, for it shares with Balwant Singh the ethic of trafficking in life stories that are not one's own, using them for "cheap thrills" and still coming out ideologically coherent on the other end. This folding of fact into fiction, of evacuating fact of its truthfulness, is made all the more interesting by Vikas Swarup's own admission that not only had he never visited Dharavi, but also that "I wasn't trying for that level of realism. That's the great thing about fiction. In my invented universe, I make the rules. Google took me wherever I needed to go. Without Google I couldn't have written the book in two months."[17] Swarup here points to a particular relationship to facts and reality which might be understood as the result of lives lived with access to television, internet, film, video but not actual understanding of proximate landscapes, in which adjudicating the difference between fact and fiction is ancillary to the pleasure produced by the feeling of verisimilitude, which has now been dissociated from any real object since no one needs to know it fully, only marginally better. This mediated understanding of competitive empiricism not only shares certain features of testing-induced memorization, but also defines the provisional and performative relationship that the petit bourgeois has to poverty: it can sympathize, but only up to a point. At the end of the narrative, the genres of realism and romance once again merge: poverty is shown to be the adventurous "green world" that it is, replete with sensuous details, but only to be abandoned for the comfort of luxury.

Realism is both the idiom in which the middle class engages in a series of self-flagellating procedures about its own economic excesses and its lack of real knowledge or concern with respect to poverty *and* the limit point of its ability to relate to the poor in anything other than a condescending way. Indeed the moral virtues of Ram Mohammad Thomas are such that winning 1 billion rupees is only supposed to be incidental to the outcome of his quest: the deflating denouement which contorts an escape from poverty into a prison of middle-class values from which the middle class has actually freed itself – service, sympathy, selflessness. But it can only do this through an important circuit in which the novel is forced to confront the fact that the reality of poverty is important only insofar as it returns the middle class to the center of the story: poverty exists or doesn't exist on the basis of middle-class sympathy and interest in the problem and not as a condition of middle-class life in the first instance. Pavan Varma, in a different context, described the worldview of this class, thus: "The educated Indian seems to labour under the illusion that there is no link between his own lack of social responsibility and the prosperity of his class and that of the community as a whole. It is this illusion that is at the core of the socially deviant behavior of large chunks of the middle class."[18] The twinning of romance and realism – which is the blurring of the boundaries which separate fact and fiction in the novel and the film – is the only way that an ideology of meritocracy and politics of sympathy can coexist, despite their necessary hostility to one another.

This, ultimately, is not the permanent worldview of the Indian middle class, but a particular ideological cul-de-sac produced between the beginning of liberalization (1991) and the Bharatiya Janata Party's routed election slogan, "India Shining" (2004), in which certain assumptions about the unending dominance and growth of the Indian middle class became commonsensical.

Massive levels of growth through that period (growth rates were still hovering around 5 percent per year with some estimates coming in at 8 or 9 percent) produced a situation in which several of the *Forbes* richest billionaires were Indians (including Lakshmi Mittal and Mukesh Ambani who make the top ten) and in which the middle class grew substantially.[19] With the evisceration of the social welfare net in India as a condition of aid and loan packages from international lending institutions, it is increasingly the super-rich who are in charge of dispensing social welfare to the very poor through massive philanthropic-cum-public relations projects: the Tata Group's Sarva Swasthya Mission Trust; Sunil Mittal's Bharati Foundation; Ambani's Reliance Foundation, to name a few.[20] But despite the renewed global interest in coming to terms with mass urban poverty, there is still an intellectual deadlock produced by the fact that the people now dispensing relief in India are the ones who rose to wealth through the dismantling of the welfare state. This class of people born under the sign of late twentieth century neoliberalism has manufactured a para-state liberalism, in which corporations (with coordinating roles assumed by the state) play the role of ensuring a certain minimum standard of life for the poorest citizens of the nation. The ideologies produced by this economic arrangement are simultaneously compassionate and hypercompetitive, using visible, conspicuous compassion to endorse aggressive acquisition.

This is what the strange union between *Q & A* and *Slumdog Millionaire* reveals: the facts which are so important to the narrative of the film and the novel ultimately only matter as long as they are able to complete the metamorphosis of neoliberal competition into liberal compassion; once the linkage between romance and realism (between utopianism and pessimism) has been secured, the specificity of the narrative no longer matters to the overall feel of either aesthetic artifact. At the end of *Q & A*, Ram Mohammad Thomas avoids prosecution for the murder of the dacoit (because no one had heard about the incident), bankrupts the quiz show *Who Will Win a Billion* after its producers are forced to pay him his winnings, frees the slum children who are forced to beg for Maman, secretly finances his best friend's movie career, marries his prostitute love interest and restores justice by bearing witness to the death of Prem Kumar. The tying up of loose ends in the novel is in sharp contrast to the clean ending of the film's love plot, since the various other plot lines in the film are merely opportunities from which Jamal Malik must escape, not problems which demand resolution. In the film, these problems are resolved through the mass democratic participation in Jamal Malik's success, symbolically cathecting his accomplishments to the rest of the country without actually redistributing his wealth. In the novel, the privatization of Ram's success is even more radical; when Ram tosses Gudiya his two-headed coin, he retorts: "I won't need it any more. Because luck comes from within."[21]

If the social phenomenon of poverty endorses both Ram and Jamal's claims to outstanding talent because of the fact of their survival, the ending of both the film and the novel have to rely on more generalized notions of merit, virtue, and accomplishment which are dissociated from general social phenomenon. The transformation of the novel into the film, both of which mobilize the generous and the contemptuous idioms which come so easily to the middle class, reveals the ways that liberalism and neoliberalism do not confront each other as real political rivals in post-reform India. The pretense of liberalism is the strongest aesthetic effect of the neoliberal fact of poverty.

But the twinning of liberal sympathies with neoliberal competition, of democracy with aristocracy, of compassion with merit, is also helpful in explaining the success of the *Slumdog Millionaire* phenomenon and the enthusiasm that spectators and critics had for the film. The intractable problem of mass urban poverty is resolved along pathways that are much easier to understand and manage for largely middle-class audiences, for whom charity has always been the flipside of self-help, in the well-trafficked form of the *Bildungsroman*. The combination of democratic and meritocratic ideologies reanimated by the film and the novel smuggle in two mutually exclusive pleasures by grounding them both in the clichéd logics of educational advancement in both its privatized and socialized forms. But it was, in fact, the timing of the film, right before the explosion of the Arab Spring and the Occupy Movement internationally and the global economic recession, which made the *Slumdog Millionaire* phenomenon a possibility; it came at the last possible moment where the promise of economic growth still held out the possibility of trickle-down largesse, or the replacement of a corrupt rich with a more magnanimous one, preferably taken from the ranks of the deserving poor. This is also what united the political demands of the Indian readership of the novel and the global spectatorship of the film: a neoliberal critique of Indian political corruption found an echo chamber with global liberal development politics. The "fact" that the novel and the film can be critiqued as "phenomenon," too, is evidence in part that the historical moment which allowed this coalition of liberalism and neoliberalism to emerge has also (thankfully) passed.

Notes

1 Stuart Jeffries, "Author Vikas Swarup on Slumdog Millionaire," *Guardian*, 15 January 2009. Online: http://www.guardian.co.uk/books/2009/jan/16/danny-boyle-india (accessed 2 September 2011).

2 See also Pierre Vitoux, "The Mode of Romance Revisited," *Texas Studies in Literature and Language* 49.4 (2007): 387–410.

3 Vikas Swarup, *Q & A* (New York: Scribner, 2005), 17.

4 Ibid., 69, emphasis added.

5 Ibid., 161–2.

6 Ibid., 227.

7 Ibid., 299.

8 Chaise LaDousa, "Nation and State: Language, School, and the Reproduction of Disparity in a North Indian City," *Anthropological Quarterly* 80.4 (2007): 927.

9 For a discussion about the relationship between middle class education and quiz shows, see also, Su Holmes, *The Quiz Show* (Edinburgh: Edinburgh University Press, 2008).

10 Swarup, 133.

11 Ibid.

12 Ibid., 139–40.

13 Ibid., 185.

14 Ibid., 188.

15 Ibid., 189.

16 Ibid., 190.

17 Mark McDonald, "A Diplomat's Unlikely Rise to 'Slumdog' Acclaim," *New York Times*, 1 April 2008. Online: http://www.nytimes.com/2009/04/02/arts/02iht-zslumdog.html?pagewanted=all (accessed 13 September 2011).

18 Pavan Varma, *The Great Indian Middle Class* (London: Penguin, 1998), 198.

19 Utsav Kumar and Arvind Subramanian, "Growth in India's States in the First Decade of the 21st Century," *Economic and Political Weekly* 67.3 (21 January 2012): 48–57.

20 For a discussion of this ideology, see Nandan Nilekani, *India Imagined: the Idea of a Renewed Nation* (New York: Penguin, 2009), 385–403.

21 Swarup, 318.

Part Three

SLUMDOG AND BOLLYWOOD

Chapter 8

SLUMDOGS, COOLIES AND GANGSTERS: AMITABH BACHCHAN AND THE LEGACY OF 1970s BOLLYWOOD IN *SLUMDOG MILLIONAIRE*

Claus Tieber

An Old Debate

The representation of India in Indian and in Western cinema has always been a heavily discussed issue. One of India's most famous film stars, Nargis, argued that director Satyajit Ray would deliver poverty to the West, when instead he should produce images of a modern India: "[*Pather Panchali*] does not represent India's poverty in its true form [...] It is not a correct image of India."[1] Ray, on the other hand, attacked the Hindi cinema that Nargis so famously represented:

> India took one of the greatest inventions of the West with most far-reaching artistic potential, and promptly cut it to size, generating images that range from the absurd to the repulsive (by way of some wonderful songs, it is true).[2]

This dichotomy of "selling poverty to the West" versus "the absurd and repulsive," of realism versus melodrama, of social consciousness versus popularity or, as D. A. Windsor puts it, "the commercial and the artistic aesthetics, the formulaic and the radical, the mythic and the real,"[3] was reproduced and mirrored in the West, as Rosie Thomas writes in her famous essay, "Indian Cinema: Pleasures and Popularity," one of the very first scholarly articles that took Hindi cinema seriously: "Western critics [...] take their cues from the Indian upper-middle class intelligentsia and government cultural bodies."[4] The "lack of realism" that Hindi cinema shares with Hollywood films in that view is compared to the different approaches and aesthetics of Indian art house cinema, especially the films of Satyajit Ray. The debate about the accurate representation of India, whose categories and arguments are created in India itself, is taken over by Western critics and scholars to denounce Hindi cinema, often in a paternalistic and more or less imperialistic way.

In the 1990s the Western image of India changed, thanks also to a significant change within Hindi cinema. The decline of communism, economic liberalization and the growth of the Indian middle class as well as a new approach to Non Resident Indians (NRIs)[5] led to a new cinematic image of India, which combined modernity and traditionalism; Western hedonism and conservative values constructed as genuine Indian ones.[6] The stories now take place in the middle class, the films targeting the Indian middle classes as well as the middle-to-upper class NRIs. It was this new image of a modern India that attracted the West. Bollywood became a well-known term but less defined; it covered dancing, food, clothes and was sold to the West as a new lifestyle trend. Films were delivering colorful pictures for stories and articles that had no interest in looking under the surface. India was no longer a place of esoteric inspiration or an exotic theme park for the adventures of Western colonialists, but a modern, urban place where East and West, the modern and the traditional, met peacefully. A new cliché of India was constructed.

A Western audience became interested in Bollywood films and Bollywood was associated with colors, love stories, a middle class setting and Shah Rukh Khan. Even more, Bollywood became a synonym for a lifestyle, consisting of dance courses and colorful clothes, music and food. Soon everything Indian or even reminiscent of India was labeled Bollywood. Western cinema, too, became interested and tried to hop on the train. *Moulin Rouge* (Baz Luhrmann, 2001) is an example often quoted for the influence of Bollywood on mainstream Western cinema. But after a couple of years, signs of Bollywood in Western cinema vanished. The hype was not able to target a big enough audience.

Slumdog Millionaire has to be contextualized before this background. The idea of a British director taking an Indian novel (or, at least, a novel written by a Non Resident Indian in English) and shooting a film with Indian actors partly in Hindi makes sense only in this short period when Bollywood and modern India became recognized in the West. But director Danny Boyle and producer Christian Colson had no stars in their film and, what is even more important, their story does not take place in the middle class as most of the successful Hindi films of the 1990s and early 2000s do. Instead, it resembles another era of Hindi cinema almost unknown to a Western audience, when slum dwellers, workers, prostitutes and gangsters met onscreen. When the film was finally released, the reception in India was very critical, or at least Western media constructed such an impression. Arguments similar to those from the Nargis–Ray debate were invoked. But the object of disappointment with a representation of India that was seen as clichéd and paternalizing was now a small British film instead of an Indian art house movie or Hindi cinema. Interestingly enough, the most famous critic of *Slumdog* was Amitabh Bachchan, who himself had played slumdogs more than once in his long career and whose persona and films are quoted by *Slumdog*. In fact, Bachchan is the single most important real person in *Slumdog*, whose influence on the film is manifold: he is a character in the film, the character of the quiz show host is modeled after him and clips of his films are shown. In narration, motives and structure, Bachchan's films of the 1970s have heavily influenced *Slumdog Millionaire*.

The Bachchan Persona

Slumdog is structured around the questions of the quiz show, *Who Wants to Be a Millionaire?* In fact, it employs a narrative structure that makes heavy use of flashbacks but puts these flashbacks in a chronological order.[7] The first question, which has to be an easy one in the dramaturgy of the show is: "Who was the star in the 1973 hit film *Zanjeer*?" The following sequence, like the other flashbacks, tells the story of Jamal's life and why he knows the answer. Jamal is locked in a shithouse while Amitabh Bachchan is coming to the slum. He escapes through the shit and, covered in it, gets an autograph of the star. Bachchan is played by a lookalike (Feroze Khan) but, in most of the shots, his face is not seen. He is introduced through a series of very short clips from his 1970s films. If I have recognized them correctly the clips are from *Don* (dir. Chandra Barot, 1978), *Coolie* (dir. Manmohan Desai, 1983) and *Ram Balram* (dir. Vijay Anand, 1980). *Zanjeer* (dir. Prakash Mehra, 1973) was Bachchan's first hit film, the one that made him a star. The clips are chosen for their extraordinary visuals and the short montage is a mix of campy looks and action scenes. More than by its sometimes extravagant '70s look, the Bachchan screen persona was defined by the social status of the characters he played, by the character's relation to his mother, his motivation to "be somebody," his lust for revenge, and his function as a representative of Bombay's and India's marginalized groups.[8] The ideology of the Bachchan persona is a point of discussion, and I will argue that it is exactly the ambiguity of this persona that made the actor the biggest star of South Asia.

Fareeduddin Kazmi uses a slightly bigger sample of Bachchan films to point out the social status of his role:

> In *Deewar*, he is a coolie in the dockyard who later on becomes a kingpin of the underworld. In *Sholay*, he is a petty crook, in *Coolie*, a coolie, in *Adalat*, a simple

> villager who is forced to flee from the village, in *Kalia*, a taxi driver, in *Mard*, a tangewala, in *Naseeb*, a waiter, in *Amar, Akbar, Anthony*, a bootlegger, in *Namak Halal*, a family servant, in *Akhri Raasta*, a small-time party worker, in *Don*, a village simpleton.[9]

Bachchan's characters are slum dwellers, workers and other poor and working class members. Their desire to become active agents is often motivated by some injustice that took place in their childhood against one of their parents. The typical protagonist of classical Hollywood cinema – active, goal-oriented, psychologically motivated, driving the plot forward with his actions[10] – was almost unknown in Hindi cinema at the time Bachchan's fame began to rise. The classical protagonist of Hollywood cinema also represents a bourgeois ideology of the subject who is able to create his own destiny, whose future lies within his own hands. Such an active agent is only possible in a more or less bourgeois, capitalist society.

There are very few Hindi films that took place in a bourgeois setting before the 1990s. The interesting point is that, in Hindi cinema, the active, goal-oriented hero was not introduced by a bourgeois character but by proletarian or sub-proletarian characters played by Amitabh Bachchan. This specificity of Indian film history should be seen in the context of the political and economic history of India. To make a long story short: the industrialization of the Nehru-era produced a growing working class but only the economic liberalization of the 1990s started the development of a quickly and massively growing middle class. For Hindi cinema, major parts of its audiences up to the 1990s were working class and lower.[11] The sociological and economic changes of the 1990s resulted in Hindi films that represented the Indian middle class and were made for them, whereas members of poorer classes, particularly slum dwellers, vanished for the most part from the screen.

In many of his films from the 1970s, Bachchan played the bad guy opposite a good brother. Good and bad personified in two brothers is a crucial motive in Hindi cinema. It has a long tradition, which can be traced back to *Mother India* (dir. Mehboob Khan, 1957). But the most famous film with two brothers signifying two opposite paths is *Deewar* (dir. Yash Chopra, 1975), one of Bachchan's most famous films. This motif can also be found in *Slumdog*, where Jamal is the good, righteous brother and Salim is the bad one, who becomes a gangster and who dies violently at the end. The character for whose love both brothers aim and who decides who is good and who is bad, is their mother. There is no character in Hindi cinema that is more important for the male protagonist than his mother.[12] This mother character not only gives and denies her love to those on the right or wrong paths but serves as a representation of India herself (Mother India), the only accepted authority, a female god for whose love the male characters are doing everything and whose punishment they fear. And, as *Mother India* shows, this punishment can be deadly.[13] In *Deewar*, the goal of Bachchan's character, Vijay, is to build his mother a home and to be loved by her. In the end he comes to the realization that all his illicit activities have led to individual wealth but cannot bring him the love of his mother.

The injustice done to his mother or father in his childhood is the motivation for an unspecific revenge for most of Bachchan's '70s and '80s characters. At the bottom of this feeling lies anger about the injustices of Indian society, corruption and the unfulfilled hopes of Independence. The angry young man, as the Bachchan persona was called, was not angry about any concrete circumstance, but his anger could be – and was – read in a political way. The examples of injustice and corruption could explicitly be seen in Bachchan's films: in *Deewar*, co-workers of the boy's father tattoo him with the sentence "my father is a thief," his mother loses her job and the family cannot afford for both brothers to go to school, so Vijay starts working as a shoe shiner to finance the education of his brother. His brother, however, cannot find a job because other applicants have better connections. Bachchan's films of the 1970s explicitly show the shortcomings of independent India. The actions of the Bachchan character are condemned but they are shown as fully justified. His anger is one of the elements that made him popular. This anger was shared by millions, not only by those who Bachchan represented explicitly but also by those who helped him on his way – narratologically speaking the "donors"[14] – who combined their destinies with his fight. Bachchan's character is helped by prostitutes, small crooks, women on the edge of society (widows, working women), Muslims and other marginalized groups. In many of his films a connection with a Muslim character is established, and in some Bachchan himself plays one (e.g., *Coolie*, *Muqaddar ka Sikander* (dir. Mehra, 1978)). The representation of Muslims in 1970s Hindi cinema is different from its predecessors as well as from its successors. While in the films from Independence (1947) up to the 1970s the religious belief of the characters was no issue at all, in the 1970s Muslims became represented. The message most often communicated in films was that all Indians belonged to one family, no matter whose religious belief they shared. The most popular example of such a sentiment is *Amar, Akbar, Anthony* (dir. Desai, 1979), with Bachchan playing the latter Christian character.

In the 1990s, not only the poor but also Muslims almost entirely vanished from the screen. Never before was Bollywood so Hindu dominated, with Hindu rituals playing an important role in many of the narratives. Ironically, the Hindu Bachchan played more Muslims in the 1970s than the Muslim Shah Rukh Khan, who mostly plays Hindu characters. It is important to emphasize the fact that *Slumdog Millionaire* not only takes place in Dharavi, Mumbai's infamous shantytown, but also features Muslims as main characters. At a time when Bollywood has created an image of a new, modern and clean India where no poor people live and where Hinduism peacefully overshadows any other religion, it is no surprise that the "usual suspects," Shiv Sena and other Hindutva organizations, criticized *Slumdog* for its depictions of Hindus.[15] Nevertheless, the most famous criticism of *Slumdog* came from Amitabh Bachchan, who played slum dwellers and Muslims himself and whose company co-produced the first Indian film about the destruction of the Babri Masjid in Ayodhya by Hindu nationalists, Mani Ratnam's *Bombay* (1995). The riots in Mumbai that followed the destruction of this mosque are also shown in *Slumdog* in the sequence when Jamal and Salim's mother is killed. (In *Bombay* two twin brothers, sons of a Hindu father and Muslim mother, get lost in the riots.)

A Slum's Eye View of Politics

The ideology of Bachchan's films from the '70s and '80s, which depict slum dwellers, the working class, Muslims and marginalized groups, is frequently discussed.[16] To understand the impact and meaning of these films, one has to add one more historical event to the context: the twenty-one months of the Emergency. In 1975, Indian Prime Minister Indira Gandhi ended democracy in India for almost two years with this state of Emergency. No elections, no parliament, no unions, no strikes or rallies were permitted, and leaders of the opposition were sent to jail.[17] Gandhi's authoritarian coup was an answer to a growing opposition, long strikes, and an increasing crime rate. The question of the legitimacy of oppression, of the justification of means is, in Bachchan's films from this period, transferred from an explicitly political context to a criminal setting with some touches of injustice and corruption to give it a broader meaning. In this context it was argued that these films, which condemn the illegal actions of the Bachchan character, would justify the Emergency and function as an argument for the eradication of organized crime by any means necessary.[18] Bachchan dies in many of these films, often shot by a police officer who is sometimes his brother, as in *Deewar*. On the other hand Bachchan, who often played the criminal in these films, built his career on such a persona, with the "angry young man" making him the "most famous man in India."[19]

One point on the agenda of the Indian government in the 1970s, especially during the Emergency, was the demolition of slums.[20] This is an issue that is explicitly depicted in Hindi films of the time and, in some cases, it is the Bachchan character who saves the homes of the slum dwellers. The Bombay riots of 1992–93, after the demolition of the Babri mosque in Ayodhya, are the historical background for the sequence in which Jamal's mother dies. They are also connected with arguments concerning the real estate value of the shanty houses. After the riots in January 1993, there were wild public speculations about the economic reasons for the rioting, with some arguing that they were directed by those who wanted the slums demolished in order to buy the land for a cheaper price and build houses on it.[21] Such a view was even found in films like *Krantiveer* (dir. Mehul Kumar, 1994). So the ideology of the Bachchan's 1970s films is more ambivalent than is apparent at first glance. On the surface they seem to sanction strong-arm tactics against criminals and simultaneously condemn the actions of the vigilante Bachchan character. At the same time, these films are also critical of the state of India thirty years after Independence and they do have a slum sensibility, an awareness that a sympathetic portrayal of a section of society constituting a large part of the mass audience was essential to their success. Ashis Nandy suggests that the films from this period reflect a "slum's eye view of politics,"[22] a phrase that effectively combines the contradictions I have described here. The slum eye's view of politics is one seen from the perspective of the slum, thereby placing the slum at the center of its narration. But a "slum's eye view of politics" sees politics only as corrupt and unjust and, at the same time, favors populist solutions. Similarly, in *Slumdog*, corruption is on display everywhere and individual solutions to broader problems are seen as justified, with the film always rooting for the underdog (in this case, the slumdog).

Bachchan, Melodrama and the Education of a Slumdog

The angry young man of the time of the Emergency went on to become a member of the Indian Parliament, had some problems with the Bofors corruption affair[23] and was remodeled as a national icon in 2000 as the host of the international quiz show modeled on *Who Wants to Be a Millionaire? – Kaun Banega Crorepati?* As Mishra states, "Nowhere has it received the kind of frenzied following that it has in India, where theaters are rescheduling their evening shows on Mondays to Thursdays so as to not coincide with the programs evening time slot."[24] In India the show continues to be associated with its first and most successful host (Shah Rukh Khan, who later also served as host for the show, never attained Bachchan's ratings).[25] Bachchan's career mirrors the history of modern India. But, for as long as it continues, it will always be closely connected with the Emergency and the subsequent curtailment of democracy in India for over a year from 1975–76, for no other film actor represented the feelings of broad parts of the Indian population so vividly at this time. While Bachchan continues to play a role in today's film industry, reworking and building on his older persona, he no longer plays outsiders and, indeed, there is no longer a series of roles that could be summarized into one screen persona such as the angry young man.

Prem, the game show host in *Slumdog*, may remind some of the most famous man in India. Prem is played by Anil Kapoor, a popular actor best known for his roles in *Mr. India* (dir. Shekhar Kapur, 1987) and *Lahme* (dir. Yash Chopra, 1991), as an Indian superhero and melancholic rich lover, respectively. Kapoor's status, however, falls flat when compared to that of Bachchan. The Prem character is an ambivalent representative of the establishment which, in the India of *Slumdog*, is seen as global entertainment industry in which individuals (contestants in this context) are treated in accordance with their ratings potential. Prem's behavior towards Jamal changes during the course of the show. At the start he makes fun of the *chaiwallah*, clearly highlighting the difference in social status between host and contestant. When he recognizes that the boy possesses the chance to win the show, he changes his attitude, attempting to direct and dramatize Jamal's growing success. Prem's changing attitude towards Jamal is neatly paralleled by that of Bachchan towards *Slumdog*. At first Bachchan criticized the film but, after it won several Academy Awards, he became one of the first to publicly congratulate composer A. R. Rahman.[26] Thus the established Bollywood star attacks the new star, the outsider, the one who reminds audiences of his younger self and, when he realizes he cannot stop the rise of this new phenomenon, jumps on the bandwagon.

As I have shown, the influence of Amitabh Bachchan, and therefore of 1970s Hindi cinema on *Slumdog Millionaire* is manifold. Bachchan's films frequently start in the present and deliver the story in flashbacks, or in one long flashback, most prominently in *Deewar*. The narrative structure may not be as elaborate as *Slumdog*'s but the bookend device is a common one in Hindi cinema. Bachchan's films tell the whole life story of their protagonists. The childhood of Bachchan's characters is shown in many of his films, as is the good and bad brother theme. Bachchan's films convey a melodramatic story within a more or less realistic setting. Melodrama in this sense does not refer to a genre but to a mode of storytelling.[27] Settings include slums and docks, coal mines and train stations, places where the poor and marginalized work and live. These settings construct a parallel India, a place that can be identified as India but that is also different from the real. Screenwriter Javed Akhtar calls Bollywood "another state within the confederation of modern India [...] Hindi cinema's culture is quite different from Indian culture, but it is not alien to us."[28]

Innocent children at the mercy of a cruel villain, such as the brothers in *Slumdog*, are a familiar theme of melodramatic narration, from Charles Dickens and Hollywood silent movies, to Hindi cinema. Melodramatic stories take place in a space that is clearly divided into binary opposites. In the Bachchan films, as well as in *Slumdog*, this division runs through one family and divides brothers from one another – the good and bad theme. The melodramatic mode of narration includes coincidences as opposed to a clear line of cause and effect. Coincidences, shown as signs of destiny, are dramaturgically crucial for Hindi cinema and also play an important role in *Slumdog*. The melodramatic protagonist is a passive, innocent character who is able to stay innocent despite all temptations. This kind of protagonist is the very opposite of the active agent of classical Hollywood cinema. Jamal wants to attain his love interest (Latika) – in this sense he is an active agent who goes on the game show to get his girl. But Jamal is also a passive protagonist who strives to remain innocent, even when his brother becomes a gangster. Thus, while in many ways the Bachchan character of the '70s is closer to Salim than to Jamal, the narrative themes of these two cinemas are the same.

Finally, the melodramatic mode of narration has a clear moral message. In the case of the Bachchan films, this would be crime does not pay, illegal means are not justified, etc. To formulate the message of *Slumdog* is not that easy. The uplifting message that anyone can make it – the rags-to-riches theme – may be part of its success at a time when this general belief has begun to erode in the West. But to find a clear moral message in *Slumdog* one has to look further. The real message of *Slumdog* is similar to that of the quiz show: that knowledge matters. This leads to the last point of this essay: the crucial difference between Hindi cinema and *Slumdog* lies in their respective approaches to education and knowledge.

The representation of education and knowledge in Hindi cinema is an issue that still waits to be fully explored in film studies. This essay is not the place to start such a discussion. But in order to show the difference in the attitude towards education between the Bachchan films of the '70s and *Slumdog*, it is necessary to take a brief look at some examples. The male protagonist in Hindi cinema of previous eras was more often than not an uneducated one. In one of the classics of Hindi cinema, *Mother India*, the whole tragedy of the family starts when a moneylender lends money with absurd conditions attached. In his attempts to stop the moneylender's exploitation, the male protagonist, Birju, learns to read and to do math. He even attends school – as an adult – in order to attain this education. But formal knowledge is unable to stop the exploitation; the moneylender's contract is evil but legal. In *Mother India* the knowledge of the upper classes is explicitly called "bad knowledge." Birju's subsequent efforts to address the injustice he is faced with are less educated and more violent. In *Deewar*, the Bachchan character as a boy polishes shoes to finance the education of his brother, whose many (unsuccessful) applications for a job demonstrate that it is not education, but connections and corruption, that get one a job.

Such a cynical attitude towards formal education can also be seen in *Dilwale Dulhania Le Jayenge*, aka, *DDLJ* (dir. Aditya Chopra, 1995), when the protagonist, played by Shah Rukh Khan, laughs and parties with his father after failing to finish college. The difference between *DDLJ* and older Hindi films is that the protagonist is no longer poor. To make a long story short: in Hindi cinema, education and wealth are not connected – education is no prerequisite for success. Only recently has Hindi cinema realized that India could have an education problem and made it the theme of the successful *3 Idiots* (dir. Rajkumar Kurani, 2009). *Slumdog*'s approach to knowledge is different. It is precisely Jamal's knowledge which wins him the money and gets him his girl. Early in the film, there is a short scene in which the brothers are brought to school against their will. Apart from this, the film demonstrates how Jamal acquires his knowledge through his life experiences. Every answer is combined with a significant episode of his life. Jamal's coincidental knowledge is not the result of a proper education but, instead, the result of a critical and negative attitude towards (formal) education.[29]

Conclusion

"Realism," as D. A. Windsor has noted, "[…] remains the predominant category by which Indian films are viewed in the West, as can be seen by the number of awards that Mira Nair's *Salaam Bombay!* (1988) [achieved]."[30] Realism also remains a powerful criterion in India itself, as can be seen in the debate between Nargis and Satyajit Ray and in the discussions about *Slumdog*. Realism as a valued artistic category seems to have more in common with the tastes and cultural beliefs of the middle classes than with those of national or regional groups. Indian cinema began to change in the 1990s. It sold middle-class characters to a middle-class audience in India and abroad. But the taste of at least part of this middle class, at home as well as in the diaspora, finally led to more realistic films; films that are closer to Hollywood than to Bollywood in the twenty-first century. *Slumdog*, as a transnational film, has to be contextualized in such a manner. It was criticized for promoting a false realism and the wrong image of India when it was seen as a British film. And it was subsequently praised as an Indian film after winning awards. *Slumdog* may fulfill common views of realism but, in fact, it is anything but a realistic film – it is a melodramatic narrative, heavily influenced by the Bachchan films of the 1970s, but with the look of twenty-first century Bollywood.

Notes

1 Quoted in Andrew Robinson, *Satyajit Ray: The Inner Eye* (London: André Deutsch 1989), 327.
2 Quoted in Robinson, 333.
3 D. A. Windsor, "Nargis, Ray, Rushdie and the real," *South Asia* 21.1 (1998), 229.
4 Rosie Thomas, "Indian Cinema: Pleasures and Popularity," *Screen* 26 (1985): 118.

5 While the ministry for Overseas Affairs was established in 2004, the cinematic image began to change with Aditya Chopra's *Dilwale Dulhania Le Jayenge* in 1995.

6 For a sociological analysis of India's middle classes and their connections to film and culture in general, see Rachel Dwyer, *All You Want Is Money, All You Need Is Love: Sex and Romance in Modern India* (London: Cassell, 2000).

7 David Bordwell, "Slumdogged by the Past," *Observations on Film Art.* Online: http://www.davidbordwell.net/blog/2009/02/01/slumdogged-by-the-past/ (accessed 28 February 2012).

8 Cf. Fareeduddin Kazmi, "How Angry is the Angry Young Man? 'Rebellion' in Conventional Hindi Films," in *The Secret Politics of Our Desires: Innocence, Culpability and Indian Popular Cinema*, edited by Ashis Nandy (London: Zed Books, 1998), 134–56; Ranjani Mazumdar, "From Subjectification to Schizophrenia: The 'Angry Man' and the 'Psychotic' Hero of Bombay Cinema," in *Making Meaning in Indian Cinema* , edited by Ravi Vasudevan (New Delhi: Oxford University Press, 2000), 238–66; Claus Tieber, "Kino im Ausnahmezustand: Amitabh Bachchan als nationaler Held in Krisenzeiten," in *Fokus Bollywood: Das indische Kino in wissenschaftlichen Diskursen*, edited by Tieber (Berlin [et al.]: Lit Verlag, 2009), 84–98.

9 Kazmi, "How Angry is the Angry Young Man?", 139.

10 Cf. David Bordwell, Janet Staiger and Kristin Thompson, *Classical Hollywood Cinema: Film Style and Mode of Production to 1960* (London: Routledge, 1988), 11ff.

11 Cf. Vijay Mishra, *Bollywood Cinema: Temples of Desire* (New York: Routledge, 2002), 134; Kazmi, "How Angry is the Angry Young Man?", 140.

12 Cf. Vinay Lal, "The impossibility of the outsider in modern Hindi Film," in Nandy, *The Secret Politics of Our Desires*, 240.

13 The title character kills her son in order to prevent him from raping the moneylender's daughter, thus preserving the rightous or *dharmic* order even if it entails filicide.

14 Vladimir Propp, *Morphology of the Folktale*, translated by Laurence Scott (Austin: University of Texas Press 2003 [1968]), 48f. See also M. Madhava Prasad, *Ideology of the Hindi Film: A Historical Construction* (New Delhi: Oxford University Press, 1998), 143f.

15 "Shiv Sena Protests Screenings of Slumdog Millionaire," *Daily News and Analysis*, 23 September 2009. Online: http://www.dnaindia.com/india/report_shiv-sena-protests-screening-of-slumdog-millionaire_1224434 (accessed 28 February 2012).

16 Cf. Kazmi, "How Angry is the Angry Young Man?"; Tieber, "Kino im Ausnahmezustand."

17 Cf. Ramachandra Guha, *India After Gandhi: The History of the World's Largest Democracy* (London: Macmillan, 2007), 493–545.

18 Kazmi, "How Angry is the Angry Young Man?", 152.

19 Jamal in *Slumdog Millionaire*, DVD. Directed by Danny Boyle. London: Pathé Productions Limited, 2009 (00.14:14).

20 Guha, *India After Gandhi*, 511.

21 Cf. Mishra, *Bollywood Cinema*, 232.

22 Ashis Nandy, "Introduction: Indian Cinema as a Slum's Eye View of Politics," in Nandy, *The Secret Politics of Our Desires*, 1–18.

23 Cf. Mishra, *Bollywood Cinema*, 154.

24 Ibid.

25 Swarup Chakraborty, "KBC: Waiting For a Facelift," *Business Standard*, 26 July 2010. Online: http://www.business-standard.com/india/news/kbc-waiting-forfacelift/402440/ (accessed 28 February 2012).

26 Cf. "Slumdog Makes India Proud," *Times of India*, 24 February 2009. Online: http://articles.timesofindia.indiatimes.com/2009-02-24/news-interviews/28018835_1_indian-cinema-rahman-slumdog-millionaire (accessed 28 February 2012).

27 Cf. Linda Williams, *Playing the Race Card: Melodramas of Black and White from Uncle Tom to O.J. Simpson* (Princeton: Princeton University Press, 2002), 42; and Claus Tieber, *Stummfilmdramaturgie. Erzählweisen des amerikanischen Feature Films* 1917–1927 (Berlin [et al.]: Lit Verlag 2011), 43–55.

28 Javed Akthar quoted in David Chute, "A Beginner's Guide to Hindi Cinema," *Film Comment* (May/June 2002): 36.

29 Editor's note: For more regarding the issue of formal and informal knowledge in *Slumdog*, see Anjaria and Anjaria's essay, "*Slumdog Millionaire* and Epistemologies of the City," included in this collection.

30 Windsor, "Nargis, Ray, Rushdie and the real," 240.

Chapter 9

"IT IS WRITTEN" (IN INVISIBLE INK): *SLUMDOG MILLIONAIRE*'S SFX AND THE REALIST OVERWRITING OF BOLLYWOOD SPECTACLE

Samhita Sunya

Identifying the "street urchin film" as a transnational cinematic genre that encompasses earlier films like *Shoeshine* (dir. De Sica, 1946) and *Oliver Twist* (dir. Lean, 1948), João Luiz Vieira notes that in recent years, this genre has come to hinge itself upon the spectacle of urban filth, poverty, and criminality that envelops abject, destitute youth rendered within an exoticized third world.[1] In the contemporary space of the "street urchin film," the mise-en-scene of the Latin American *favela* becomes interchangeable with that of the Asian slum – an equation facilitated by a common denominator of spectacular cinematic alterity that wholly dislocates the oppressive world of the street urchin from the realities of the so-called first world.[2] Consolidating the Third World as alien, as a powerful and distant vortex that brims with decay, the space of the street unfolds as one that is nonetheless visually arresting in its raw appearances and rough edges. Tying aestheticized representations of the slum to contemporary, transnational youth cultures of fashion and music, e.g., commercial rap, Vieira explains:

> [the street urchin films'] key innovation lies in focusing on native excluded youth as authentic subjects of, and shareholders in, this transnational rap culture. The international impact and the 2009 Oscar consecration of Danny Boyle's *Slumdog Millionaire* comes as no surprise then: its authentic *favela* locations, the use of a young and largely inexperienced cast who were asked to improvise dialogues and even actions, a cool soundtrack creating a musical landscape at once local and global, and its frenetic editing style are all part of an aesthetic package ostensibly inspired by *City of God* to ignite an effect of instant reality.[3]

Invoking the importance of "a cool soundtrack [in] creating a musical landscape at once local and global," Vieira hits on the necessarily *audio-visual* space and the "effect of instant reality" conjured by an identifiable genre that includes films like *City of God* (dir. Meirelles and Lund, 2002) and *Slumdog Millionaire* (dir. Boyle and Tandan, 2008). Just as transnational hip hop and rap culture is equated with the urban poor who are implied to be its "most authentic shareholders," *Slumdog*'s citations of not only hip hop but also of Bollywood reinforce the film's credibility in documenting the realities of contemporary Bombay.

Among the more pejorative connotations of Bollywood – a term for Hindi-language popular cinema that gained currency in tandem with 1990s globalization – is that the cinema is a Bombay-based derivative of Hollywood. Despite the non-realist, performative elements for which Hindi popular cinema is well-known, *Slumdog*'s invocations of Bollywood are easily subsumed into an "effect of instant reality," authenticating the diegetic space of a fictional narrative that collapses into the film's documentary and ethnographic genre proclivities. After all, how does the thickly layered score by synthesizer-guru and popular Indian film music director A. R. Rahman jive with *Slumdog*'s much-touted location shooting, location sound and ostensible investment in well-researched, gritty portrayals of the urban realities of the slum? How does a pulsating, flamboyant song-and-dance sequence become an appropriate cadence to the film's impossibly romantic narrative outcome, as Jamal is reunited with his beloved upon winning a game show precisely because he is able to recall several, horrific, exploitative experiences that he and the other slumdog characters have suffered?

I pose the leading questions above to emphasize the extraordinarily seamless integration of upbeat, stylized, audio-visual spectacle – coded by a hybrid fusion of hip hop and Bollywood elements – in a film whose realism is not only graphic and jarring, but also quite heavily emphasized in the Euro-American press reportage that comprises the film's extra-cinematic tale. These press accounts underscore the film's effect of realism as when, for example, a sensational story reported that the father of the child actress Rubina Ali was willing to sell her to undercover reporters from *News of the World*, a British tabloid. The reporters posed as a wealthy couple, visited the family living in the slums, and expressed interest in adopting Rubina in exchange for a large sum of money, after which the story was run.[4] The father's side of the story – that he was just being polite and did not, for a moment, actually consider selling his daughter to the couple – remained irrelevant, as *Slumdog*'s realism was itself strong enough to both underwrite the tabloid piece and overwrite the father's side of the story.

In a different vein, another set of news stories dramatically portrayed *Slumdog* as an underdog film that succeeded against all odds, which seemed to only give further credence to the film's fantastic narrative in an obvious parallel. As journalistic accounts lauded *Slumdog*'s commercial success and deplored the horrific conditions of Indian slums, they backed the film's strong investments in a discourse of cinematic realism. I characterize cinematic realism as an effect of immanence that is produced through the naturalization, or overwriting, of a film's more or less laborious processes of construction, such as screenwriting, casting, scoring, shooting, editing and production design. This overwriting often occurs through a series of realist styles and genre conventions that are coded to be taken at face value, such as those of documentary, newsreel footage or neorealist cinema. What is interesting about *Slumdog* is that alongside its realist and even documentary proclivities, the film's aural and visual invocations of Bollywood – perhaps counterintuitively – complement *Slumdog*'s "effect of instant reality."

Film semioticians Christian Metz and Georgia Gurrieri's keen characterization of "offscreen sound" as both a faulty misnomer and wonderfully insightful term – since technically all cinematic sound is offscreen, emanating from speakers and not from the screen – reveals the extent to which sounds and images produce meanings out of their relationships with one another, often in a hierarchical manner that privileges the image.[5] Michel Chion underscores sound-image relationships with his term "synchresis," placing emphasis on both the temporal synchrony of audio-visual elements and the dynamic synthesis by which their meanings unfold through cinematic media.[6] Attentive to the fact that neither the form nor the technological apparatus of cinema is solely visual, but properly audio-visual, the above insights urge methods of film analysis that destabilize an additive model, which assumes parallel meanings encoded by separately-analyzable sound and image tracks. Instead, one requires analytical models that investigate the meanings that emerge out of the perpetual embrace of audio and visual elements, as images and sounds thoroughly infuse and mutually constitute one another as nodes of intelligibility in film texts.

Classical French film theorist André Bazin, dubbed the "high priest of realism," argues that the advent of deep-focus (depth of field) cinematography revolutionized cinema to a much greater extent than the coming of "talkies," i.e., synchronous sound, the former contributing much more to Bazin's conception of a "total cinema" of immanence.[7] According to Bazin, this total cinema fulfilled a destiny initially foretold by Plato's cave and later prophesied by the development of perspective in Renaissance painting, with cinema's arrival heralding the unique, hitherto elusive ability to reproduce and render the world in art. For Bazin, depth of field could preserve the ambiguity of reality, epitomized by post-war Italian neorealist film and Orson Welles' *Citizen Kane* (1941), while "the talkie sounded the knell of a certain aesthetic of the language of film [...] What it turned its back on was metaphor and symbol in exchange for the illusion of objective presentation."[8] It is precisely that which Bazin identifies as an "illusion of objective presentation," coded as the authenticity of the third world mise-en-scene and its occupants, that comprises the contemporary street urchin film and that yields the "effect of instant reality" noted by Vieira.[9]

Bazin lyrically professes his faith in a total cinema wherein:

> Only the impassive lens, stripping its object of all those ways of seeing it, those piled-up preconceptions, that spiritual dust and grime with which my eyes have covered it, is able to present it in all its virginal purity to my attention and consequently to my love. By the power of photography, the natural image of a world that we neither know nor can know, nature at last does more than imitate art: she imitates the artist."[10]

Bazin's classical conception of an absolutely realist cinema seems to beg for what has become an aphorism in postmodern critical theory – that is, a critique that maintains the untenability of an immanent representation of reality (not to mention that Bazin's conception seems to beg for an equally obvious feminist critique of an idealized, feminized metaphor for a cinema described as pristine, passive and virginal – and also so natural as to transcend even nature, also rendered as a "she"). In arguing that "[n]eorealism knows only immanence," Bazin's criteria for defining neorealism as "more an ontological position than an aesthetic one" is its anti-theatricality, lack of artifice, minimalist editing and reliance on no means of expressivity other than that of the ultimate, uncontaminated mise-en-scene of nature as it is distilled by the mechanical function of the camera and rendered through the unique, indexical properties of the photographic medium of cinema.[11] Bazin further asserts, "*Ladri di Biciclette* [*Bicycle Thieves*] is without a doubt the ultimate expression of neorealism," and, to be sure, the beauty, simplicity, and tenderness of Vittorio De Sica's 1948 classic has subsequently inspired several "new wave" and auteurist filmmakers all over the world. Bazin attributes the film's profundity to its nonprofessional actors, its mise-en-scene of the working-class space of the modern industrial city and its preservation of an unadulterated ambiguity that is endemic to reality-as-nature, which in turn accounts for the film's transcendence and universal appeal.

Perhaps less obvious than a general critique of Bazin's belief in the absolute immanence of a particular kind of neorealist cinema would be one that notes the discrepancy between Bazin's recognition of synchronous sound's role in formulating an "illusion of objective presentation" – an observation that was likely to have been directed at the Hollywood "talkie" – and his elision of sound's role, particularly at the level of scoring, in the Italian neorealist films that he cites.[12] In fact, the orchestral score for *Bicycle Thieves* by Alessandro Cicognini garnered the prestigious Miglior Commento Musicale (Best Score) from the Italian Syndicate of Film Journalists in 1948, and one is hard pressed to deny either the expressionist tendencies of music in *Bicycle Thieves*, or the fact that music is not at all natural to the film's mise-en-scene. In terms of the former, one observes that in the final sequence of *Bicycle Thieves*, ominous, staccato horns accelerate and swell into a full orchestral wave of trilling chords, which poignantly narrativize Antonio's fraught desperation that culminates in his theft of a bicycle. The poor man is spotted and apprehended almost immediately, and the score recedes for a moment before it resumes with a minor, lilting adagio led by strings, guiding an effect of pathos that ensues from Antonio's public shaming in front of his young son Bruno. While Bazin may not have been entirely deluded in his exaltation of *Bicycle Thieves*' lyricism, his nostalgia for cinematic "metaphor and symbol" (transcendence, perhaps?) in the face of the talkie's "illusion of objective presentation" fails to recognize, on the one hand, that synchronous sound was endemic to the effectiveness of his beloved Italian neorealist classic that, on the other hand, consequently presents but its own "illusion of objective presentation," as would any other purportedly realist account.[13]

The manner in which the artifice of scoring is naturalized to the supposed immanence of Bazin's total cinema is entirely symptomatic of Christian Metz's assertion that there is no such thing as offscreen sound, but that such a term indicates the extent to which sounds are interpreted vis-à-vis the image onscreen. In terms of scoring and nondiegetic sounds, one hardly expects (or even thinks to expect) to ever see the sound source onscreen, and, in fact, the effect of such sounds largely depends upon being overwritten and made unnoticeable by the image or narrative – much like cuts in the classical Hollywood style of invisible editing – and subsumed into the overall naturalized coherence of the diegesis, or world of the film.[14] That Bazin entirely displaces the impact of the score (that, too, a critically-acclaimed score) in a film like *Bicycle Thieves* onto a pure indexicality of the image is indicative of sound's frequent invisibility in both the construction of meanings through cinematic media, and in scholarly writings about cinema.

Bazin favored a minimally interventional filmmaking practice that would capture the pristine mise-en-scene of natural settings and natural lighting, appearances, and acting styles over Soviet filmmaker Sergei Eisenstein's well-known espousal of montage as a structuring principle for a cinema that forwarded an ontology of conflict and dialectical movement, producing meaning in the juxtaposition of shots via editing.[15] Furthermore, Eisenstein and other Soviet filmmakers were proponents of the contrapuntal use of sound, whereby sound would similarly clash, rather than harmonize and neatly synchronize, with the image.[16] Thus, despite their vastly different conceptions of cinema, both Bazin and Eisenstein highly deplored the coming of sound as it established a dominant, Hollywood style of invisible editing that seamlessly synchronized sounds with a series of moving images from which they appeared to naturally emanate.

The more contemporary writings of Michel Chion, too, voice regret over the fact that the coming of sound has not heralded a plethora of audio-visual practices and formations, but has instead entrenched an extremely narrow range of ways in which sound operates through cinematic media.[17] Paying attention to audio-visual relationships that are present in individual films seems to constitute an antidote to the tendency to leave sound elements out of critical discussions of cinema, and such attention could easily invigorate discussions over potential alternatives to current regimes of audio-visual practices that are themselves under-theorized. Even then, however, the ways that meanings unfold through audio-visual relationships is not fully intrinsic to a cinematic moment, but beholden to genre conventions and genealogies of cinema that are extrinsic to an individual film or film fragment. The range of elements that are incorporated into *Slumdog*, the film's realist underpinnings that posit its diegesis as contiguous with the contemporary space of third world slums, as well as the film's transnational contexts of production and reception, allow opportunities to examine the invisible role of sound in cinema, particularly in realist constructions of space. Through an analysis of *Slumdog*, this essay also considers the manner in which audio-visual aesthetics are narrativized, or subject to certain contextual associations, that in turn yield particular effects.

Framed by a popular, international, television game show and characterized by a fast-paced, rhythmic style of editing, *Slumdog* contains graphic depictions of urban poverty, extended sequences of Hindi dialogue subtitled in English, outdoor location shots, outdoor location sounds, "authentic" child actors from Bombay slums and little-known adult actors. Scored by synthesizer-wizard Rahman, the film includes a "Paper Planes" music-video montage featuring UK-based, alternative hip-hop artist M. I. A., an upbeat "Jai Ho" song-and-dance finale and a Bombay-underworld setting with a host of gangster characters, fairytale romance, and rags-to-riches plot that are collectively reminiscent of 1970s Hindi popular cinema.[18] Looking at two promotional posters for *Slumdog*, one might not immediately recognize that they are advertising the same film (Fig. 9.1 and 9.2). One presents a film in bold colors that is ostensibly a (perhaps teen) romance, and the other appears to advertise, in much more subdued tones, some sort of indie documentary about poor, Third World children, with the easily identifiable Taj Mahal in the background serving as a giveaway clue. Despite the juxtaposition of such a wide range – indeed, extremes – of stylistic and narrative elements, *Slumdog*'s diegesis holds together with an astonishing degree of coherence.

Figure 9.1. Poster for *Slumdog Millionaire*, ostensibly a love story.

Figure 9.2. Poster for *Slumdog Millionaire* with the appearance of an indie documentary.

If the contemporary, transnational genre identified by Vieira as the "street urchin film" accounts for this coherence to a certain extent, then a look at other extra-cinematic contexts such as press bytes and promotional materials may further clarify the codes that scaffold *Slumdog*'s legibility.[19]

On the eve of *Slumdog's Millionaire*'s 22 January 2009 release in India, following its successful run through film festivals and theatres in North America, Europe and Australia, the Travel section of the UK *Telegraph* ran the headline, "Slumdog Millionaire: On the Trail of Mumbai's Slumdogs." The article, by travel writer Nigel Richardson, begins, "The film *Slumdog Millionaire*, which opens in India tomorrow, holds a mirror up to Mumbai – and the subcontinent's most vibrant city may not be entirely comfortable with what it sees."[20] Richardson goes on to describe the film's boosting of a controversial "niche market in tourism – the slum tour," on which he then offers a first-hand report, having himself traveled to Bombay and even embarked on such a tour. A link directs online readers to a slideshow of images that depict the realities of these slums, and four out of the fourteen images are stills from the film, not including a photograph of an enormous poster advertising the theatrical release of *Slumdog* in India, in front of which are two passersby (Fig. 9.3).[21]

Figure 9.3. An online slideshow accompanies a 22 January 2009 column in the "Travel" section of the UK *Telegraph*.

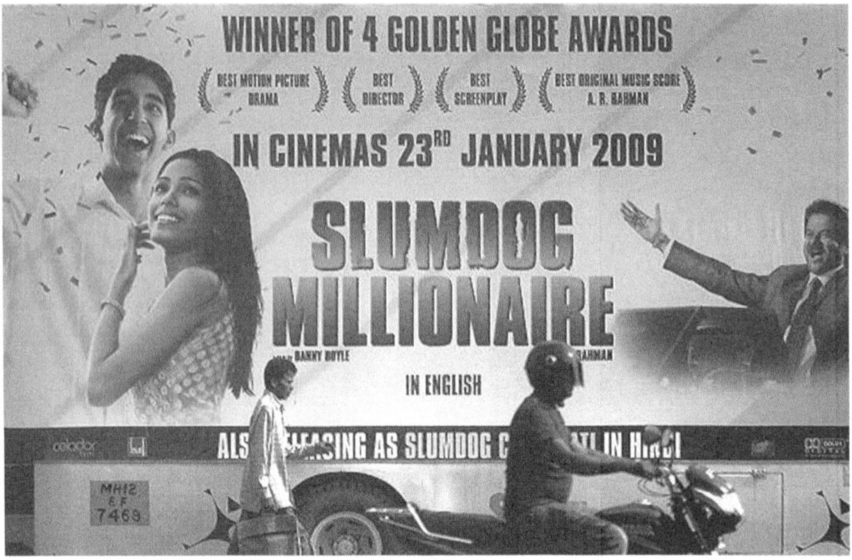

The caption for this particular photo, one among the fourteen that comprise the online slideshow, echoes the first line of the travel piece: "Having taken the British box office by storm and collected four Golden Globes, *Slumdog Millionaire*, which opens in India on Friday, holds up a mirror to Mumbai's underbelly."

That the release of *Slumdog* in India serves as the context for a British newspaper's travel column on the condition of slums, and the industry of slum tourism in Bombay explicitly indicates the degree to which the film's representation of slums was taken at face value, as in fact "hold[ing] up a mirror to Mumbai."[22] A month later, after *Slumdog* swept eight Academy Awards, the *New York Times* printed the headline, "Starless Movie's Starry Night," underscoring the fact that the lead actors were all little-known or unknown, most notably the child actors from the slums who were cast in the film. But what of popular Indian film actor Anil Kapoor, who plays the game show host in *Slumdog*, and what of critically acclaimed Indian actor Irrfan Khan, hardly a stranger even to American film audiences, as he was also cast in *The Darjeeling Limited* (dir. Wes Anderson, 2007) and *The Namesake* (dir. Mira Nair, 2006), not to mention the enormously popular Indian composer and music director Rahman? Furthermore, David Carr, the author of the article, not only describes *Slumdog* as "starless," but goes on to imply that its magical success lay in its ability to offer surprises and prove, in the wake of Hollywood's dominance, that "global imperatives go both ways," for "[w]hen a film with a British director, Indian actors and French co-financing goes home with eight Oscars, it's hard not to see a message."[23] However, Carr later asserts that "while *Slumdog* might have been conjured elsewhere, its DNA is Hollywood to the core," and he concludes, "Hollywood's efforts to globalize its content as well as its business have been a train wreck for the most part, but for a stagnant industry under duress at home, the rest of the world is waiting for their stories to be told as well."[24]

The above *New York Times* piece not only makes a complete elision of three, important figures of Indian cinema in its description of *Slumdog* as "starless," but also implies that the film's success lies in "its DNA [that] is Hollywood to the core," ultimately suggesting that Hollywood may do well to travel to other parts of the world that are "waiting for their stories to be told," just as the story of India/Bombay was given voice by *Slumdog*. If this is indeed the model for "global imperatives go[ing] both ways" – that Hollywood should certainly tell the rest of the world's stories, that there is no need to acknowledge or know anything about other film practices and industries, and that whenever a good story is told, it is surely "Hollywood to the core" – then the discourse of global exchange wears thin as anything but a veneer for a renewed, chauvinistic Hollywood-centrism.

Together, the *New York Times* piece and the travel feature in the *Telegraph* reveal an assumption that the rest of the world would do well to have itself, and all of its issues, interpreted by Euro-American–led cinematic initiatives such as that of *Slumdog*. Yet, a contradiction persists in the recognition of *Slumdog*'s story as fantastic and improbable, and simultaneously one among many stories actually out there in "the rest of the world," which are just waiting to be told – by Hollywood in particular.[25] One is confronted with a hierarchy that privileges the domain of Euro-America as the storytellers and producers of knowledge, and the rest of the world, their object. Caught in this discourse, the industry known as Bollywood, as a sign of contemporary Bombay that is associated with the spectacular, fantastic, and improbable, becomes an invocation that authenticates and subsumes *Slumdog*'s stylized, hybrid-fusion, audio-visual attractions into its neat, realist – but fun and commercially viable – packaging.

In the original version of the film, subtitled Hindi dialogue is spoken through its early portions. Just as establishing shots are meant to visually orient the spectator within a particular diegetic space, the subtitled non-English serves as sort of establishing sound that aurally marks the authenticity of the film's space as that of a real, third world slum. Apart from the sound of non-English dialogue, the very presence of subtitles, associated not only with art cinema, documentary, and ethnographic film, but also with televised world news footage and the ever-present ticker, further plots the film's space along geographic coordinates.[26] Eventually, the film switches over to English entirely, and from there, one deduces the film's intended, English-speaking spectator – but a spectator who is invested enough in the film's authenticity to have followed subtitled dialogue for a sizeable chunk of time. In fact, a widespread criticism of *Slumdog* from Indian audiences was that it seemed extremely odd for characters that grew up in a slum to have somehow come to possess an ability to converse in English (in addition to the complaint that the unfamiliar term slumdog sounded offensive, carrying overtones of British colonial attitudes that condescendingly regarded Indians as dogs).[27]

The invisible and highly paradoxical manner in which the film's scoring and song sequences lend further credence to its realist portrayal of the slum becomes especially evident in the product description for the hit soundtrack-album, whose first three notes are worth reproducing in full:

> In composing the music for acclaimed director Danny Boyle's intoxicating new film *Slumdog Millionaire*, A. R. Rahman has conjured *the sound of a city*, fusing the frenetic scramble of daily life in Mumbai [Bombay], India into *beautiful fugues that ride upon the dust clouds kicked up by its everyday people.*
>
> From the movie's first frames – with children racing through alleyways, knocking over merchants and pottery, police kicking loose clay roof tiles, disrupted birds fluttering from gutters – we hear the sound of their commotion made manifest in "O […] Saya." It's a *rumbling hybrid of Bollywood and hip-hop*, a brand new collaboration between Rahman and M. I. A. It's the kind of cinematic moment where image and sound coexist. And that's only the first five minutes.
>
> *Filmed in the streets and slums of Mumbai, India, Boyle needed just the right music to compliment the film's cinema verité urban realism.* He turned to internationally renowned composer A.R. Rahman (a huge star in South Asia – selling more than 100 million albums worldwide and 200 million cassettes – Rahman is one of the world's top 25 all-time top selling recording artists). The *film's score is central to the propulsive modern grit* that pervades the story, but is *also a nod to classic Bollywood productions where the music is front and center.* And loud. Says Rahman, "We wanted it edgy, upfront. Danny wanted it loud."[28]

Rahman's synthesizer-heavy music becomes naturalized as "the sound of the city" and carries, to use Bazin's words, the "paradoxical intention not to produce a spectacle which appears real, but rather to turn reality into a spectacle."[29] While Bazin is once again discussing *Bicycle Thieves*, his privileging of neorealism's immanence recalls that neorealist cinema and other post-war "new waves" did, indeed, become the foundation for a domain of global art cinema, inspiring other "new waves" of neorealist cinema that were in turn "discovered" (and continue to be discovered) in far corners of the world and exhibited at film festivals, whereupon their respective, neorealist-torch-bearing filmmakers have since been anointed as eminent auteurs.[30]

Among these new waves was cinéma verité, a 1970s French new wave style of documentary that tended to use hand-held cameras and acknowledge the presence of the filmmaker and camera in an intentionally stylized filmmaking practice that sought truthfulness and objectivity. Witnessing the official description of Rahman's score for *Slumdog* as "just the right music to compliment the film's cinema verité urban realism," one notes that *Slumdog* is heavily coded by a stylistic genealogy of documentary and (neo)realist cinema. As the album's product description goes on, the score's "nod to classic Bollywood productions where the music is front and center" explicitly links *Slumdog*'s invocation of contemporary Hindi cinema as an authenticating device for the film's realist, "propulsive modern grit," among other stylized elements such as the "Paper Planes" montage, which seem to be at odds with the film's realism. Classic Bollywood, however, is an oxymoronic term – Bollywood is a term that only gained currency in the late 1980s and'90s, whereas the classical moment of Hindi cinema is has been pinned as that of the 1950s and '60s. *Slumdog* does reference certain *classic* Hindi films, albeit ones from the post-Golden Era of the 1970s, which saw the rise of actor Amitabh Bachchan as the "angry young man" and have since been enshrined as milestones.

Rahman himself is a crossover music director from the Chennai-based Tamil language cinema industry, and his initial breakthrough arrived with the soundtrack he composed for the Tamil film *Roja* (Ratnam, 1992), which shot to immense popularity. After *Roja*, Rahman's fame escalated through a series of collaborations on other successful films whose songs were hailed as the work of a genius, including *Kadhalan* [Tamil] /*Muqabala* [Hindi] (Shankar, 1994) and *Bombay* (Ratnam, 1995).[31] Rahman made his Bollywood debut as the music director for the Hindi film *Rangeela* (Varma, 1995), which was followed by a series of subsequent, enormously popular Hindi film soundtrack-albums, including those that Rahman composed and arranged for the films *Dil Se* (Ratnam, 1998), *Taal* (Ghai, 1999), *Lagaan* (Gowariker, 2001), *Saathiya* (Ali, 2002), *Swades* (Gowariker, 2004), *Rang De Basanti* (Mehra, 2006), *Guru* (Ratnam, 2007), and *Jodhaa Akbar* (Gowariker, 2008).

As a music director who had become a star in his own right well before the release of *Slumdog*, Rahman is tightly associated with the sound of the "new" Hindi cinema of the 1990s, known for production practices and digital recording workflows that broke with an established, characteristic sound and respective set of studio processes that had dominated the industry for several decades. Known for endorsing Apple studio products like Apple Logics, Rahman has accrued for himself the star image of a quiet, solitary and eccentric genius who is technologically savvy, highly spiritual in his adherence to Sufism, and worldly in his knowledge and enthusiasm for incorporating influences from Western genres like rap and metal into synthesizer-rich music that simultaneously draws on the instrumentation and genres of East Asian, Latin, Middle Eastern and Indian folk as well as classical music.[32]

Hindi film music has, since its earliest moments, been immensely eclectic in incorporating a wide range of influences, and Rahman's musical signature is not constituted by fusion per se, but by a particular kind of electronic fusion and layered sound that has been coded as global for a texture that reverberates with its indebtedness to digital technologies. Thus, while the official description of *Slumdog*'s soundtrack claims to give classical Bollywood a nod, the description's conflation of Rahman's contemporary Bollywood music with the music of not only the 1950s–1960s classical moment of Hindi cinema, but also the 1970s era of Amitabh Bachchan movies, only indicates the lack of specificity and the flattened discourse through which *Slumdog* gives this classic Bollywood a nod.

The "Paper Planes" montage sequence in *Slumdog* features Rahman's remix of UK-based artist M. I. A.'s hit song, drawing on the twin subtexts of Rahman/classic Bollywood and hip-hop/urban youth culture in a way that, once again, naturalizes this music to the diegetic space of India/the urban poor. Capitalizing on the genre of the hip hop music video and that of the Bollywood musical interlude, the film indeed features, to return to Vieira's description of *Slumdog* in terms of the genre of the street urchin film, "a cool soundtrack [that creates] a musical landscape at once local and global [...] all part of an aesthetic package ostensibly inspired by *City of God* to ignite an effect of instant reality."[33] The product description of the album nods in agreement: "It's a rumbling hybrid of Bollywood and hip-hop, a brand new collaboration between Rahman and M. I. A. It's the kind of cinematic moment where image and sound coexist."[34] It is worthwhile to dwell, for a brief moment, upon the purported allure of a "cinematic moment where image and sound coexist" – for in what kind of contemporary cinematic moment do image and sound *not* coexist? The soundtrack's claim thus highlights an ostensibly organic relationship between the sound-space of *Slumdog* and the visual space of the "cinema verité urban realism" from which its sounds emanate.

Given the film's powerful metadiscourse discourse of realism and authenticity, I re-examine a question that I posed early on: How does a pulsating, flamboyant song-and-dance sequence become an appropriate cadence to the film's impossibly romantic narrative outcome as Jamal is reunited with his beloved upon winning a game show precisely because he is able to recall several, horrific, exploitative experiences that he and the other "slumdog" characters have suffered? An implausible narrative of star-crossed lovers who triumph over

Figure 9.4. The improbability of Jamal's success is implied in the film's opening moments (00:01:28).

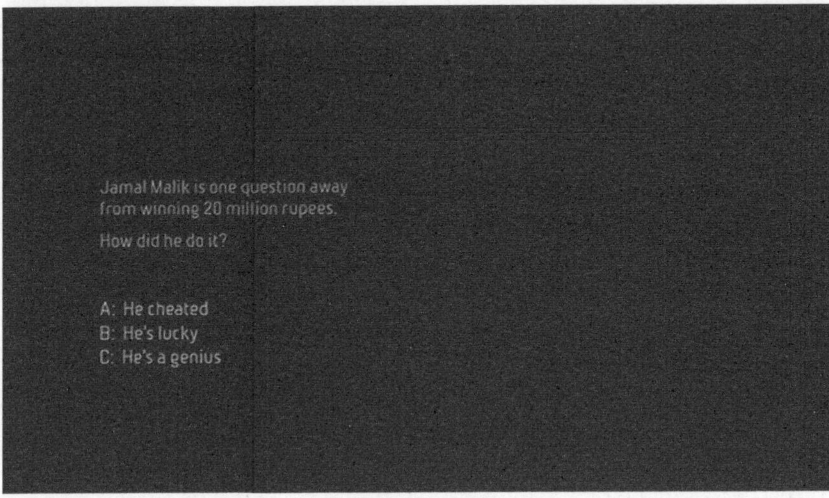

Figure 9.5. Jamal's success is foreshadowed as fate (00:01:32).

their circumstances, are united against all odds and spontaneously burst into a rousing song-and-dance number constitutes a stereotypical Bollywood recipe, and as earlier invocations of both Bollywood and hip hop flag the authenticity of *Slumdog*'s diegetic space, its fairytale romance and finale song-and-dance occur as additional invocations of Bollywood that work to the same end.

The triumphant outcome of the film's narrative that culminates in its rousing Jai Ho sequence takes on yet another layer amidst the underdog film's commercial success that was touted as similarly miraculous, having apparently been "written," or destined against all odds. The visual display of the text, "It is written," foreshadowing the protagonist Jamal's exceptional success in life and love at the outset of the film (Fig. 9.4 and 9.5), conveys a sense of a future that is destined and natural, and simultaneously "written" in the sense of having been orchestrated – presumably by a higher order or transcendent, universal agent. "It is written," one could explain, concerning three different yet related destinies thus foretold: (1) that *Slumdog*'s protagonist Jamal would emerge as a winner within the film's diegesis; (2) that the film itself would emerge as a victor in its worldwide success; and (3) that, à la Bazin, an immanent, realist, total cinema would emerge as a messianic hero in the quest for the medium's raison d'être. With regards to each of these destinies, I find it illuminating to ask not *whether* it was written but *how* it was written – what underwrote these destinies as such and what alternatives were overwritten in the process.

The narrative logic that juxtaposes the integrity of Jamal's moral character with the tragic figure of his brother Salim implies, for example, that Jamal's own forthrightness pulls him along towards his destiny, the fulfillment of which gives way to the celebratory Jai Ho sequence. The implication that one's own character can lead him/her to success, however unlikely, forecloses a consideration of the larger histories and geopolitics that produce the oppressive circumstances of modern slums, for which an individual slum dweller's moral character may be no match. The tale of *Slumdog*'s success in Euro-American contexts has been spun as the triumph of an underdog, reinforcing the very logic of its narrative – that if something is good enough, it will surely win. The film's underdog story, however, unfolds at the expense of ignoring the sizeable Indian audiences among which the film was far less successful, as well as the industry of Hindi popular cinema and the fact that three of its extremely well-known figures play significant roles in *Slumdog*. One of these figures, Rahman, declared in his speech at the Academy Awards, "all my life, I had a choice of hate and love. I chose love, and I'm here."[35] Onlookers might have aligned Rahman, in that moment, with the fictional character of Jamal, giving credence to the film's diegetic romance and the film's own underdog success, and believing that one's fortune is indeed beholden to his/her moral integrity. This is despite the fact that Rahman, already a hugely popular and sought-after composer within and beyond South Asia well before the success of *Slumdog*, could have hardly been considered an underdog at the time. Finally, to privilege a teleology of (neo)realism as the epitome of the medium's potential is to narrow the range of ways in which to imagine, write, and tell stories, and to privilege a particular genealogy of film practices at the expense of multitudinous alternatives that are reduced to mere footnotes, much as the specificities and histories of Hindi filmmaking practices are reduced in *Slumdog* to stereotyped Bollywood conventions that serve to authenticate its representation of India/Bombay.

Bazin's conception of a total cinema of immanence is a powerful desire, as well as an impossible one. By imagining that this total cinema was the outcome of a teleological development that was initiated by Plato's cave and forwarded by the development of perspective in Renaissance painting, Bazin's narrative reveals a limited, Eurocentric vision for cinema's potential. Cinematic realism, while it can be many different things, is necessarily an effect that ensues from giving oneself over to the indexical properties of the medium – a transaction that may occur as a trained response to certain conventions, such as those of neorealism or documentary. Bazin's own lack of attention to background scoring is indicative of the extent to which music, for example, is an element that is rendered invisible, as its meanings and effects appear intrinsic to image. Scoring and other aural elements are crucial not only in producing emotional effects, but also in constructing a diegesis that seems believable, authentic, and natural. This naturalization of the score to the indexicality of the image, with which it shares no intrinsic connection, is paradigmatic for the workings of cinematic realism, as the indexicality of the image overwrites the film's audio-visual constructed-ness. In terms of *Slumdog*, such an effect of realism is reinforced by extra-cinematic press narratives, and by the movie's affinities to other films that coalesce into a genre of contemporary street urchin films – many of which are styled as documentaries – that dedicate themselves to chronicling the realities of destitute youth in Third World slums.

SFX as a shorthand term may indicate either special effects or sound effects, and the two are often closely associated with blockbuster genre films that promise a full-throttle cinematic experience. While *Slumdog* is not considered a special-effects film in common parlance (precisely because a special effects film is usually understood as a Hollywood-genre-based, animation, or CGI film that foregrounds and revels in its own effects or "tricks"), I find it useful to ponder this categorization. It is not, after all, that a film like *Slumdog* lacks high production values, did not avail itself of sophisticated technologies, or is by any means sparse in its sound design or scoring. The difference, I would argue, is that the film's coherence is structured by a realist discourse that overwrites other values, making invisible its own writing or painstaking, complex construction. Sound effects are recognized as being crucial to special effects films, again, to the extent that the shorthand SFX denotes either special effects or sound effects. Sound indeed plays a crucial role in producing the blockbuster special effects of colliding spaceships and roaring monsters, as well as the "effect of instant reality" in films like *Slumdog*, as processes of scoring, sound design, recording and editing are overwritten by a discourse of immanence that renders these sounds as organic and authentic, as givens with respect to the gritty, realist image.[36]

While sound effects are usually held as being separate from both music (i.e., the film score and film songs) and dialogue, both the Hindi dialogue and the score (ostensibly a nod to classic Bollywood productions, as is the final Jai Ho sequence) operate in *Slumdog* as markers of authentic space. It is useful, then, to certainly consider the above elements as speech and music, respectively. However, one might simultaneously position them as aural effects that contribute to an urban soundscape of local dialects, car horns, crowd noises and police sirens as they are subsumed into the audio-visual spectacle of Bombay's slums and overwritten by cinematic genealogies and discourses of realist representation, and by the extra-cinematic narratives that reinforce the film's purported authenticity.

Vieira wonders, "how then [might] these films avoid representing the so-called Third World subjects merely as 'The Other'? How [might] these filmic texts succeed in representing the dynamism of a more transnational economic reality [...]?"[37] Howsoever the street urchin films that Vieira identifies, including *Slumdog*, fall short in "representing the dynamism of a more transnational economic reality" by indulging an "anachronistic specular regime in which the Third World is constructed for, and subjected to, the gaze of the First World," we may, at the very least, train ourselves to recognize transnational cinematic genealogies, relationships and codes such as that of the street urchin film genre that Vieira identifies, and the contexts in which these codes gain traction. The processes and narratives by which these audio-visual forms accrue their meanings then become apparent – and audible – rather than remaining invisible in their illusory transparency.

Notes

1 Rick Altman takes an approach to genre that is simultaneously semantic and syntactic, i.e., attentive to common themes and tropes (structures of meaning), as well as devices and elements that are present as content. With Vieira's identification of the "street urchin film" as a genre, for example, syntactic structures could include all-pervading despair, resilience in the face of extreme difficulty, etc., while its semantic structures could include Third World settings, hip hop and rap music, racialized youth, depictions of filth, garbage, criminality, violence, poverty, etc. See Altman, "A Semantic/ Syntactic Approach to Film Genre" *Cinema Journal* 23.3 (1984): 6–18; and Vieira, "The Transnational Other: Street Kids in Contemporary Brazilian Cinema," in *World Cinemas, Transnational Perspectives*, edited by Ďurovičová and Newman (New York: Routledge, 2009), 242.

2 *Favela* is a Portuguese word that designates a shantytown on the outskirts of large cities in Brazil. It can also refer to an urban slum more generally.

3 Vieira, "The Transnational Other," 240.
4 Zubair Ahmed, "Father Denies Slumdog Child Sale," *BBC*, 20 April 2009, sec. South Asia. Online: http://news.bbc.co.uk/2/hi/8008359.stm (accessed 10 August 2012).
5 Metz and Gurrieri, "Aural Objects," *Yale French Studies* 60 (1980): 28.
6 Chion, *Audio-Vision* (Columbia University Press, 1994), 63.
7 "BFI/ Sight & Sound, The Innovators 1950–1960: Divining the Real," British Film Institute, August 1999. Online: http://www.bfi.org.uk/sightandsound/feature/176 (accessed 1 August 2012); Bazin, "The Myth of Total Cinema," in *What Is Cinema?* (Berkeley: University of California Press, 1967), 23.
8 Bazin, "The Evolution of the Language of Cinema," in *What Is Cinema?*, 38.
9 Vieira, "The Transnational Other," 242.
10 Bazin, "The Ontology of the Photographic Image," in *What Is Cinema?*, 15.
11 Bazin, "De Sica: Metteur-En-Scene," in *What Is Cinema?*, 64, 66.
12 Bazin, "The Evolution of the Language of Cinema," 38.
13 Ibid.
14 Often, it is difficult to make the distinction between nondiegetic and diegetic sounds. For example, background music may often be classified as nondiegetic because it does not emanate from a source that is within the diegesis. At times, however, there may be ambiguity over whether sounds are nondiegetic, or whether they are coming from within the mind of a character onscreen, whose psychological state is being expressed – in which case these sounds could then be classified as diegetic. For a discussion of diegetic vs. nondiegetic sound, in terms of sound and space, see Bordwell and Thompson, "Sound in the Cinema," in *Film Art: An Introduction* (New York: McGraw Hill, 2008), 278–9.
15 Eisenstein, "Beyond the Shot," in *The Eisenstein Reader*, ed. Richard Taylor (London: British Film Institute, 1998), 88.
16 Eisenstein, "Statement on Sound," in *The Eisenstein Reader*, 81.
17 Chion, *Audio-Vision*, 170.
18 In a personal communication, Chris Maroulakos, the managing editor of San Diego-based music blog owlandbear.com, has described M. I. A.'s music as "mall-friendly rebel rap."
19 Vieira, "The Transnational Other," 227.
20 Richardson, "Slumdog Millionaire: On the Trail of Mumbai's Slumdogs." *Telegraph: Travel* (London), 22 January 2009. Online: http://www.telegraph.co.uk/travel/destinations/asia/india/4306996/Slumdog-Millionaire-on-the trail-of-Mumbais-slumdogs.html (accessed 1 August 2012).
21 Ibid.
22 The 4th Edition of *Frommer's India*, a comprehensive travel guide, actually references *Slumdog Millionaire* in its section on "Dealing with Beggars": Children are maimed to up the ante by making them appear more pathetic (a reality, you will recall, that is dealt with on quite a visceral level in the Oscar-winning film *Slumdog Millionaire*)," Bruyn et al., *Frommer's India* (London: John Wiley & Sons, 2010), 118.
23 Carr, "Oscar Night Is Starry Night for the Starless "Slumdog Millionaire,'" *New York Times*, 23 February 2009, sec. Arts. Online: http://www.nytimes.com/2009/02/24/movies/awardsseason/24bagg.html (accessed 1 August 2012).
24 Ibid.
25 "Slumdog Millionaire: Mumbai's Real Slumdogs." *Telegraph: Travel* (London), 22 January 2009. Online: http://www.telegraph.co.uk/travel/picturegalleries/4307256/Slumdog-Millionaire-Mumbais-real-slumdogs.html?image=6 (accessed 22 June 2009).

26 Regarding the crossover success of the Chinese-language film *Crouching Tiger, Hidden Dragon* (Ang Lee, 2000) in the United States, Ďurovičová observes: "[P]re-production focus groups [were] established [...] to determine whether the presence of subtitles could be made acceptable for mainstream US distribution. The green light came from the first generation whose reading skills had been honed by the continuous 'breaking news' creep-line and stock market ticker at the lower edge of their television screens, and by perceptual multitasking at their PC terminals." See Ďurovičová, "Towards a History of Cinematic Translation," in *World Cinemas, Transnational Perspectives*, 106.

27 Wax, "Kids in Oscar-nominated 'Slumdog' Remain in India Slums." *Houston Chronicle*, 4 February 2009. Online: http://www.chron.com/entertainment/article/Kids-in-Oscar-nominated-Slumdog-remain-in-India-1729360.php (accessed 1 August 2012).

28 Rahman, *Slumdog Millionaire* (Interscope Records, 2008); emphasis added.

29 Bazin, "De Sica: Metteur-En-Scene," 67.

30 In presenting the category of "art cinema" as one that shifts and is laden with ambiguity, Galt and Schoonover note: "We can illustrate this ambivalence by considering one of the ways in which new art cinema objects enter into the field: the discovery of an emergent national new wave via two or three films in the international film circuit [...] And the thrill of discovery for these audiences eagerly consuming the next big thing repeats a fantasy at the heart of art cinema: that of making the transformative discovery of neorealism." Examples of auteurs "discovered" in this way would include Satyajit Ray, Mohsen Makhmalbaf, Abbas Kiarostami, and more recently, Cristi Puiu. See Rosalind Galt and Karl Schoonover, "Introduction," in *Global Art Cinema: New Theories and Histories* (Oxford: Oxford University Press, 2010), 3–26.

31 Critic Arul Mani notes, "Much has already been written about the manner in which Rahman invested the business of composing film music with mystique [...] All we need to add to this discussion are a couple of reminders. One, of the fact that he returned music to primacy over lyrics, and that very often this mastery is underlined by sound signatures, which remind us clearly of who is boss, of whose work we are listening to. These are often nonsense syllables and can go kola-ha-kola-ha-kolakola as in the refrain to 'Uppu Karuvadu' from *Mudhalvan/Nayak* or better still, be as beautifully bizarre as the somewhat Turkish sounding buyakk-buyakkusha from 'Aha Tamizhamma' in *Kangalal Kaidhu Sei*." See Mani, "The Taming of Rahman," *Tehelka - India's Independent Weekly News Magazine* 8.8 (26 February 2011). Online: http://www.tehelka.com/story_main48.asp?filename=hub260211The_Taming.asp. (accessed 1 August 2012).

32 A. R. Rahman is widely known among his fans as a Sufi. For example, the song "Khwaja Mere Khwaja" that was composed for the film *Jodhaa Akbar* (Gowariker, 2008) is in the genre of *qawwali*, a genre of ecstatic songs associated with certain South Asian Sufi-Islamic orders, and the song praises Hazrat Moinuddin Chishti, one of the most renowned South Asian Sufi saints. An unpublished Master's thesis that contextualizes A. R. Rahman and the music that he composed for *Slumdog* within global circuits of consumption observes that among a wide base of fans, Rahman is perceived as a solitary genius, and that Rahman's music is recognized and heralded (see above note as well) for its sonic lushness: "For the most part, Rahman has developed a particular 'sound' defined by his use of the latest technology involving digital sampling, computer software, keyboard synthesizers and a fully-equipped home studio. Rahman's film music is hybridic – Indian film music that essentially adheres to global popular music trends." See Stephanie Jackson, "Beyond Kitsch," 58.

33 Vieira, "The Transnational Other," 242.

34 Rahman, *Slumdog Millionaire.*
35 Quoted in Amit Roy, "Greatest Bolly Tale Told in Cannes," *Telegraph* (Calcutta), 17 May 2011. Online: http://www.telegraphindia.com/1110517/jsp/frontpage/story_13992215.jsp (accessed 1 August 2012).
36 Vieira, "The Transnational Other," 242.
37 Ibid., 227.

Part Four

SLUMDOG'S RECEPTIONS

Chapter 10

WHY THE SUN SHINES ON *SLUMDOG*

Anandam Kavoori

I originally wrote this soon after the Oscar awards in 2009, hounded by two questions: Why *Slumdog Millionaire*? Why now? This essay examines the recent success of *Slumdog Millionaire* (hereafter *Slumdog*) by undertaking a *contextual* reading of the film based on its expected appeal for American audiences (where the author resides). It recommends that we read *Slumdog* as the arrival of a specific kind of cultural hybridity, a process begun in earlier texts. It then outlines how such a reading of hybridity must be placed within three interrelated contexts of American political, economic and social life that helped the film achieve its place in the sun.

Slumdog garnered numerous accolades. Journalistic accounts of its success typically focused on its feel-good storyline, its effervescent music score (by A. R. Rahman, one of India's most prolific and creative composers) and the freshness of its unknown cast of actors as primary factors in its success. Built into such accounts was a narrative of implausibility, the rags to riches story that has taken the film from straight-to-DVD distribution to the Oscars. These were all important elements but, I suggest, proximate causes, not ultimate ones. In what follows, I suggest some entry points for a more complete discussion of the film.

Hybridity

For American audiences, *Slumdog* represents one point – after the Oscars a very important point – in a wider journey of cultural transference and cross-fertilization that is often described using the term "hybridity." These include at least three separate developments in the mainstreaming of non-Western cinema. The first is the development of diasporic cinema, where the cultural concerns of the homeland are recast in the experience of the diaspora and watched by both diasporic and mainstream populations (such as the film

My Big Fat Greek Wedding (2002)). The second is the expansion of non-Western *national* cinema into the global marketplace, reflecting wider trends in patterns of cultural assembling and distribution that come with an integrated (global) marketplace. Bollywood, the dominant popular cinema in India, now speaks to a global market using plot lines of diasporic love, cosmopolitan angst and a reflexive engagement with traditional values. The third is the development of what is often termed "crossover cinema," where the specifics of ethnicity are recast within wider narrative concerns of a global kind – the material needs of a middle class; the coming of age narrative; the experience of postmodern ambivalence; the centering of the self as the vehicle for fulfillment (the film, *Bend It Like Beckham* (2002), represents such a development).

Each of these elements in the creation of hybridity is present in *Slumdog*. To illustrate: Dev Patel, the film's British-Indian lead actor, represents both diasporic arrival and national aspiration; Freida Pinto, the Catholic-Indian actress, presents a discourse about Indian national identity – her status as a novice actress merging with her onscreen innocence which, in turn, coalesces with the idea of a new nation on the world stage, speaking through a minority (Christian) woman. Bollywood speaks through the entirety of the film, not just in the dance at the end of the film (as the credits roll) but in the narrative premise of destiny, the pursuit of love, the eros of the Indian male and in the final staging of personal sacrifice for familial good. Needless to add, *Slumdog* is not a Bollywood film, it is a classic crossover text, using the specifics of Indian locale to speak to wider (global) concerns of personal responsibility in a heartless world; the need for agency in an alienated society and, perhaps most critically, the renewal of love as a medium for understanding the self.

These thematic connections are only a beginning – a closer reading of the scenes of the film (in terms of shot composition, score, visual style and textual composition) uncovers a wealth of such connections and it can be unarguably stated that the appeal of *Slumdog* lies in the emotive register of these scenes. While space does not allow for a detailed listing of these scenes, three stand out for their visual/lyrical directness. The first, and perhaps most important one, is the scene in the latter third of the film, of Latika (Freida Pinto) standing at the platform, her face bathed in sunlight, looking up at Jamal (Dev Patel). This is the emotional climax of the film, its visual center where intimacy and its impossibility are cinematically centered. Jamal, looking at her from the above, positioned at a location where he can see her but cannot physically reach/rescue her, places this scene at the film's heart. The second scene that stands out is where one of the orphan's eyes is burnt out so that he can be successful as a blind beggar. Powerfully understated, it provides audiences with an uncomplicated formula for reaction – throwing up, an act undertaken on their behalf by Jamal's brother Salim as he witnesses this scene. Acting as the climax of the first third of the film, it sets up the narrative topology of the rest of the film – a world of cruel, inhumane brutality where love is a frivolous, irrelevant detail. Finally, the scene in the bathroom where Jamal looks at the letter "B" written on the mirror by the TV game show host (Anil Kapoor), who hopes that, by providing him with the wrong answer, he will lose. Jamal sees it as a ploy, a cruel gesture by a cruel world and chooses the correct answer, ensuring that he wins the round and is on his way to becoming a millionaire. What stands out here is the visual language of representation – a rapidly disappearing smudge on a mirror, evoking the fragile trajectory of success for individuals in a Bombay slum. Such a textual reading of scenes is important and necessary to understand the pleasures the film provides but, in the end, remains an incomplete gesture towards asking wider hermeneutic questions about the context in which the film can be read. In what follows, I will suggest there are three such contexts that American audiences drew on in propelling the film to the Oscars.

Politics of Class (It Could Be the US)

The current global economic crises may be just "globalization gone awry" (for those holding a market liberalization approach) or the "end of capitalism" (for its critics). Whatever the accurate prognosis of the current crises, there is one thing few can quibble about: the development of a profound, persistent ambivalence amongst (Western) film audiences about their lives when they step outside the film theatre. It is this sense of collective angst that fuels a wider unstated feeling in western societies – that their moment in history may be gone. As consumer confidence drops, cinema attendance rises, taking with it texts that speak to the crises of capitalism. *Slumdog* is a many-sided economic parable – a treatise about the excess of greed, a vision about hard work and luck, a story about the uses of violence for material gain and so on – but more than anything else, it provides a space for understanding the permanent effects of a global economic downturn: endemic, structural poverty. For Western audiences, the beautiful/ugly landscape of the Indian slum, with its cruel, hard-worn residents, evokes not just a Dickensian landscape but a litmus test for their own feelings about an American future – losing their homes, their livelihoods, forced to come to terms with the incomprehensible – in which *everyone* is one paycheck away from poverty. One may go further and argue that an important part of understanding the success of *Slumdog* is American audience's understanding of its own place in the arbitrary workings of capitalism, a reliable index of which is the widespread anger at bank bailouts, the outpouring of consternation at a single woman who chose to have eight embryos implanted and, more recently, with the rise of the "Occupy Wall Street" protests and the reactionary rhetoric of the Tea Party movement.

The State Rises to the Occasion

In close tandem with the first context – the global economy – is the question of the role of the state in capitalism's moment of crises. Here there appear to be two contradictory discourses that *Slumdog*'s success seems to draw on. The first is the idea of personal responsibility and agency that the young children in the film represent, and the second is the role of the state as the prime arbitrator of salvation. In the latter case, the film's villains – Mumbai gangsters who blind children and make them beg for a living – represent the distorted state, using its subjects for gain. The opposite end of this spectrum is occupied by a key figure against whom the film must be read: the current American president, Barack Obama. While concerns of race dominate journalistic discourse about Obama, I want to focus on what he represents as a political touchstone. Here his identity is segmented into a wider discourse about the role of the state – the mobilization of collective hope and succor, both financial and emotional, for a nation. The "Obama effect," as seen in the success of *Slumdog*, works as follows: the film uses the same discursive strategy, hope, as the text of its storyline, as the vehicle through which the film itself became marketed/ narrativized and, finally, as the context in which it was read. One may speculate that as American audiences (and critics) looked for hope through the televisual construction of Obama, this construct spilled over to the other texts they watched, and what emerged was the creation of a discursive energy around the text of the season, something that spurred it all the way to the Oscars. Looking back in late 2011, what stands out is the liminality of that moment captured by the Oscars. Today, as Obama faces the very real possibility of losing the upcoming election, it is important to note the end of this narrative arc. As *Slumdog* fades from the quick-to-forget public memory, so does Obama as the story arc he represented disappears into the quicksand of political expediency.

What We Look Like Now

A final context for American audiences lies in the contemporary (Western) rendition of ethnicity, in all its constitutiveness – cultural, religious and gendered. The term hybridity appears value neutral but, as with all matters of culture, rarely is. *Slumdog* must be seen within the context of immigration wars in the United States, the religious conflict around diasporic Islamic communities and, finally, in the emergence of Latino consciousness and political power. Simply put, *Slumdog* allows for an understanding of ethnicity at a safe distance. As a crossover text, it works admirably in fashioning a space for common understanding – the quiz show, *Who Wants to Be a Millionaire?* (the ultimate text of consumption, it sets up the obvious answer: everybody!) – regardless of culture and ethnic background. Working in this common space is an uncommon culture – that of India. India's bottomless repertoire of symbols, clothes, landscapes, foods, cultural practices and norms are the texts through which such an understanding of ethnicity is constructed – but at a distance, preserving its ethnic/exotic integrity, even as it is centered in the marketplace.

Hidden not too far below this consumption of ethnicity is an unspoken concern with Latino identity, where one kind of brown is accepted (from afar and on one's own terms) but the other is constructed as a problem. It is no accident that, at the 2009 Oscars, Penélope Cruz had to both center and efface her Latino identity in her acceptance speech. This is an important part of how *Slumdog* needs to be read. It bears reminding that the entire crew of *Slumdog* drew attention to a narrative of (Indian) ethnicity marked through comments about the Indian nation and national identity. Finally (and perhaps cynically), the ethnicity that *Slumdog* offers suffers from the "Paul Simon syndrome," where the work of cultural extraction is left to metropolitan media brokers and practitioners looking worldwide for a good story and a career boost. In such a reading, the placement of the slum children center stage at the Oscars is an illusion – smoke and mirrors for the circulation of capital.

Having said that, there remains this social fact: *Slumdog* went where no text about the Third World has gone before – to the center of the mediated world, Hollywood, where the images, ideas and constructs that shape our (global) lives are created. This is indeed a matter of celebration – *Jai Ho!*

Chapter 11

SLUMDOG CELEBRITIES

Priya Jaikumar

Three child actors from British director Danny Boyle's *Slumdog Millionaire* (hereafter *Slumdog*) (2008) walked the red carpet at the Kodak Theater in Los Angeles, for the Oscar ceremony on 22 February 2009. The celebrated feel-good film about a boy from the slums of Mumbai, India, swept the Oscars. It won in eight categories, taking home the award for best motion picture and best director of the year. In what was equally meaningful to Indians, it won for best original song and score, credited to A. R. Rahman and Gulzar, veteran composers of India's mainstream film industry. It was a picture postcard moment for the triumphant promise of transnationality in cinema. Much was made of the fact that, as for its protagonists, the odds were stacked against this film. It had a small budget by Hollywood standards (at an estimated $15 million), was shot partly in Hindi with no known actors and set almost entirely in Dharavi, the largest slum of Asia. By way of pitching for its success and explaining its timeliness, Fox Searchlight, one of *Slumdog*'s distributors collaborating with producer Warner Brothers in the US and Celador Films and Film 4 of the UK, pronounced *Slumdog* "Obama-like" in its "message of hope in the face of difficulty."[1]

On Oscar night, *Slumdog*'s six young actors were undoubtedly an unusual presence. They look wonderful in a photograph (Fig. 11.1) that tempts us with the seductive neoliberal promise of egalitarianism ("If these kids from India can win, we must be an equal opportunity society/ industry"). Equally and in an opposite way, it tempts us to distance ourselves from the machinery of fame, putting at risk the potentially breakthrough desire to make structures malleable to change ("If these kids from India can win, they are just part of a promiscuous commodity culture granting them their Warholian 15 minutes"). Celebrity culture thrives on voyeuristic self-validation and disenchantment as configurations of feelings to attach to narratives of a personality's ascent to fame and disappearance into oblivion. I want to track these emotive configurations

Figure 11.1. The young stars of *Slumdog Millionaire* on Oscar night.

surrounding *Slumdog*'s child actors as a series of disjunctures around the idea of celebrity across the contexts of the US, the UK and India.

Disjuncture is Arjun Appadurai's word to rethink the world outside the center-periphery model, as an irregular scalar global landscape of connections and difference across the realms of economy, culture and politics.[2] The film and its child stars animated debates that expressed links between communities and debates within nations. The participants and platforms of the debates are as interesting as its content. The title, *Slumdog*, was one cause for protest, with cases filed in the Gujarat High Court against the word "dog" (the Hindi equivalent "kutta" being a term of abuse). Protesters were, ostensibly, roused by Hindu right organizations looking for electoral publicity through nationalism. Slum organizers like Jockin Arputham of the National Slum Dwellers Federation of India were also offended by the term. In opposing foreign investors interested in demolishing Dharavi and raising high rise, low cost apartments (a move also opposed by Prince Charles's Foundation for the Built Environment, an unlikely ally), Arputham said: "I am a slum dweller, not a slumdog."[3]

The issue of novelty was another bone of contention. A writer for the *Guardian* (UK), quoting the absence of poverty in Bollywood films about globe-dancing elites, hailed *Slumdog* as novel in subject and perspective.[4] Critics in the US and India countered the claim on both counts, noting that India's slums have been depicted in commercial Indian films (such as *Parinda* (1989); *Satya* (1998); *Black Friday* (2004); *Company* (2002)). Boyle's film was a fantasy romance evoking 1970s Indian films, they noted, full of coincidences, morality tales and reunions, but lacking the choreographic finesse of Bollywood's dance finales.[5] Complicating global ignorance of the variegations within India's domestic cinema was the fact that Danny Boyle watched *Black Friday* and *Satya*, and cast Saurabh Shukla (writer of *Satya*) as the film's torturing cop. Was this a knowing cultural wink or poaching? What was the flow of aesthetic influences here? How does a focus on the celebrity accruing to *Slumdog*'s child actors impact these questions?

The photograph has some answers. It depicts six young faces with, to use a concept from the film, different *destinies* of stardom scripted into their social space. Each plays the characters of Jamal, Latika and Salim at various stages of life. Loveleen Tandan, credited as co-director of the film, suggested to Boyle that they scout for talent not merely in India's "parks, residential areas, football grounds, line-dancing classes," but look at "slums, streets and non-governmental shelters."[6] The use of Hindi, the film's realism and the city's energy are linked to this production decision, leading to the use of a digital movie camera and sync-sound to convey immersion and speed in the 360 degree space of external locations. Mohammed Azharuddin and Rubina Ali (front row, left and middle) were selected from Mumbai's shanty towns to play the young Salim and Latika respectively. Ayush Khedekar (front right), son of a Bombay Port Trust employee, was young Jamal. The others were from English speaking schools, with Tanay Chheda (rear right) already a star in Aamir Khan's *Taare Zamin Par* (2007) and Farhan Akhtar's *Don* (2006).

Two of the actors lack access to the upward mobility available to the other *Slumdog* children and adolescents. Whereas US broadcasts of the Oscars focused on the children's darling status, the blogosphere has been rife with stories of their abjection: their homelessness in contrast to the film's lucrative transglobality.[7] In the Oscar broadcasts, the children are adorable; online, the children are framed by stories of razed homes and sales into prostitution rings. Both popular television and blogs, dominated by opinion rather than fact, have been premised on the indistinguishability of the children from each other, relative to their difference from the universe inhabited by the telecasting or blogging narrators. Any effort to look at the image of the young *Slumdog* cast must be based on disaggregating the characters from the actors, and the actors from each other, to account for how each child may have encountered the red carpet and the film's narrative against his/her own experiences and future expectations.

Ali and Azharuddin's silence when faced with Ryan Seacrest's patter offers a commentary on the surreality of the moment for them.[8] This surreality also has an audience. Nine year old Rubina Ali has already published a memoir, *Slumdog Dreaming: My Journey to the Stars*.[9] Highlights from the book include her escape from and return to the slums. Ali also reputedly discusses Nicole Kidman as "strange" for avoiding the Indian sun. This news appears with links to "More Famous Catfights" on the *US Weekly* site.[10] A girl from Mumbai's slum at the Oscars is made explicable through alliances between the spectatorial spaces of Western paternalism, girly trash-talk, and *schadenfreude* at the inescapable clutch of poverty. The visual and moral functions of abjection are inextricably linked in today's global culture of the confessional but, despite memoirs, blogs, and internal narratives, it remains impossible to speak of the intractable experience of a child subject to these visual and moral regimes. Familiar encasing discourses (paternalism, voyeurism, confessionals) are one way to mitigate the obscurity of the children, which the film must alleviate as well. This it does with the transnationally familiar television format of *Who Wants to Be a Millionaire?*, produced by UK's Celador Productions, which co-financed *Slumdog* through sister company, Celador Films. The Indian version, *Kaun Benega Krorepati?* has been hosted by Amitabh Bachchan (superstar of the 1970s and 80s, who appears in the film) and Shah Rukh Khan (reigning megastar since the 1990s, who introduced *Slumdog* at the Golden Globes).

Unlike Khan, Bachchan condemned *Slumdog* in his popular blog for getting "global recognition" by portraying India as a "third-world, dirty, underbelly [...] nation," even though the West also has a seamy side.[11] The *Guardian* denounced Bachchan with equal stridency: "Having failed miserably at cultivating a western audience [in *The Last Lear*, 2008], it must hurt him to be so monumentally upstaged by white folk on his home turf. The bitter truth is *Slumdog Millionaire* could only have been made by westerners."[12] The question "Whose view does this film represent?" is important, but leads to a belligerent impasse that hides the partial truth of both sides, and a focus on the children clarifies this. The *Guardian* is right: Ali and Azharuddin would never be cast in a commercial Indian film. Bachchan is right: equivalent British social groups – underclass immigrant kids from council housing, mainly South Asian Muslims – do not have a chance at the same success. *Slumdog*'s children are palatable to the production of global celebrity because they participate in several familiar visual regimes: of children living in Third World poverty, of universal romance, and a liberal meritocracy. The film's *punctum* to the meritocracy narrative is that Jamal's success at the game show comes from knowledge gleaned by street life. This, for Boyle, is India's schizophrenia: inescapable poverty simultaneous with a fantastic inner life of emotions and ambitions promoted by Bollywood and globalization. So Boyle shows slums, and makes them fantastical.

If *Trainspotting*'s Scotland had the worst shit-hole toilet scene followed by pure *photogenie*, when the protagonist dives into luminous fluids for his suppository fix, *Slumdog*'s shit-hole does not lead to a new cinematic vision. The cosmically mobile camera is not rooted in any singular subjective experience but offers an exhilarated objectification of its surroundings. This vision has boosted "reality," or "slum tourism," in India, with foreign tourists eager to see Dharavi.[13] Like the quarrels, the connections made by the film – some inhabitants of Dharavi welcome tourists; some Indians see an opportunity to attract more US companies – have not led to structural or perspectival transformations. A joyous photograph of the children at the Oscars chastens us to think that such high expectations are not the point. The trouble is the image nevertheless sneaks in claims to a new global order of empathy and interest in the ordinary person.

Notes

1 David Lim, "What, exactly, is *Slumdog Millionaire?*" *Slate*, 26 January 2009. Online: http://www.slate.com/articles/arts/the_oscars/2009/01/what_exactly_is_slumdog_millionaire.html (accessed 20 July 2009).

2 Arjun Appadurai, "Disjuncture and Difference in the Global Cultural Economy," *Public Culture* 2.2 (Spring 1990): 1–24.

3 Robert Booth, "Charles declares Mumbai shanty town model for the World," *Guardian*, 29 February 2009. Online: http://www.guardian.co.uk/artanddesign/2009/feb/06/prince-charles-slum-comments/print (accessed 3 August 2009).

4 Nirpal Dhaliwal, "Slumdog Millionaire could only have been made by a westerner," *Guardian*, 15 January 2009. Online: http://www.guardian.co.uk/film/filmblog/2009/jan/15/danny-boyle-shows (accessed 22 July 2009).

5 See Lim's article from *Slate* magazine cited above [note 1], and Namrata Joshi, "All it Boyles down to," *Outlook* (India), 26 January 2009. Online: http://www.outlookindia.com/article.aspx?239565 (accessed 22 July 2009).

6 Kevin Maher, "Oscar 2009: Loveleen Tandon-the unsung hero of *Slumdog Millionaire*," *Times* (London), 21 February 2009. Online: http://entertainment.timesonline.co.uk/tol/arts_and_entertainment/film/oscars/article5772395.ece (accessed 30 July 2009).

7 Various threads from *The Huffington Post* lead to articles, blogs and commentary on *Slumdog Millionaire*'s children. As a start, look at Katherine Thompson's post on 18 May 2009, "'Slumdog Millionaire' Kid Ayush Mahesh Khedekar Does Cannes." Online: http://www.huffingtonpost.com/2009/05/18/slumdog-millionaire-kid-a_n_204929.html (accessed 22 July 2009).

8 A video of the interview is on *The Huffington Post*. Rubina clearly articulates her name and falls silent. See "Ryan Seacrest and the 'Slumdog Millionaire' Kids Interview (Video). Online: http://www.huffingtonpost.com/2009/02/22/ryan-seacrest-and-the-slu_n_168979.html (accessed 22 July 2009).

9 The memoir was released on 16 July 2009 by Transworld Publishing and Random House. It is available on amazon.com.

10 "Slumdog Star calls Nicole Kidman 'Strange,'" *US Magazine: Celebrity News*, 16 July 2009. Online: http://www.usmagazine.com/news/slumdog-millionaire-star-slams-nicole-kidman-2009167 (accessed 22 July 2009).

11 Amitah Bachchan's Official Blog. http://bigb.bigadda.com/ (accessed 22 July 2009).

12 See Dhaliwal review in the *Guardian*, above [note 4].

13 See "Slum Tourism in India," *Shubh Yatra*. Online: http://www.shubhyatra.com/maharashtra/slum-tourism.html. You can book discount tour packages through several websites.

Chapter 12

SLUMDOG MILLIONAIRE AND THE NEW MIDDLEBROW

Robert Koehler

Danny Boyle's *Slumdog Millionaire* is the film of the moment for the "new middlebrow" – the audience able to perceive momentous changes in the world and culture when they're reported in, say, the *New York Times*, but that wouldn't have the slightest clue that the most thrilling new rushes of creative filmmaking since the nouvelle vague originate in the apartments and editing rooms of Manila, Kuala Lumpur, Barcelona and Buenos Aires. This new middlebrow has a fresh object of adoration in Boyle's entertainment, since it quite conveniently summarizes and expresses so many wishes, hopes and romantic yearnings of the West toward what is perceived as the troubled East, with today's West resembling nothing so much as the West of the Sixties and its taste for turning Indian style into various forms of Hippie Chic. *Slumdog* is paisley cinema, pure and simple. Boyle's feverish, woozy, drunken and thoroughly contrived picaresque also conveniently packages misperceptions about India (and the East) that continue to support the dominant Western view of the Subcontinent. This makes the film a potent object to examine not only what is cockeyed about an outsider's view (particularly, an Englishman's view) of India, but even more, what is misperceived by a middlebrow critical establishment and audience about what comprises world cinema.

Suitably then, the creative godfather of *Slumdog*, more than Bollywood musical fantasies, is Charles Dickens. Certain Bollywood tropes are obediently followed, such as the innocent hero rising above terrible circumstances, the determined pursuit of a love against all odds and that stock Bollywood type, the snarling (often mustachioed) nemesis. But, including the much discussed group-dance finale, these are tropes included almost by necessity and play onscreen in a notably rote fashion. They are alien to Boyle, which is why the Dickens model is more culturally and even cinematically germane when addressing the issues inside *Slumdog*. Dickens's picaresque novels about young underdog heroes struggling and managing to eventually thrive in social settings weighed heavily against them were grist for, first, Vikas Swarup's novel, *Q & A*, and then, Simon Beaufoy's loosely adapted screenplay, which greatly compresses the novel's episodes and sections, renames characters and – as outlandish as the final film is – actually tones down the adventure's more incredible events and coincidences.

If Dickens's milieu was the early years of the Industrial Revolution, the film's setting is the new era of globalism in which India is undergoing its own revolution. Jamal (Dev Patel) is Pip, Nicholas Nickleby and Oliver Twist rolled into one; a lad who by sheer gumption has managed to land a spot as a contestant on the hugely popular *Who Wants to Be a Millionaire?* even though he's a humble (but oh-so-smart) *chai wallah* (or tea servant) at a cell-phone sales center. When he's first seen on screen, though, Jamal is in trouble: a fat cop is abusing him in a police station, though that's nothing next to the electrocution he receives from the chief inspector (veteran Indian actor Irrfan Khan), who's convinced that Jamal has cheated on the show. How, his caste-based logic goes, could a slumdog like Jamal have won ten million rupees (and only have been one question away from winning 100 million) without cheating? Even the most scurrilous and bigoted of Mumbai cops likely wouldn't go all Abu Ghraib on a poor teen boy for cheating on TV, and this is just the start of the film's endless supply of stunning exaggeration-for-effect gambits that are more like a two-by-four upside the head than anything that might be termed in polite company as dramatic touches. Boyle appears to have absorbed this exaggeration into his directorial bloodstream, since, in at least the film's first half and lingering long into the second, he indulges in a rush.of shots filmed with an obsessively canted camera, the technique lovingly nurtured by Orson Welles to convey states of eruption and dislocation, but grievously abused by Boyle through repetitive excess until it reeks of desperation.

So, we get it: Jamal has everything stacked against him, as he must convince these thugs with badges how he knew the questions thrown to him by the show's supercilious and remarkably condescending host, Prem (Anil Kapoor), and he will – it is written – prevail. From here, the rest of the movie comprises Jamal's case, which begins with the wildly implausible notion that Jamal remembers more or less everything in his life inside the framework of a Dickens novel, and ends with his endless and, um, dogged pursuit of his only true love, the beautiful (can she be anything else?) Latika (Freida Pinto). Of course, wild implausibility has been Boyle's general stock-in-trade for some time, beginning with his *Clockwork Orange* pastiche, *Trainspotting* (which followed his Hammer pastiche, *Shallow Grave*, and preceded his Roland Emmerich pastiche, *The Beach*, a film so awful that it would have killed many lesser

Figure 12.1. Jamal, Latika and Salim as Mumbai street kids.

Left to right: Jamal (Ayush Mahesh Khedekar), Latika (Rubina Ali) and Salim (Azharuddin Mohammed Ismail) are street kids in Mumbai in *Slumdog Millionaire*.

mortals' directing careers on the spot, and nearly killed Boyle's). *28 Days Later* was intrinsically implausible – about zombies apparently ready to race Usain Bolt in the Olympics – but so burly, aggressive and spectacularly rude that it didn't allow a moment's pause for reflection. Is Boyle's last movie, *Sunshine*, about a space crew on a mission straight for the sun, any more ridiculous than *Slumdog Millionaire*, which suggests that a little Muslim boy raised in Mumbai's worst hellholes can become rich and famous? (Well, maybe a little more.)

Because *Slumdog* isn't conceived as a genre piece with its own built-in conventions (horror, sci-fi) but is rather a self-consciously contrived picaresque situated in the real world of Indian class structure – Muslim/Hindu religious conflicts, underworld crime rings and pop media – the sheer impulse to push the story into a frothy romance functions as a betrayal of its fundamental material. In the end, when Jamal has won (because, as the viewer is reminded more times than is worth counting, his victory is destined to happen), he becomes India's new superstar, its latest populist hero, a seeming sensation, a bolt out of the blue. So where is he? Squatting ever so quietly, alone, unmolested, unnoticed by anyone in Mumbai's central train station, where he spots Latika, also alone, and where they then run to each other and break into a Bollywood-style number. The effect of this scene turned the first audience at Telluride, based on eyewitness accounts, all goofy in the head. ("I wanted to run outside and scream and holler at the mountains," one starry-eyed survivor told me.)

It's hard to argue against such sentiment or reaction; for sure, early viewers of Julie Andrews running down that Austrian meadow in *The Sound of Music* were similarly nutty. Some are just mad for *Slumdog Millionaire* – including far, far too many critics – and they won't hear a discouraging word. As the cult-like object of many in the new middlebrow, *Slumdog* receives no criticism and some express outright shock when their beloved new movie is broken apart, knocked or dismissed as what it is – a really, really minor movie with really, really big problems. Similarly, the score by composer A. R. Rahman, a crafty and fairly cynical Bollywood hand, is bogus Indian music from top to bottom, with an excess of quasi-hip-hop stylings, electronic beat patterns and vocalese gumming up the works and sounding like the kind of backgrounds one might hear in a TV travel advert. So, the closing number is bogus Bollywood following on the heels of bogus social drama.

The problem, for the fresh-scrubbed middlebrow and for the rest of us, is that if the real thing isn't known – that is, genuinely Indian cinema – how can we judge the Fox Searchlight facsimile? Really, though, *Slumdog* is fun, so let your quibbles just drift away, sit back, relax and let it spill all over you like a nice mango lassi. That's certainly the refrain of too many of the post-Telluride reviews, which recognized Boyle's brazen manipulations and absurd storytelling jumps of marginal logic for what they were, but still joined in the cheering (a word that I counted in at least ten reviews).[1] And they're right; it is fun – fun as a cultural fabrication to question. Consider this overlooked yet central aspect of the film's many conceits: *Slumdog* uses TV as a national arena, and precisely as the medium wherein Jamal not only escapes his class, but (when the show is reviewed on tape during the police station interrogation) uses it as a tool to justify his existence. The film at once reinforces the myths of reality game show TV as actual rather than manufactured suspense and as a machine for getting rich quick, while – in total contradiction – suggesting that TV can also be a partner with the police in torture. As at so many other points, Boyle and Beaufoy try to have it both ways: Jamal proves his mettle by deploying his life experiences in order to be the ideal game show star, while the show itself (via Prem, who says that he "owns" the show and reveals that he's also from the slums) collaborates with police to persecute and torture Jamal, even though Prem also knows – an important point – that Jamal isn't cheating. The basis for arranging for Jamal's arrest is a collapsing house of cards on close inspection, since the arrest is not only a surprise to the show's producer, but couldn't have possibly been managed by Prem, who has after all been on the show during airtime.

Perhaps Prem is jealous of his fellow slumdog? An interesting, even profound, character point – one that's right there, hanging like ripe narrative fruit, and which would have been even more interesting had Beaufoy and Boyle bothered

Figure 12.2. Jamal and *Millionaire* host Prem Kumar.

Jamal (Dev Patel, left) and *Who Wants to Be a Millionaire?* host Prem Kumar (Anil Kapoor) in a scene from Danny Boyle's *Slumdog Millionaire.*

to pluck it. The Dickensian sensibility, with its ironies and coincidences, is imposed here but never truly developed and only selectively applied. Dickens's picaresque tales, laden with social criticism and narrative athleticism, never fail to point a harsh finger at unjust authority (something Boyle is clearly uncomfortable doing) through a romance of the hero's ultimately improbable triumph over odds (something Boyle bases his whole movie on, culminating with the ersatz Bollywood finale). As a result, the exchanges of colonialism in *Slumdog Millionaire* are too delicious not to notice. In a single film we have: the celebration of the export of a British game show to the Indian viewing public; a narrative structured on the show itself and the (British) Dickens picaresque; a disastrously tone-deaf and colorblind depiction of the world experienced by Muslim lower classes, decorated in gloriously erotic and lush colors as perhaps only a European-based director and cinematographer (the usually brilliant and ingenious Anthony Dod Mantle) could manage; and a British-themed call center as the opening of opportunity and upward mobility for Jamal.

In its expressly liberal intentions to depict an India in which a single Muslim boy can win a nation's heart, *Slumdog Millionaire* massages the Western viewer's gaze on a country and culture s/he barely knows, save for a vague sense of cultural exports like the occasional Bollywood movie or song. Perhaps especially now, after the fearsome attacks by Islamist extremists on Mumbai's most cherished institutions and on Western tourists, Boyle's film is just the soft pillow for concerned Western viewers to plump their heads on; surely, there's hope, when even a Muslim lad who is abused, scorned and rejected can recover his dignity, win the girl and thrive in a world free of terror. It's precisely the India of which Westerners, starting with its former British masters, heartily dream; an India where everything is possible.

The Indian reality, of course, is far more complex, and it has taken filmmakers of sublime artistry and a subtle grasp of the huge Indian spectrum like Mani Ratnam, Shonali Bose, Buddhadeb Dasgupta, Girish Kasaravalli and Murali Nair to express that complexity on screen. Opportunities for lower classes to free themselves from the old constraints are indeed greater now in India than ever before, largely through the jobs created by the nation's exploding high-tech and manufacturing sectors, which have literally created a middle class where one barely existed. That new middle class is full of Jamals, using the new social streams fostered by computers and the Web to find types of work that simply never existed before in the Indian economy. The now infamous call centers – an aspect Boyle's film hardly glances at – are mere slivers of this new economy. But it is new, and therefore has only just begun to make its presence felt in a nation of such vast stretches and distances of geography, culture, religious traditions and economic status.

It's here that Boyle's vision of India goes truly south, since it reinforces his target audience's general ignorance of reference points in Indian cinema. An affectionate nod in an early sequence to the Bollywood spectacles starring Amitabh Bachchan is typical: his enduring superstar status aside, the particular Amitabh movies visually cited in *Slumdog Millionaire* are actually too old for Jamal – a lower-class boy born in the late eighties – to have seen (except, perhaps, on videotape). The brief Amitabh film reel in *Slumdog* is more properly seen as reflective of Boyle's own personal memory bank of the Bollywood movies seen in his youth, and therefore useful for Boyle's purposes, since Amitabh remains the one Bollywood superstar widely known in the West. (He's also something of an insider's joke here, since he was the original host of the Indian *Millionaire* show entitled, *Kaun Banega Crorepati?* (*Who Will Become a Crorepati?*).) *Slumdog Millionaire* may be minor, but in one way it's important: it serves as the ideal vehicle for the new middlebrow's perception of what makes up world cinema. For starters, as a non-Indian movie with Indian actors (professionals based in the UK and India, plus newcomers and nonprofessionals), dialog, settings and music, it provides a comfortable substitute for a genuine Indian film (say, by the abovementioned, neglected and under-seen Ratnam, Dasgupta or Nair). The new middlebrow can thus say they've covered their current Indian cinema; after all, they've seen – and enjoyed – *Slumdog Millionaire*.

Boyle's film has been celebrated as an expression of globalization, and it's certainly true that the story itself couldn't exist in a world before globalization took effect in once-protectionist India, and that Jamal's progress is globalization incarnate. But a truer manifestation of globalization is the explosion of world cinema itself, and how the past decade and a half has seen the spread of national cinemas to an unmatched degree in the art form's history. This has been possible only through the combined forces of globalization and the absorption of previous experimentation in film grammar and theory; the ways in which local filmmakers in their local conditions have responded to the challenges of making cinema on their own terms has made the current period probably the most exciting ever from a global perspective.

India is an interesting example in this regard, since its many languages and regions have produced a wide range of filmmaking styles and voices, most of which continue to struggle (like Ratnam, who himself dances between more genres and forms than Steven Soderbergh) to be seen abroad. We're living in the midst of a paradoxical climate, however: just as world cinema and its locally-based voices (and not glib, fly-by-night tourists like Boyle) are more aggressively active than ever, and more exciting in their expressions, the outlets in the US for this work are shrinking. Distributors, burned by too many subtitled films that bomb at the box office, have narrowed their shopping lists at festivals and markets. Alternative outlets, from festivals to pay-per-view, can contain only so many titles. Video is the last refuge, meaning that cinema made by artists ends up being seen (if at all) on TV.

Boyle is obviously keenly aware of this condition in his own film about characters raised speaking Hindi: he manages to compress the Hindi dialogue into about fifteen minutes' total running time (a fraction of the full running time of 116 minutes), and then offer up subtitles for the Hindi in distractingly snazzy lines of text that dance all over the screen like a hyperkinetic TV ad – apparently the perfect solution for otherwise worldly minded folks who hate reading subtitles. In the future, *Slumdog Millionaire* might be seen as a talisman of a potentially degraded film culture, in which audiences were sufficiently dumbed-down to accept the fake rather than the real thing, and in a new middlebrow haze, weren't able to perceive the difference.

Note

1 See, for example, the compilation of reviews listed on the Rotten Tomatoes website: https://www.rottentomatoes.com/m/slumdog_millionaire/(accessed 11 November 2012).

Chapter 13

SLUMDOG COMPRADOR: COMING TO TERMS WITH THE *SLUMDOG* PHENOMENON

Ajay Gehlawat

Every time a film about India made by a Western director gains critical acclaim in the West, two related phenomena seem to also occur: the greatest hits of negative stereotypes are brought out and served up in the film (think poverty, squalor and general backwardness), even as the "usual suspects" emerge to tout its merits. I am referring, of course, to the comprador class of critics; those native-born, self-styled authorities who are summoned to validate the authenticity of the work at hand and to defend it against the potential critiques of their brethren. With the Oscar winner, *Slumdog Millionaire* (2008), one witnesses the re-emergence of both phenomena. In such instances a third phenomenon also frequently occurs, namely, the referencing of the last instance of such a cinematic "milestone" – in this case, Richard Attenborough's *Gandhi* (1982) – as a marker of how far we (as a Western/ global culture) have come.[1] Hamid Dabashi has noted the recurrence of the comprador phenomenon in recent times:

> Given the transnational disposition of the globalised empire, a crucial function of its ideological foregrounding is predicated on the role that expatriate intellectuals can play. [...] In the immediate aftermath of 9/11, comprador native intellectuals were actively recruited to perform a critical function for the militant ideologues of the US Empire. Their task is to feign authority, authenticity, and native knowledge and thus to inform the US public of the atrocities that are taking place throughout the world, in the region of their native birth in particular, by way of justifying the imperial designs of the US as liberating these nations from the evil of their own designs.[2]

While proponents of *Slumdog* may argue that, at most (i.e., at worst), the film is "harmless fun" or "just entertaining" or "only, after all, a *film*," it is precisely such a veneer of innocuousness that *Slumdog*'s proponents summon to defend it from subsequent criticism. The film's director, Danny Boyle, has also expressed this sentiment, noting in an interview with Fareed Zakaria, that "it's an entertainment, in the end. It's not a documentary."[3] The best-case scenario, as framed by *Slumdog*'s fans, is even more problematic, namely, arguing that the film actually *engages* with serious issues (the slums, poverty, corruption), raising awareness and, in the process, functioning as *more* than "merely" a work of art. Anand Giridharadas, for instance, claims that *Slumdog* "shows a much more realistic version of life in India than films traditionally have."[4] Even better for proponents (to have the best of both worlds) would be to see *Slumdog* as simultaneously being a fun, entertaining film that addresses serious issues. Dennis Lim notes this tendency to have its cake and eat it, too, calling *Slumdog* "a slippery and self-conscious concoction" that "has it both ways. It makes a show of being anchored in a real-world social context, then asks to be read as a fantasy."[5] This would arguably provide the Western fan with the greatest satisfaction, leaving intact his/her complacency about patronizing such films. Furthermore (to come full circle), having witnessed the "global" success of the film, Western fans can reaffirm their belief in the West's unique ability to produce such successes.

Another phenomenon linked to this last sentiment can also be traced to the emergence of *Slumdog*, namely, the misconception in the West of what constitutes a Bollywood film, as well as the subsequent reappropriation of this latter moniker (itself appropriating the system which now attempts to "steal it back"). Thus *Slumdog* is heralded as both "the new Bollywood" and "turn[ing] Bollywood on its head."[6] It is precisely in the summoning of this term – ironically now used as a marker of authenticity – that the compradors come in, for who better to speak on Bollywood than Indians?[7] These compradors can even be relied upon to go one step further and argue that, even as *Slumdog* is just as entertaining as a Bollywood film and, in many ways, resembles one, it goes further than any Bollywood film has, or can, in addressing the "social ills" of India.[8] Here we begin to see the emergence of the first of several contradictions: on the one hand, it is the style of the Bollywood film that prevents it from such (serious, social) engagement; on the other hand, it is precisely such a style that *Slumdog* emulates in engaging with such issues. It is precisely such a contradiction which makes possible the reemergence of what Dabashi describes in reference to the United States' response to 9/11 (the so-called global war on terror) or, indeed, what the 2009 Oscar Awards ceremony provided, namely, the image of the benevolent white man surrounded by grateful brown children, being honored for his noble effort.[9]

There seem to be at least three invocations at work in the case of *Slumdog*, then: one, that of the "slum" (read: "real India") and, thus (as a byproduct of this), the "good intentions" of the Western filmmaker – in this case, Danny Boyle; two, that of Bollywood (read: "real Indian cinema"); and thus, building upon these two, three, that of the film's "authenticity" (read: a film about "real India" made in a "real Indian" way). In order to better understand how *Slumdog* circulates within such a Western discourse, it is necessary to first examine the underlying premises of these three invocations, as well as their interrelations, in some detail.

The Slum

In his Introduction to *The Secret Politics of Our Desires*, entitled, "Indian Popular Cinema as a Slum's Eye View of Politics," Ashis Nandy claims that "the right metaphor for the Indian popular cinema [...] turns out to be the urban slum."[10] In developing this metaphor, Nandy describes the conditions of the slums in Bombay and Calcutta, circa the late 1990s, noting that "nearly half of metropolitan India today lives in slums," and "if their present rates and patterns of growth continue, both cities will become 80 per cent slum by the year 2010."[11] While Amitabh Bachchan is correct in claiming that slums exist the world over (including within the heart of the so-called First World), the sheer magnitude of the numbers involved in the case of India is indeed overwhelming.[12]

The slum in many ways comes to define India in the Western popular imagination. As Mark Magnier notes, there is a long cinematic history chronicling the West's fascination – one might even say, fixation – with this paradigm. Films such as Louis Malle's documentaries for French television, *Phantom India* and *Calcutta* (1969), Mira Nair's *Salaam Bombay!* (1988), *City of Joy* (1992) and the documentary, *Born into Brothels* (2004), display the ongoing appeal of images of the slum – the slum-scape, one might say, paraphrasing Arjun Appadurai – in Western films focusing on India. The fact that native-born directors also engage in this phenomenon is both an acknowledgement of the slumscape's appeal to Western audiences and a testament to the savviness of comprador-*auteurs* such as Nair, who claims that "any approach is fine, as long as their [the audience's] bums are in the chairs."[13] Both *Salaam Bombay!* and *Born into Brothels* were nominated for Academy Awards (for Best Foreign Language Film and Best Documentary, respectively), with *Brothels* winning the prize in 2005. In many ways, then, such films – stemming back to Malle's documentaries and including *Slumdog* – provide what Shyamal Sengupta calls "a poverty tour" for Western audiences.[14] Furthermore, in the case of *Slumdog*, this is a poverty tour-as-music video, providing brief, rapidly-edited bursts of shocking slum imagery to the pounding, pulsating beats of

A. R. Rahman's techno-fusion soundtrack. In an interview, Rahman claimed that, with regard to *Slumdog*'s soundtrack, "[Boyle] said no sentiment. And no cello. He didn't want anything depressing. Some scenes are unbearable, and then the music comes in."[15]

Slumdog, in other words, is not E. M. Forster's poverty tour, in which the filth of the Indian slum "deters all but the invited guest."[16] With *Slumdog*, there tends to be no monotony in "everything that meets the eye"[17] – instead, in Rahman's words, "one is pushed from a cliff and then [given] wings to fly."[18] Indeed, following Alice Miles's labeling of *Slumdog* as "poverty porn," one could say the slum in *Slumdog* is aestheticized and invites the Western viewer to enjoy said aestheticization.[19] David Denby has also noted this approach, arguing that "Boyle has created what looks like a jumpy, hyper-edited commercial for poverty – he uses the squalor and violence touristically, as an aspect of the fabulous."[20] If the slum is what *Slumdog* finds fascinating, then the latter's slummy style may be what, more often than not, draws the ire of its detractors. Slumming the slum, *Slumdog*'s slumlord supplants this site with a simulation, so that even as India emerges (yet again) on the international scene, it finds itself, like the film's protagonist early on in the narrative, literally mired in (its "own") shit. Naturally the prime consumers of this "visual salad of glowing rotten fruit" are Western audiences.[21] (*Slumdog* was not released in India until the day after it was nominated for Best Picture at the Academy Awards and, as Latha Jishnu notes, it has thus far failed to become a hit there, with the Hindi version of the film almost a flop.[22]) Nandy's claim that "most well-wishers of these [slum-dwelling] classes like to serve as the latter's mouthpieces in the belief that they use the wrong language to interpret their predicament," thus takes on new resonance with the *Slumdog* phenomenon.[23] The ensuing issue becomes how Boyle's imagined slumscape is credited with appropriating an Indian form.

Bollywood

As a way of beginning this discussion, it should be noted that, despite Bollywood's global popularity, it has yet to make significant inroads with the majority of the non-Indian population in the United States. More often than not, films such as *Monsoon Wedding* (2001) and *Bride and Prejudice* (2004) are thought of as Bollywood productions in the West.[24] The differences between such films and actual Bollywood films, however, are worth noting. To begin with, the typical Bollywood film is nearly three hours in length (as opposed to the two-hour length of films such as *Wedding* and *Bride*), and typically features five to six song-and-dance sequences. These sequences, along with playback singing and sound, feature frequent costume and scenery changes as well as intricately choreographed dance movements that combine a range of Western and more classical Indian styles. Meanwhile *Slumdog*, coming in at two hours, features a grand total of one song-and-dance sequence at the very end (technically during the end credits), in which the male and female leads, accompanied by a host of background dancers, perform a (stationary) line-dance in one setting: the platform of a train station. How and why, then, is *Slumdog* heralded as "borrow[ing] the narrative and aesthetic elements of Bollywood" or, indeed, as being a Bollywood film?[25]

Bollywood, according to comprador critics, is defined by its logical loopholes and "feel-good factor."[26] Critics subsequently find similar structuring – "all [the] classic elements of popular Indian cinema"[27] – in *Slumdog*. Yet what ultimately informs *Slumdog* (more than the Bollywood narrative/form) is the game show format. While both formats (Bollywood and the game show as manifested in *Slumdog*) generally engage in narrative ruptures and departures, the nature of these ruptures (or, of this rupturing) significantly differs in these cases. Whereas, in the typical Bollywood film, the most frequent narrative disruptions – the song-and-dance sequences – bear no direct relation to the story, *Slumdog*'s narrative breaks subserve the game show storyline, in the sense that each of the main character's recollections provides him (and the viewer) with an answer to the question he faces. In this sense, while the Bollywood rupturing (via song-and-dance sequence) works to defamiliarize and disorient both the narrative and the viewer, the departures (read: Jamal's recollections) in *Slumdog* demystify and reorient both film and viewer, explaining, as it were, the present scene through the flashback.[28]

This narrative reassurance is crucial to understanding *Slumdog*'s success with Western audiences. As screenwriter Simon Beaufoy noted, "we felt if we could bring them [the audience] back to the safety of *Who Wants to Be a Millionaire?* they would be comforted and go off on another dangerous journey into another culture."[29] While actual Bollywood films are generally criticized by Western critics and audiences for their lack of narrative plausibility, *Slumdog*'s narrative structure is praised as clever, even by those who otherwise dislike the film. Heera Kulkarni, for instance, director of an Indian arts and culture group in Northern California, argues that "there is more to India than this part of India" (i.e., that *Slumdog* depicts), however, she acknowledges that the film carries an "exceedingly good story line."[30] One might rearticulate the distinction between Bollywood and *Slumdog* by saying that the latter's departures ultimately reaffirm the telos of its filmic plot, while the song-and-dance sequences in Bollywood remain essentially outside of the narrative proper and are not necessary to it. It is in this sense that the sole song-and-dance sequence in *Slumdog* comes, without coincidence, at the *end* of the film, i.e., after its story has completed. Its position can no longer disrupt the narrative, and it serves instead as a form of narrative coda. In this sense, the static nature of the dance – dancers and camera remaining essentially stationary on the station platform – doubles that of the narrative. There are, in other words, no "absolute loopholes" in *Slumdog*'s narrative logic – rather, the film remains faithful to its game show format, whose Q & A structure keeps both film and viewer on an essentially linear journey.

Finally, there is what film critic Anupama Chopra calls "the feel-good factor" of *Slumdog*.[31] While this is undoubtedly true (*Slumdog* indeed contains such a factor, as do many Bollywood films), as noted previously, the *Slumdog* viewer is led to feel good, paradoxically, via the aestheticization of the slum-scape, presented both as something exotic and familiar/-ized. Jamal's ability to leave this setting behind at the end also contributes to the feel-good factor of the film, in that it conveys the essentially transitory nature of such slumminess, that is, that it can be escaped (here we see the resurfacing of the Horatio Alger/ Dickens narrative, repeatedly referenced by critics in their discussions of *Slumdog*).[32] In Bollywood films dealing with the slum, on the other hand – for example, those featuring Amitabh Bachchan from the 1970s – the protagonist's rise comes in tandem with the rise of the slum (i.e., its dissolution). In *Trishul* (1978), for instance, Bachchan's character, Vijay, cleans up the slum (singlehandedly) and constructs new housing complexes in its place. If one feels good, then, it is not because Bachchan can leave (or has left) the slum but, rather, because he remains and transforms it from within.[33] This may indeed invest Bollywood films (at least those of the 1970s that *Slumdog* is allegedly almost an homage to) with "a vision of a desirable society or a lost utopia."[34] However, this is in direct contrast to the dystopian vision *Slumdog* provides of the slum, as a source of lurid fascination and a place to escape. Before coming to terms with what this fascination/ escapism entails, I would like to briefly examine the third invocation made by (and for) *Slumdog*.

Authenticity

As noted earlier, one of the interesting ironies of the *Slumdog* phenomenon is how it has made Bollywood a marker of its authenticity. This use of Bollywood becomes particularly intriguing in terms of Sumita Chakravarty's metaphor for this cinema, one of "impersonation."

> Concentrated within this metaphor [impersonation] are the notions of changeability and metamorphosis, tension and contradiction, recognition and alienation, surface and depth: dualities that have long plagued the Indian psyche and constitute the self-questionings of Indian nationhood. Indian cinema, caught in the cross-currents of this national dialogue and contributing to it,

> has made impersonation its distinctive signature. This is more than a matter of reinforcing truisms that films impersonate life; characters impersonate real men and women; the film-viewing experience impersonates dream. Impersonation subsumes a process of externalization, the play of/on surfaces, the disavowal of fixed identity.[35]

Bollywood (as its moniker suggests) simultaneously references a multiplicity of identities and repudiates any one, essentialized form other than, paradoxically, one of impersonation. With *Slumdog*, then, we see popular Western cinema impersonating popular Indian cinema which, in turn, impersonates popular Western cinema. How to gauge authenticity in this funhouse of mirrors? One way is by distinguishing between the forms of impersonation *Slumdog* and Bollywood engage in, as well as how these differing forms, in turn, create different approximations of the so-called real India.

According to Vamsee Juluri, professor of media studies at the University of San Francisco, *Slumdog* "brings it down to earth."[36] As noted earlier, much has been made of the authenticity of *Slumdog*'s setting, which comprador critics have described as both "real" and more realistic than Bollywood.[37] Indeed, it is precisely by removing Bollywood's "filtered lens" that *Slumdog* becomes more authentic (read: brings it down to earth) in its depiction of India, according to these critics. One might paraphrase this, however, along the lines of Chakravarty's and Lim's earlier characterizations of Bollywood and *Slumdog*, respectively, by saying that *Slumdog* replaces one impersonation of India (that of Bollywood) with another – "a simulation of 'the real India,'" as Lim puts it.[38]

Another way in which *Slumdog*'s authenticity is forged is by the invocation of "real Indians" and their collective response to the film's multiple Academy Awards. Writing in the *Times* the day after Oscar night, Somini Sengupta effectively articulates this particular strategy at the outset of her article: she begins by noting that the film's "depictions of filth" fueled "protests," but then, "on Monday, as India woke up to news of the spectacular wins, [by *Slumdog* at the Academy Awards], this movie-mad country went 'Jai Ho.'"[39] In other words, whatever problems Indians may have had with the film have magically melted away with its garnering of Oscars. The movie, Sengupta asserts, "was embraced as India's own," a sentiment also voiced by the film's co-director, Loveleen Tandan, in Sengupta's earlier piece, when she claimed that "for us [Indians], it's almost like a validation of our celebration of cinema [...] It [*Slumdog*] feels like it's ours."[40] In this way, India is made to speak for *Slumdog* via its compradors, even as *Slumdog* is seen as speaking for the real India, i.e., the one overlooked by Bollywood. Rather than a reappropriation of *Slumdog* by Indians, this strategy may be described as an appropriation of India's own by *Slumdog*.

In the process, members of the Motion Picture Association of America become the ultimate arbiters of authenticity in this global arena. Such a formulation also maintains the First World–Third World hierarchy in which, yet again, the East looks to the West for direction and approbation. Such a relationship was also in evidence the last time an "Indian" film won at the Oscars. One witnesses the emergence of the third phenomenon described at the outset of this study in newspaper columnist Vir Sanghvi's claim, the day after *Slumdog*'s Oscar wins, that "even when *Gandhi* won the Oscar for Best Picture all those years ago, we never felt that it was India's victory;" *Slumdog*'s success at the Academy Awards, however, in Sanghvi's view, is a "breakthrough for India."[41] Thus, in comparison to *Gandhi*, *Slumdog*'s Oscar wins are said to mark the true arrival on the world stage of authentic India. It is precisely in line with such a formulation that Anil Kapoor, the Bollywood actor who plays the game show host in the film, can claim, "India has made a clean sweep here"; the office of India's prime minister, Manmohan Singh, can assert, "the winners have done India proud"; and comprador-*auteur* Shekhar Kapur can argue that *Slumdog* is "the most successful Indian film ever."[42]

Whose *Slumdog*?

Having examined the underlying premises of the invocations made on *Slumdog*'s behalf, the question we must now address is: for whom? In other words, who owns *Slumdog* or, to be more precise, whose interests do such invocations serve? Even as spokesmen for Fox Searchlight Pictures, which ended up buying *Slumdog*, told *New York* magazine that "the film is Obama-like" for its "message of hope in the face of difficulty," there is another, earlier political relationship that needs to be examined in greater depth, namely, that of India and the United States during the eight years of the former administration.[43] In a visit to the White House in September 2008, Prime Minister Manmohan Singh told then-President George Bush, "this may be my last visit to you during your presidency, and let me say, Thank you very much. The people of India deeply love you."[44]

Why so much love? During the ongoing US-led global war on terror, or GWOT, as it is occasionally called, India and the US have developed "a natural partnership," in which Bush elevated India to the status of "strategic ally." In 2006, it also moved to create an exception in global nuclear nonproliferation treaties, by proposing that India be allowed to keep its military stockpile of nuclear weapons and simultaneously be given access to US technology and fuel for its civilian nuclear reactors, setting a clear double standard in terms of nuclear nonproliferation policy.[45] This agreement has led to increased collaboration between the two nations, with companies from either country gaining increased access to the other's markets. As Giridharadas notes, industries in both countries now have a "vested interest" in "deepening ties" – in Afghanistan, for instance, Indians and Americans are collaborating in nation-building.[46]

Yet, as Giridharadas also notes, India's closer ties to the US have also caused anger amongst much of the poorer Indian population, whose members are denied entry to the US market even as Indian software engineers are given easy access.[47] In the Western view, as Shekhar Deshpande notes, India has two distinct elements: poverty and call centers.[48] Yet there is another lucrative area of collaboration between India and the US that has, until recently, been denied access to American businesses: the cinema industry. India is famous for being one of the few nations in the world to boast of its own thriving film industry (Bollywood) which does not rely on nor allows itself to be usurped by Hollywood. Yet this, too, may be changing. As Deshpande notes, *Slumdog* may merely be the most successful in a series of burgeoning joint ventures between the US and Indian film industries, following Sony/Columbia Pictures' 2007 release of *Saawariya*, Walt Disney's 2008 collaboration with Yash Raj Films on the animated release, *Roadside Romeo*, and Warner Brothers' release of the 2009 film, *Chandni Chowk to China*.[49] Giridharadas has speculated, following political scientist David Singh Grewal's argument that "when empires wane, they live on [...] by embedding their values, systems and standards in a presumptive heir," that India may indeed become such an heir to waning American hegemony in the twenty-first century.[50] Another way of formulating this, however, would be to say that India may become the United States' comprador, thus extending US power rather than signaling its diminution.

Even as I write these words, Gandhi's glasses have been auctioned off in Manhattan to the tune of $1.8 million. In many ways, the account in the *Times* reads like a *Slumdog* narrative: "After intense protests from India's government and the Indian press, Mohandas K. Gandhi's eyeglasses [...] were sold [...] for $1.8 million at an auction in Manhattan, after last-minute attempts to halt the sale."[51] A synecdoche quite unlike the pince-nez of *Potemkin*, Gandhi's $1.8 million glasses serve as an apt paradigm for viewing *Slumdog*, and for *Slumdog*'s mode of viewing India. In them, we see how an Indian culture is commoditized and sold (the auction also included a slide show of Gandhi, complete with a recording of piano music). Adding to the controversy of the sale, the glasses' owner, one Mr. Otis of Los Angeles, offered to donate the glasses to India if the Indian government agreed to increase its spending on the poor.[52] Here, then, we also see a form of "benevolent blackmail" or, perhaps, ransom, in which cultural artifacts become bargaining chips in the ongoing exchange between East and West. In the case of *Slumdog*, of course, the cultural artifact on display is the slum (and its inhabitants). Yet, just as

Gandhi's glasses are no longer the same once $1.8 million has been paid for them, the slums of *Slumdog* are no longer "real India" but, indeed, "a white man's imagined India."[53]

All of this is not to deny the existence of the Indian slum but, indeed, to question how it is consumed by Western audiences and how it continues to circulate for such consumption. Salman Ali, a twelve-year-old boy who lives in the Mumbai slum, claims he would love to appear on a game show like *Slumdog*'s protagonist. Yet, however hard he tries, Salman says, he never gets ahead. Whenever a film crew begins to shoot in the slum, he tries to get their attention, however he is never chosen to be in the film.[54] Boyle has claimed that he is "not a politician," however, one would be remiss not to notice how *Slumdog* has been positioned (by comprador critics) as a form of cultural critique, despite or because of Boyle's best intentions.[55] In this sense, it is also somewhat difficult to believe that the director was truly "astonished" at the film's reception, particularly in America, given that *Slumdog* has been tailor-made for precisely such an audience.[56] As Ashis Nandy has noted, popular cinema does not merely shape and become shaped by politics, it "constitutes the language for a new form of politics."[57] *Slumdog* does precisely this by employing "a well-honed psychological technique: creating a lovable or at least tolerable strangeness by projecting predictable elements of a once-known world on to the strange and distant."[58] By aestheticizing the slum, Boyle contains and channels it along "more acceptable paths," namely, those leading to all the awards ceremonies in the West, where it has been hailed, in part, as precisely what its director denies it to be, i.e., a form of political critique.

In the process of articulating such a critique (of India, of its slums and its popular cinema) Boyle paradoxically draws upon – or, lays claim to – the very elements being critiqued to inform his vision. Boyle's central thrust, for instance, "was to capture [...] as much of the city [Mumbai] as possible," as "you cannot ignore that part of life in Mumbai – nor would I want to."[59] Similarly "crucial" for Boyle is that his film be seen as "a Bollywood film in the sense that virtually all the cast and crew are from Bollywood," yet also, crucially, not as a Bollywood film, in the sense that, "it is a good story."[60] Boyle's language here is telling, in particular his metonymic substitution of Bollywood for India. Despite Boyle's claims, however, his lead actor, Dev Patel, is British and his accent has been noted by several critics.[61] Similarly, though Boyle promotes *Slumdog* as "a hybrid of good things working together," three questions immediately arise: what type of "hybrid" does *Slumdog* constitute, what does "working together" precisely entail and for whom does the film "work"?[62]

Slumdog's producer, Christian Colson, for instance, has noted the difficulties the Indian cast and crew had in dealing with what he calls "the militaristic style of a British operation."[63] Similarly, as the earlier segments of this essay have demonstrated, *Slumdog* remains an essentially Western film (rather than a hybrid) – its resemblance to Bollywood is, as Dennis Lim notes, "superficial."[64] Yet, in the process of being an essentially British operation with the superficial veneer of hybridity, an answer to the remaining question (of whom such a concoction works for) is provided. Boyle claims that, while making the film, people in the Indian slums asked if he intended to display their poverty, "because that's what Westerners always do."[65] His response has indeed been not to remain mired in India's poverty and squalor but, paraphrasing A. R. Rahman, to soar above it, occasionally swooping down to get a graphic glimpse but never missing a beat, as it were. This is a film, after all, to be consumed by Western audiences and it is precisely for such an audience that the film works (as a superficially hybrid production). It is also in this sense that the film is ultimately not so much about the real India as it is about the West's own conceptions of India and its atavistic desire for an earlier, simpler narrative.[66] Here we see the reformulation of what Nandy described as the familiar into the lovably (or at least tolerably) strange, even as this reformulation reaffirms the essential(ist) difference between the First and Third Worlds.

One wonders what Danny Boyle meant when he called *Slumdog* a "very subversive" film.[67] Roughly eighty years ago, a young German playwright wrote of attempts to "renovate" the existing theatre without changing its "culinary character." A new form of entertainment, however, the dramaturge concluded, needed to reckon with "new appetites."[68] *Slumdog*, while making claims to a new recipe, employs the same (old) ingredients in serving up the spicy, ethnic dish that satisfies, rather than takes away, its intended consumer's appetite. If the proof of the pudding is in the eating, then *Slumdog*'s success demonstrates both the West's insatiable hunger for the glowing, rotten fruit of India and the willingness of comprador critics to dish out praise for such strange (yet familiar) concoctions. "From monkey brains to slumdogs might not seem like a giant evolutionary step," writes one, "but in Hollywood terms it's really a miracle."[69] "I wanted to be a little more angry about it, but I wasn't," claims another, adding, "it's been a long time since *Gandhi*."[70]

Notes

1 There tends to be some slippage between these terms (Western/ global), especially in the American imaginary. It is precisely within the interstices of such slippage that the American Academy Awards take place and, as we will see, a film such as *Gandhi* or *Slumdog* is said to "speak for" those not in attendance, i.e., Indians.

2 Hamid Dabashi, "Native Informers and the Making of the American Empire." *Al Ahram Weekly*, 1–7 June 2006. Online: http://weekly.ahram.org.eg/2006/797/special.htm (accessed 2 February 2009).

3 Boyle quoted in Fareed Zakaria, "Slum Voyeurism?" *Newsweek* (International Edition), 30 January 2009. Online: http://www.newsweek.com/id/182341 (accessed 30 January 2009).

4 Anand Giridharadas, "Horatio Alger Relocates to a Mumbai Slum." *New York Times*, 17 January 2009. Online: http://www.nytimes.com/2009/01/18/weekinreview/18giridharadas.html (accessed 26 January 2009).

5 Dennis Lim, "What, Exactly, Is *Slumdog Millionaire*? Is it a) a portrait of the real India, b) a Bollywood-style melodrama, c) a fairy tale or d) a stylishly shot collection of clichés?" *Slate*, 26 January 2009. Online: http://www.slate.com/id/2209783/pagenum/all/ (accessed 26 January 2009).

6 Sandip Roy, "The New Bollywood." *San Francisco Chronicle*, 22 February 2009: 16.

7 Some of these include the *New York Times*' Somini Sengupta, who claims that "despite the director's strenuous denials, it [*Slumdog*] could well be a Bollywood film"; Shekhar Deshpande, who claims "*Slumdog Millionaire* is an 'Indian' film in the sense that it borrows the narrative and aesthetic elements of Bollywood"; and Anupama Chopra, who calls *Slumdog* "pure Bollywood in its feel-good factor, the fantastical story line and the absolute loopholes in logic." See, respectively, "Extreme Mumbai, Without Bollywood's Filtered Lens," in the *New York Times*, 11 November 2008; "A Million Slumdogs Now," in *Little India*, 13 February 2009; and "The New Bollywood," in the *San Francisco Chronicle*, 22 February 2009.

8 Sengupta's piece in the *New York Times* provides a good example of this trend, beginning with its title and also when the author points out that "*Slumdog* is decidedly not Bollywood in one crucial aspect: It was shot on the streets of Mumbai," thus rendering it, in her opinion, more "realistic" than Bollywood films which employ "more exotic locales (Brooklyn, for instance)." See "Extreme Mumbai, " 11 November 2008. Online: http://www.nytimes.com/2008/11/16/movies/16seng.html (accessed 2 February 2009).

9 Here we see an instance of the "fantasy sequence" that the Bush administration envisioned as it planned its incursion into Iraq – a fantasy, again, in no small part promoted by the comprador intelligentsia. Who better to make the case for an invasion of Iraq than an Iraqi?

10 Ashis Nandy, "Introduction," in *The Secret Politics of Our Desires: Innocence, Culpability, and Indian Popular Cinema*, edited by Nandy (New Delhi: Oxford University Press, 1998), 2.

11 Ibid., 3.

12 On his blog, Bachchan writes: "Let it be known that a murky underbelly exists and thrives in the most developed nations." See Deshpande, "A Million Slumdogs." The numbers associated with film production and exhibition in India are also staggering, with over 800 films released every year and over ten million tickets sold every day. See Manjunath Pendakur, "India," in *The Asian Film Industry*, edited by John A. Lent et al. (Austin: University of Texas Press, 1990), 230; and Pendakur, *Indian Popular Cinema: Industry, Ideology and Consciousness* (Cresskill: Hampton Press, 2003).

13 *Cinema India! TimesTalk* Panel, Asia Society, New York, 17 April 2004.

14 Sengupta quoted in Mark Magnier, "Indians Don't Feel Good About *Slumdog Millionaire*," *Los Angeles Times*, 24 January 2009. Online: http://www.latimes.com/entertainment/news/la-fg-india-slumdog24-2009jan24,0,1162547.story (accessed 2 February 2009).

15 Rahman quoted in Sandip Roy, "Composer is up for multiple Oscars," *San Francisco Chronicle*, 22 February 2009: 19.

16 E. M. Forster, *A Passage to India* (New York: Harcourt Brace Jovanovich, 1984[1924]), 1.

17 Ibid.

18 Rahman quoted in Roy, "Composer is up…"
19 Alice Miles, "Shocked by *Slumdog*'s Poverty Porn," *Times*, 14 January 2009. http://www.timesonline.co.uk/tol/comment/columnists/alice_miles/article5511650.ece (accessed 26 January 2009).
20 David Denby, "Curious Cases: This Year's Oscar Picks." *New Yorker*, 9–16 February 2009: 119.
21 Ibid.
22 Latha Jishnu, "Slumdogs and fat cat bankers." *Business Standard*, 28 February 2009. Online: http://www.business-standard.com/india/news/latha-jishnu-slumdogsfat-cat-bankers/09/10/350372/ (accessed 1 March 2009).
23 Nandy, "Introduction," 13.
24 On nearly every occasion when I have mentioned Bollywood to Americans of non-Indian backgrounds, they respond, if at all, by citing films such as these.
25 Deshpande, "A Million Slumdogs, and Sengupta, "Extreme Mumbai," respectively. While Anthony Lane finds "the energy" in *Slumdog*'s end credits dance sequence (which he labels "a Bollywood dance number") "difficult to resist," Dennis Lim notes that "the limp dance number that closes the film lacks both the technique and the energy of vintage Bollywood." See, respectively, "Now Playing," in the *New Yorker*, 2 February 2009: 18, and Lane's original review, "Hard Times," in the *New Yorker*, 24 November 2009: 130; as well as Lim's "What, Exactly, Is *Slumdog Millionaire*?"
26 Chopra quoted in Roy, "The New Bollywood," 16.
27 Sengupta, "Extreme Mumbai."
28 For more on Bollywood's narrative rupturing, and how this differs from the strategies employed by Hollywood, see Ajay Gehlawat, "The Bollywood Song and Dance, or Making a Culinary Theatre from Dung-Cakes and Dust," *Quarterly Review of Film and Video*, 23.4 (2006): 331–40.
29 Beaufoy quoted in Roy, "'Slumdog's Beaufoy wrote from the heart," *San Francisco Chronicle*, 22 February 2009: 17.
30 Carla Meyer, "'Slumdog Millionaire' isn't as big a winner…in Sacramento's Indian community," *Sacramento Bee*, 13 February 2009: 26.
31 Chopra quoted in Roy, "The New Bollywood," 16.
32 See, for instance, Giridharadas, "Horatio Alger Relocates to a Mumbai Slum."
33 It is ironic, given this difference, that *Slumdog*'s co-director, Loveleen Tandan, calls *Slumdog* "almost an homage to the '70s masala potboiler of Indian cinema." See Sengupta, "Extreme Mumbai." For more on the Amitabh Bachchan films of the 1970s, see Fareeduddin Kazmi's "How Angry is the Angry Young Man? 'Rebellion' in Conventional Hindi Films," in *The Secret Politics of Our Desires*, 134–55.
34 Nandy, "Introduction," 11.
35 Sumita S. Chakravarty, *National Identity in Indian Popular Cinema, 1947–1987* (Austin: University of Texas Press, 1993), 4.
36 Juluri quoted in Roy, "The New Bollywood," 16. It remains a bit unclear what precisely is "brought down to earth" here – one assumes the representation of "India" in cinema. One might recall Rahman's description of his soundtrack for *Slumdog* at this juncture (see note 18). As a way of synthesizing these two characterizations of *Slumdog*, one might say the film is saved from coming to earth by its wings.
37 Chopra quoted in Roy, "The New Bollywood," 16; Sengupta, "Extreme Mumbai"; Deshpande, "A Million Slumdogs Now." In the latter piece, Deshpande claims, "The film [*Slumdog*] is steeped in realism," and "once the realism of reality hits the screen, Bollywood

squirms." See http://www.littleindia.com/news/125/ARTICLE/4509/2009-02-13.html (accessed 21 Feburary 2009). See also notes 4 and 8.

38 Chakravarty, *National Identity*, 4; Lim, "What Exactly is *Slumdog Millionaire*?"

39 Sengupta, "India Celebrates a Hollywood Victory." *New York Times*, 23 February 2009. "Jai ho," as Sengupta goes on to note in her article, roughly translates as "Let there be victory." It is also the title of Rahman's Oscar-winning song from the film. Online: http://www.nytimes.com/2009/02/24/world/asia/24india.html (accessed 24 February 2009).

40 Sengupta, "India Celebrates," and "Extreme Mumbai." At the same time, as Sengupta notes, "*Slumdog*, of course, is not an Indian film. It was backed by two American studios" ("India Celebrates").

41 Sanghvi quoted in Sengupta, "India Celebrates."

42 See Sengupta, "India Celebrates," and Magnier, "Indians Don't Feel Good."

43 Quoted in Lim, "What, Exactly, is *Slumdog Millionaire*?"

44 Giridharadas, "India Has a Soft Spot for Bush." *New York Times*, 11 January 2009, 4. Note, again, the invocation of "the Indian people."

45 Ibid. Even as India, which never signed the Nuclear Nonproliferation Treaty, was rewarded with access to US nuclear fuel and technology, Iran, which did sign the Nuclear Nonproliferation Treaty, was slapped with US sanctions and identified as a member of the so-called axis of evil.

46 Ibid. Interestingly enough, the game show, *Who Wants to Be a Millionaire?* has just been licensed in Afghanistan. See Jishnu, "Slumdogs and fat cat bankers."

47 Giridharadas, "India Has a Soft Spot."

48 Deshpande, "A Million Slumdogs Now."

49 See Deshpande, "A Million Slumdogs," and Michael Dequina's online review of *Chandni Chowk to China*. http://www.imdb.com/Reviews/417/41766 (accessed 1 March 2009).

50 Giridharadas, "India Has a Soft Spot."

51 A. G. Sulzberger and Sewell Chan, "Gandhi Items Are Sold for $1.8 Million." *New York Times*, 5 March 2009. Online: http://cityroom.blogs.nytimes.com/2009/03/05/india-rejects-owners-proposal-on-gandhi-items/?ref=world (accessed 5 March 2009).

52 Sulzberger and Chan, "Gandhi Items."

53 Shyamal Sengupta quoted. in Magnier, "Indians Don't Feel Good."

54 Magnier, "Indians Don't Feel Good."

55 Boyle, "10 Questions for Danny Boyle." *Time*, 19 February 2009. Online: http://www.time.com/time/magazine/article/0,9171,1880635,00.html (accessed 21 February 2009).

56 Ibid.

57 Nandy, "Introduction," 12.

58 Ibid.

59 Boyle, "10 Questions."

60 Boyle; and quoted in Sengupta, "Extreme Mumbai." The only actor "from Bollywood" in the film is the game-show host, Anil Kapoor.

61 Somini Sengupta, for instance, points out, "though he is a fine actor, Mr. Patel's accent gives away who he is: a Briton of Indian origin. Not a kid from a Mumbai slum." See "Extreme Mumbai."

62 Boyle, "10 Questions."

63 Colson quoted in Sengupta, "Extreme Mumbai."

64 Lim, "What, Exactly, is *Slumdog Millionaire*?"

65 Boyle, "10 Questions."

66 Anthony Lane, for instance, calls *Slumdog* "an old-fashioned crowd-pleaser." See his "Hard Times," 130.

67 Boyle quoted. in Miles, "Shocked by Slumdog's Poverty Porn."

68 Bertolt Brecht, "The Modern Theatre is the Epic Theatre," in *Brecht on Theatre: The Development of an Aesthetic*, translated by John Willett (Methuen & Co.: London, 1964 [1930]), 33.

69 Roy, "Seeing India through a foreign lens," *San Francisco Chronicle*, 22 February 2009, 18. Roy goes on to say, "some Indians still cringe because all the West ever seems to see of India is poverty. But others, like me, are just happy that onscreen Indians get to love, scheme, maim or get rich – but for their own sakes."

70 Juluri quoted. in Roy, "Seeing India." Juluri's further claim that *Slumdog* "was about finally being recognized," provides an instance of "all those Indians who view the approbation of the West as the ultimate litmus test." See Ashis Nandy and Vinay Lal, "Introduction: Popular Cinema and the Culture of Indian Politics," in *Fingerprinting Popular Culture: The Mythic and the Iconic in Indian Cinema*, edited by Nandy and Lal (New Delhi: Oxford University Press, 2006), xi.

Chapter 14

THE LIFE-CYCLE OF *SLUMDOG MILLIONAIRE* ON THE WEB

Thomas Elsaesser and Warren Buckland

Introductory Note

In the spring of 2009, Thomas Elsaesser asked his graduate seminar to jointly undertake a specific case study – of the British made, Hollywood-produced, India-claimed, surprise hit *Slumdog Millionaire* (2008) – in order to reconstruct the various discourses that are involved in locating and stabilizing the authorial, generic, ideological and national "identities" for a contemporary independent film of the kind that shows up at film festivals and makes up the loose category of "world cinema." In this case, the seminar chose a film that started its life as an underdog but gradually emerged as a festival favorite. First spurned by the majors, even orphaned and sold as DVD-fodder by its parent production company, Warner Bros, *Slumdog Millionaire* went on to become a multiple Oscar-winner, an "issue" film and an international classic.

The purpose of the case study was to look at the way the meaning, title, perception and identity of such a hybrid festival film can (sometimes unexpectedly) change over a particular time period in the act or process of reception, especially if one factors in not only critics and commentators but nationally and linguistically specific, globally connected internet social networks and fan communities. Reception becomes not just meaning-making but involves acts of appropriation, of owning and disowning. These become integral parts of a film's identity and nationality, which are thus no longer pre-defined and static but evolve across dynamic processes of interaction, contestation and debate that internet tools now allow us to follow and track in real time. In place of the reception history of a film, we therefore propose to speak of its life-cycle, to indicate the multi-dimensional, fluid and dynamic processes which now must complement the analysis of the meaning or intention ascribed to a film by various communities, interest groups and experts.

For the purposes of studying such a life-cycle, Elsaesser proposed the following four layers as research tools for reception studies:

1. Raw data culled from statistics (like Google's "Insight for Search")
2. Data gathered from users on (nationally, linguistically and regionally specific) blogs, list-servers, chats (incl. IMDb users' reviews)
3. Critics' taste and classification (e.g., external reviews listed on IMDb, Rotten Tomatoes, Metacritic, Factiva.com)
4. Scholars' conceptualization and systematization (trans-national cinema, postcolonial studies, etc.)

In a separate move, Warren Buckland developed (in conjunction with Elsaesser) a research project called "Data Mining World Cinema." This project develops the first three layers of research tools (but especially layer 1) which Buckland initially applied to David Lynch's *Inland Empire* and to *Slumdog Millionaire*.[1] The following essay brings together Elsaesser and Buckland's attempts to data mine the web and databases of newspaper reviews to determine the reception and life-cycle of *Slumdog Millionaire* during its circulation around the film festival circuit and its initial release.

The results are still tentative and provisional, since *Slumdog Millionaire* was initially chosen as much to test the internet tools and the effects of layering the data as it was to generate new and unexpected insights into the film itself.

***

Our study took, as its starting point, Janet Staiger's agenda for reception studies as expressed in her book, *Interpreting Films: Studies in the Historical Reception of American Cinema*. For Staiger, reception studies researches "the history of the interactions between real readers and texts, actual spectators and films."[2] The interactions take the mediated form of newspaper reviews and feature articles. Rather than privilege one review over others, Staiger studies the range of interpretations and evaluations found in the reviews and provides explanations for the reasons behind those variations. Taking into consideration Staiger's emphasis on the *history* of interactions, we focused on the historical context in which *Slumdog Millionaire* (2008) was initially promoted, discussed and received, a context dominated by bloggers, online reviews and especially internet users actively seeking information on the film. Yet such information is now so vast that it is difficult to perceive or comprehend. For example, one author mentions that even as far back as 2008 there were over one trillion websites,[3] while comScore.com, which measures internet traffic, estimated that in the United States alone, internet users conducted a total of

19.5 billion search queries in August 2011, with Google coming out on top with 12.5 billion searches.

Online Reception Studies

In the last fifteen years, the web has established new and distinct conversation networks between geographically dislocated publics. A dispersed audience for a new film release, for example, can be connected via the web, blogs or social networking sites. As we bring together the disciplines of film studies and computer science, combining statistical methods and semantic analysis, we in fact build and expand upon the seminal work of literary scholar Franco Moretti,[4] who reconfigures literary study by drawing upon quantitative history, geography and evolutionary theory. That is to say, our project uses the web not simply as a source of information but, in an additional, reflexive move, also as an object of study in relation to traditional humanist and hermeneutic methods of analysis. Every time users of the web go online, post blogs or interact on social networking sites, they leave electronic traces of their behavior, clues to their preferences and evidence of their activity. This has created a wealth of electronic data consisting of social opinion and news but also soft data such as rumors, likes and dislikes. Given that films are cultural objects where hard and soft data converge as a matter of course and that value judgments tend to be volatile, it seems especially promising to employ digital technology to analyze this data generated around films released at film festivals throughout the globe. If we can indeed track how such data spreads on the web and distil from it an image or profile of a film's reputation, then our project has the potential to alter the way film studies scholarship gathers and processes information in the study of a film's reception. By digital technology, we mean web data mining software, which identifies patterns, trends and anomalies in huge amounts of electronic data on the web.

What tools, techniques and methods can data mining offer to film studies? The simplest software to use has been created by Google, called "Insights for Search" (Google has also developed a search engine that searches blogs). Google collects and saves all search queries, creating a huge database of people's information-seeking habits, that is, their interest in a particular topic or issue, and their search for information about it on the web via Google's search engine. "Insights for Search" makes freely available to researchers a representative sample of this search query data.

In film studies research there is, at present, a sharp divide between those interpreting films, in view of their symptomatic or allegorical meanings, and those concentrating on providing contextual or background information, whether technical, relating to the makers or focusing on audiences. This project tries to bridge these gaps by shifting the approach and subsuming the different methods under the general heading of data, all of which is of potential significance, once layers of pertinence have been identified and a film is treated as a living being or organism. However, so far, there are no guidelines regarding either how to tackle the new scale of data, or how to exploit the potential power of data mining software, most of which has been developed for commercial, i.e., marketing, ends, rather than for the kind of holistic analytics we have in mind.

A certain circumspection and procedural caution is therefore in order. The primary dimension of our research, which belongs to the first layer of reception studies, involves analyzing search engine queries centered on the film's title and the director's name. Search engine queries are thus a natural starting point about a film's perceived identity, its relevance to different discourses and its reputation among communities of fans and experts. Since festival films are particularly mobile and their reputation fluctuates and accumulates over time, the focus on film festivals seems justified, especially when also following a film's initial (art house) release and afterlife (as a DVD and in the scholarly literature). All of this activity can now be tracked online and interpreted in a communication/interaction context. Laura A. Granka points out that "online digital media affords researchers with a naturally robust platform on which to track actual user behaviors in an immediate and inexpensive manner."[5] A search engine query, however banal it may seem, represents an individual's desire to seek out additional information on a film, suggesting s/he already has some knowledge of it. Studying the relation between online information regarding a film and more traditional forms of information dissemination, such as print newspapers or television (what Granka calls the "offline-online dynamic"), is therefore necessarily a complementary task. In the end, the object of study is very traditional – word-of-mouth, although we need to recognize that it has now moved online. Dina Iordanova notes that "on-line word-of-mouth gradually becomes the make-or-break focus of marketing efforts. It can push up a small independent feature as easily as it can cut the revenues for a multi-million production."[6] Word-of-mouth has always been recognized as a decisive although elusive influence on the success or failure of a film; now, with data mining technology, this elusive phenomenon (in the form of search engine queries) can be measured. We will measure word-of-mouth around *Slumdog Millionaire*, using Google's "Insights for Search" and data gathered from the web by users, by mining the databases of traditional print newspapers and identifying the different academic debates that emerged in the wake of the film's increasing popularity.

Layer 1: Google "Insights for Search"

> Google "Insights for Search" [...] provide[s] a daily insight into what the world is searching for on Google, by showing the relative volume of search traffic in Google for any search query.[7]

Shimshoni, Efron and Matias point out that some Google searches are predictable, especially relating to seasonal health (search terms such as "cold" and "flu" increase in the autumn and winter, for example), while other trends are less predictable, such as soft news stories and entertainment. Can we automate reception studies to enable film scholars to sample the huge, inclusive array of online messages about new films, and to follow the dynamics of those messages? This dynamic ranges from the predictable to the unpredictable, and one advantage of this research is that humanities scholars do not simply find what they are looking for (the predictability of hermeneutics) but discover something completely new (the unpredictable). As a starting point, we can use Google's "Insights for Search" to see how many searches have been carried out for a particular term.[8] Figure 14.1 represents the "Insights for Search" graph for the search term "Slumdog Millionaire" in quotation marks, the time range narrowed to twelve months, from May 2008 to May 2009. The graph shows the number of times this film title was entered into Google as a search term. The graph gives a visual representation of that interest. There is an initial small peak during September 2008 (labeled E), and much larger peaks during the Oscar buzz in January and February (C and B on the graph). We will have a closer look at the initial peak in a moment. The graphs are useful for giving us analogue visual information, information that instantly shows us the rate of interest in the film over time.

The bottom half of Google's "Insights for Search" gives additional analogue visual representation of where, geographically, interest in the film is to be found (Fig. 14.2). It will come as no surprise to discover India at the top of the list. And below that are the top ten search terms entered into Google. After the film's title, the soundtrack seems to be quite important, followed by searches that are looking for the movie online to download.

We can return to that small peak in September 2008 and narrow our search to the beginning and end of that month. This yields Figure 14.3, where (as with all searches) the greatest search is normalized to 100. Interest seems to be building up gradually during the month, suddenly peaking right in the middle.

To investigate further, we looked at the Google pages dated September 1–30 2008 (using the Julian calendar system[9]), and discovered that most of them were newspaper sites. We decided to look at the newspaper articles in a

Figure 14.1. "Insights for Search" graph for "*Slumdog Millionaire*" (May 2008–2009).

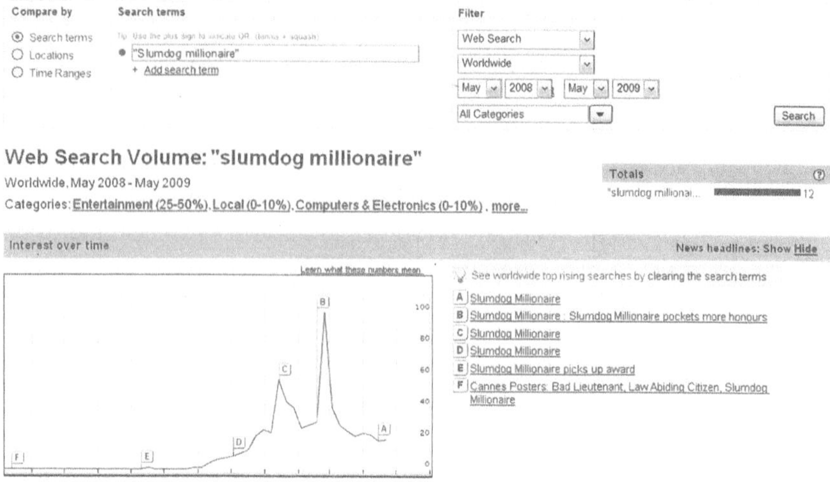

Figure 14.2. Regional interest and top ten search terms for "*Slumdog Millionaire.*"

massive database, Factiva.com, since not all electronic versions of newspapers are freely available on the web. Factiva.com (owned by Dow Jones) represents a collection of more than 25,000 authoritative sources – newspapers and newswires from around the globe. As of October 2011, Factiva has over 34,000 news articles that reference Danny Boyle's *Slumdog Millionaire*, the

Figure 14.3 "Insights for Search" graph for "*Slumdog Millionaire*" (September 2008).

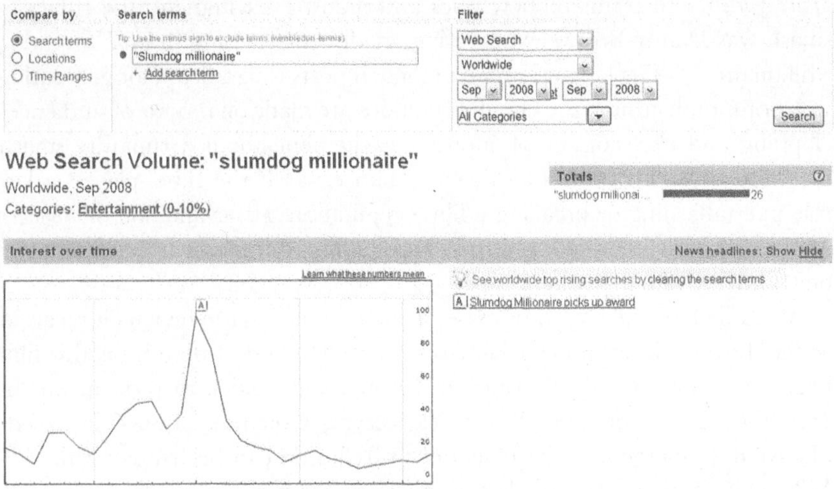

earliest dating back to a short note on the film on 23 March 2007 from the *Hindustan Times*, followed one day later by a feature article.[10]

The graphs of layer 1 indicate, first of all, that a timeline of search queries does indeed provide a robust platform for identifying moments of increased interest and attention, which can be correlated with events either directly involving the film or debates or issues generated by the film in the public sphere. Furthermore, the geographical distribution of the queries indicates that the film proved to be of special interest, as one would expect, in India, Sri Lanka, Nepal, Bangladesh and Pakistan, but also in places where the Indian diaspora is present as a significant demographic or cultural factor: the United Arab Emirates, Singapore, the US, Canada and Hong Kong. The real surprise is the relative lack of interest in Britain, the film's (and the filmmaker's) country of origin.

Layer 3: Newspaper Critics

By examining newspapers (as represented in electronic databases), we jump to layer 3 of the reception studies model (we discuss layer 2 below). There was a steady stream of articles on *Slumdog Millionaire* towards the end of the Telluride Film Festival. On 1 September 2008, Christine Kearney wrote for *Reuters* that "British director Boyle's new 'Slumdog Millionaire' earned praise after it packed the larger festival cinemas with audiences who clapped and cheered as the credits rolled."[11] On the same day, Todd McCarthy wrote in *Daily Variety*: "In terms of new titles and industry excitement, the runaway smash was Danny Boyle's exhilarating, madly entertaining drama 'Slumdog Millionaire.'"[12] The language used in these reports is significant for generating word-of-mouth around the film. Reputations are made on reports of audiences clapping and cheering, or of industry excitement about a runaway smash hit. McCarthy, who was *Variety*'s chief film critic at the time, played a key role in establishing or breaking a film's reputation. His evaluation of *Slumdog Millionaire* as an exhilarating, madly entertaining drama set up interest at its next film festival, in Toronto.

We can chart the day-to-day rise of the film during the reviews it received at the Toronto International Film Festival. The word-of-mouth for this film began at Telluride, which critics at Toronto were quick to pick up on. In *USA Today* on 3 September, Susan Wloszczyna wrote that "a possible crowd-pleaser has emerged, if the reactions at Telluride can be trusted: Slumdog Millionaire."[13] Here, we see that positive word-of-mouth was already part of the film's reputation – Wloszczyna not only discussed the film, but also its previous reception. On 8 September, Michael Phillips of the *Chicago Tribune* wrote:

> "Come on! It's a really good movie!" Baz Bamigboye of the London Daily Mail was telling me – ordering me, in fact – as we exited the packed Saturday press screening of "Slumdog Millionaire," a slick, dazzlingly crafted crowd-pleaser from British director Danny Boyle. Shot largely in the slums and tumult of Mumbai, it's the first widely acknowledged popular success of the 33rd Toronto International Film Festival, which continues through Saturday.[14]

Film reviewers are keen to discover new hits. By September 8, Phillips was touting *Slumdog* as "the first widely acknowledged popular success" of the Toronto International Film Festival. He was keen to emphasize the packed screening and to label the film a crowd-pleaser. It is unusual for him to quote the praise of a fellow film reviewer – Baz Bamigboye, who filed his own review in the *Daily Mail* on 12 September, praising *Slumdog* as "a fantastic picture, full of heartbreak, fun, and energy – and most importantly, passion."[15]

The following day, 13 September 2008, seven newspapers and trade journals announced that *Slumdog Millionaire* had won the Cadillac People's Choice Award in Toronto. The Factiva database shows how the story then spread to twenty-four other publications the following day (Sunday, 14 September) and a further twenty on the Monday – mainly the mainstream press around the globe picking up the story. The peak on the Google "Insights for Search" diagram takes place on 14 September, implying that people searched for the film's title after reading these news accounts of the film's success. The online search was therefore fuelled by the trade press and newspapers, based primarily on the film's winning of an award, making the story a suitable one to be picked up. Nonetheless, the story fell quite rapidly, spreading to only seven more publications on Tuesday, 16 September.

But the film did not just disappear. It regained its place at the forefront of print journalism and on the web towards the end of 2008 by raising a number of contentious discussion points, including: Fair pay for child actors; whether the film was too Indian or not Indian enough (was it an Indian film or a Western version of an Indian film? This question raised issues of neo-colonialism); the reception of the title in India (calling a slum dweller a "dog" is an extreme form of insult), as well as the semantic tension in the title, where the opposites (slum/millionaire) are combined; the fan community's reaction to the music (especially to A. R. Rahman and M. I. A.); the representation of a major city in terms of glamour and crime (and the impact of the latter on tourism); whether this was a typical Danny Boyle auteurist film (in terms of style and themes) or a hybrid product of commercial calculations; and the role of religion, violence and poverty in the film (especially the gratuitous glamorization of poverty, summarized in the phrase "poverty porn").

Slumdog became intricately bound up with these issues. In terms of music, both Rahman and M. I. A. are global artists; M. I. A. has lived in Sri Lanka, London and Brooklyn, and Rahman has composed music for television, film, commercials and plays all over Europe and North America. M. I. A. is considered a kind of multi-national "Indi" hip-hop star, while Rahman is the great diplomat of Bollywood music, who is considered a genius for his eclectic tastes and the styles he brings into the compositions. In India there was the question of whether Rahman needed something like the Oscars to legitimate his craft and Indian music in general.

Many of these issues soon polarized into irreconcilable oppositions, ensuring continued discussion of the film, thereby keeping it in the spotlight. The phrase poverty porn took on special importance, as we can see from the "Insights for Search" graph for the term (see Fig. 14.4). Although the earliest reference to *Slumdog* and "poverty porn" is Kim Voynar's blog review of the film at the Telluride film festival on 31 August 2008,[16] the term poverty porn did not become an issue until 14 January 2009, when Alice Miles, writing in the *Times*, took an Emperor's new clothes stance and argued that the film was vile: "it is not a comedy, is not uplifting, and is poverty porn because it glamorizes India's poverty and violence, and turns it into entertainment for Western audiences."[17] This began a backlash against the film leading up to the Oscar awards ceremony of 22 February 2009 (the date which coincides exactly with the peak of the web searches for "poverty porn" in Figure 14.4).

Figure 14.4. "Insights for Search" graph for "poverty porn" (October 2008–2009).

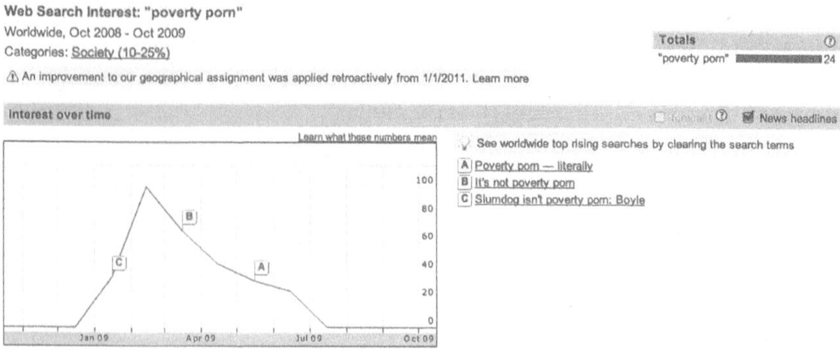

Between Miles's story on 14 January and the Oscar wins on 22 February, no less than sixty-five newspaper articles from around the globe (primarily from the UK, India, Canada, the US and South Africa) could be found on Factiva.com discussing *Slumdog* in terms of poverty porn. The *Independent* ran a story called "'Smear tactics' threaten to halt Slumdog's Oscar march,"[18] blaming rivals in the Oscar race for the negative campaign. During January–February 2009, poverty porn became a catchphrase and suddenly changed the film's perception in the media. This one phrase altered the whole dynamic of the debate around *Slumdog*, polarizing it into those who continued to perceive it as an upbeat comedy and those who argued that it was vile and exploitative.

Layer 2: Web Users

In his graduate seminar, Elsaesser was able to involve students from various countries who in turn asked friends back home to also monitor websites that were discussing *Slumdog*. Much of web-based research is limited to searching English-language data, whereas, in this case, we were able to draw on no less than eleven different linguistic domains to aggregate and process relevant information. The students provided the following summaries (written in February 2009, i.e., just prior to the Academy Awards), which represent the second layer of our reception studies model:

- **Thailand:** *Slumdog* is already available through downloading and purchasing pirate copies. Boyle is well-known in Thailand because of *The Beach*, which was shot in Thailand and generated not just local interest but also jobs and training opportunities. Nonetheless, *Slumdog* is being interpreted as a Bollywood film. The absence of Western characters has led the film to be praised as an indigenous film. Discussion furthermore centers on the relationship between the brothers (a familiar motif in Thai films as well) and the presence of fate versus free will. The soundtrack by Rahman and M. I. A. is loved by critics and fans.

- **Turkey:** *Slumdog* is widely available for downloading. Discussion tries to locate the film within Bollywood and Hollywood, but also Turkish cinema – all three genres being very familiar to Turkish audiences. There are references made to India as an outsourcing site ("call centers"). Also, in relation to global Hollywood, parallels are drawn to *Midnight Express* (a British film showing Turkey and Turkish prisons in a bad light).
- **Greece:** ninety-five percent of the hits on the web centered on awards and prizes given to the film. Blogs commented on form and style of the film, and *Slumdog* was repeatedly called a Danny Boyle film. The criticism was that it was escapist. Interestingly, *Slumdog* was often treated as a "low budget" film that was triumphing over big Hollywood. Quickly available on bit-torrents *Slumdog* generated much user activity: There were lots of downloads of Greek subtitles of the film, which suggests that fans were keen to make the film their own by sharing their language skills. Much appreciation for the music but, in general, there was little discussion of postcolonial issues or of the film's social-geopolitical implications regarding the representation of India as an emerging superpower.
- **France:** Many commentators consider *Slumdog* a kind of Dickens story remixed in Hollywood ("Oliver Twist with Indian sauce").[19] Danny Boyle films India "as it is." Lots of culinary metaphors in the reviews. "Above all, a captivating portrait of today's India, miserable, violent, full of splendor. The film doesn't give you time to catch your breath and leaves you exhausted and euphoric." "What energy, what life, what a will to survive among these kids who grow up in front of our eyes. The director shows us India as it bubbles and boils, repellant and ravishing, sublime and beautiful. The cinematography is superb, the music carries us right into the story, and one feasts, swallows and gorges on the spectacle with gusto." The film was also perceived as a marvelous modern fairytale one wants to believe in, like children, told at an infernal pace and which concludes, to our greatest joy and satisfaction, with a colorfully choreographed finale, like a genuine Bollywood film.[20]
- **Germany:** Controversy generated around whether *Slumdog* is the "pride or shame of India." Also, whether it is an "Indian film." The issue of "poverty porn" was picked up, literally: there were protests in front of the multiplexes and guerilla takeovers of cinemas. Despite this, the film is predicted to be a big success, because it is a surreal fairy tale and an "achievement narrative." Also, discussion of Boyle and how he is able to distil the archetypal elements of Hollywood and Bollywood. Blogs note that *Slumdog* is bound to generate

controversies, has unresolved problems and asks big questions – without answering them.

- **Russia:** By February 2009 the film had only officially been released in a few select cities. By contrast, illegal downloading was widespread and easy, sparking much commentary, review and opinion on the Russian internet. Some comparisons between *Slumdog* and *Last King of Scotland*, as well as the Serbian film *Time of the Gypsies*. The reviews on the whole are not politicized. Boyle is popular in Russia, and auteurist arguments point out his preoccupation with money, violence and with characters from sub-cultures and the underworld. The film is seen as a major breakthrough for Boyle since *Trainspotting*.
- **India:** Discussed initially by expatriates. Boyle is not really responding to whether it is an Indian film. Reviews/blogs comment on the mixture of Hollywood-Bollywood and it is precisely the mix that makes it so good. There is some access to the film in India because a percentage of the films that show in "the slums" have to offer cheap seats. Also, the discourse around the term "slumdog" has been written about. Some protests around megaplexes about the film.
- **Japan:** The film will be released in April [2009] in Japan. The *Slumdog* website just came up. Ewan McGregor is always paired with Danny Boyle. The lead female actress is seen as a kind of star in the film. Indian food and Bollywood films were big in Japan ten years ago. This alone will make it a "must see film" in Japan.

  A Japanese-American respondent was all too aware of the perils and controversies concerning representation and perceived "authenticity": "We understand that leveling criticism against Boyle simply for not being Indian and creating a work that to some extent depicts 'India' would be somewhat close to criticizing Japanese-British novelist Kazuo Ishiguro for writing *The Remains of the Day* or Taiwanese-American director Ang Lee for directing *Brokeback Mountain*. But that is the point: I do not believe Boyle's *Slumdog* comes close to being as important as either one of these works, because *Slumdog* has less of an inextricable link to its setting than they have."
- **China:** There is a marked difference in the reception of *Slumdog Millionaire* in three territories: mainland China, Taiwan, Hong Kong. Bootlegged copies are available on bit-torrents but bloggers from Hong Kong encourage their readers/users to wait for the "big-screen" experience.

  Warner Bros Taiwan uses a more "literal" translation (Pinmin baiwan fuweng; Millionaire from the Ghetto), while Warner Bros Hong Kong tries to be "creative" by naming the film (Yibaiwan ling yi ye; One Million and One Nights). The title is a takeoff on One Thousand and One Nights. It has the effect of "grafting" the historical "British" imagination of "India" (mis-recogniized as "Persia" in this case) onto the contemporary "Hong Kong" imagination of "India," or the "poor Asia." The title quite literally puts "Orientalism" under erasure, thus layering multiple playing fields for the spectators/ readers/ users to re-imagine the power-position they have with a supposedly "Anglo-American" film.

- **Iran:** There are bootleg copies of *Slumdog Millionaire* in circulation. But so far, these are screen shot versions (illegally shot with a camcorder during a theatrical screening), and most people do not watch these versions. They wait for the demo version (bootlegged from promo DVDs, usually for Academy Award considerations). These better quality DVDs are subtitled in Farsi and are very popular here. Early indications are that the film will be a success. A review in Farsi from an Iranian living abroad:

  > "*Slumdog Millionaire* is a fresh, powerful and engaging film with a simple but strong universal story of rags to riches. What makes it special is that it is a perfect mixture of all that is Indian (beauty, intensity, color, vibrancy, violence, poverty) and the best of British filmmaking (first and foremost as an industry and then as an art form). The catalyst is of course the sort of money and technique that only British or American filmmakers can throw at such a film. This film could have easily been made by Bollywood and it would have just been another typical, run of the mill Indian film. In the hands of an able and talented British filmmaker with a big budget, *Slumdog Millionaire* has turned into a successful fusion of Indian drama and English art."

- **South Korea:** *Slumdog* will be released in March [2009], amidst high expectations and hype. There was a lot of press about "dog" being the term that the British would call Indians during the colonial period. The pirated version is available online and there are efforts to create subtitles. One review written by a famous blogger in Korea says that it is a very smart film, renegotiating many discourses. For example, the game structure is both present in the plot and relates to the spectatorial act of viewing the film.

The commentaries from the different countries and linguistic regions are at this stage too general to yield fine-grained insights; it would take a separate article to do them full justice. Nonetheless, a number of leads are suggestive; for instance, bloggers relate the film strongly to their own national agendas (especially Thailand and Turkey), finding unexpected analogies or connections, which shows that reception is often local and driven by specific interests without ignoring global intentions, foreign origins or multi-national contexts. A major discovery has been the interest in subtitling, which fans undertake as a collective activity of learning and appropriation, quite separate from the distributor subtitling the film for commercial release. Testing their English language skills or using foreign films to acquire English brings independent films closer to Anglo rock and pop – a well-tested way of honing one's language skills through performance and emulation.

In Europe, commentators are most sensitive to the charges of exoticism but national clichés are also confirmed, for instance, when France shows a tendency towards using culinary metaphors or tourist imagery, while other countries are more wary of the Orientalist trap. By contrast, Hong Kong and Taiwan commentators are keen to put some distance between their own national sensitivities and those of Indians, re-assigning the Orientalist element by the choice of translation for the title. As in India, "dog" is felt to be unacceptable but in addition, the issues of poverty, crime, politics, media and religious conflict are taken out of their realist, contemporary frame and placed into the fairy-tale setting of a "Thousand and One Nights," despite the geographical inappropriateness.

Layer 4: Scholarly Discourses

We can identify a number of film-historical and critical discourses into which *Slumdog Millionaire* was quickly inserted, and where its unusual characteristics helped to challenge accepted categories as well as reaffirm their novel uses. Five of these discourses are worth briefly listing: auteurism/*mise-en-scène*/style; postcolonial versus postmodern; narrative logic versus game logic; gender and psychoanalysis; bio-power/bio-politics/control societies.

The auteurist discourse, mise-en-scène/style

What does it mean to call *Slumdog Millionaire* a Danny Boyle film? The auteur is now a trademark and brand, and the Boyle brand connotes: elaborate soundtrack, flashy and/or hand-held camera-work and musical rhythm determining the editing ("MTV aesthetics"). However, themes are also still identified with the auteur: in the case of Boyle, these themes include money; children and adolescence; protagonists that are violent, depraved and usually thought of as unsympathetic; and a predilection for sub-cultures in urban environments.

As a possible (second) auteur of the film, the nominal co-author Loveleen Tandan is rarely mentioned. Neither does Vikas Swarup, the author of the novel on which the story is based, play a role outside India. By contrast, the co-screenwriter Simon Beaufoy (*The Full Monty*) is frequently cited for his creative input, while the most serious contender for co-authorship is undoubtedly cinematographer Anthony Dod Mantle, bringing with him a reputation from *Festen* and other Dogme films (including six with Lars von Trier), and thus balancing the charge of MTV aesthetics. The Boyle–Dod Mantle partnership is often compared with the creative team of Wong Kar-Wai and his cinematographer Chris Doyle, hinting at contemporary authorship being less a matter of self-expression and more the creation of a look and a style which, in turn, signify a stance and an attitude, also often (mis)identified as postmodern.

There is, however, a high degree of reflexivity attached to the auteur today, which is reminiscent of postmodernism: Boyle often addresses the spectator with a conspiratorial gesture of knowingness about his/her expectations as both fan and expert in Bollywood conventions, tourist clichés of India, romantic clichés and melodrama ("boy meets girl, boy loses girl, boy gets girl"). It is an art film, in other words, "slumming" in several commercial genres. In addition, by the time of its multiple Oscar nominations, the film's own history was reflexively doubled in the presentation of the story and the director's self-presentation: part of the film's mythology became that "it almost didn't make it into the cinemas," which is to say, it was itself a slumdog/underdog in the world of big boys–big business film distribution, winning through chance, chutzpah and luck. Boyle, too, became a millionaire, because he knew all the answers to the questions of what makes a successful transnational indie film today.

The postcolonial discourse

Within academia, the more common approach to the film than postmodernism seems to have been postcolonial theory, especially the tropes of the subaltern and of hybridity.[21] As to the latter, the film cultivates hybridity and in-betweenness at several levels. It cannily combines television and cinema (in the production of the film but also in the film itself as the TV program is at the heart of the narrative); it self-consciously places itself in the lineage of films about the British Empire but does not opt for the heritage Merchant-Ivory line and, instead, follows Mira Nair's films, themselves playful hybridizations of Bollywood, itself a hybrid tradition. Also, the subaltern theme in the relation between Scotland and England (so prominent in *Trainspotting*) is recast and filtered through the subaltern relation that British Asians experience vis-à-vis Britain, but now projected back on the relation between Mumbai slumdwellers and the new Indian middleclasses. Many of the postcolonial themes are encapsulated in the questions posed by the quiz master and the personal associations that lead Jamal to give the right answers: The Three Musketeers, Benjamin Franklin, a Bollywood actor, Hindu gods, national epics, cricket, London topography and street names.

However, the film is also mindful of its international/global audiences, and especially the popularity of Bollywood films: many stereotypical Bollywood situations are present: enemy brothers, the single-minded pursuit of the "love of one's life," the ups and downs of the quest. Other motifs are stereotypical of Hollywood, notably the coming-of-age story format. Finally, art house themes are also touched on: the English novel (Dickens), Italian neorealism (children) and Latin American magic realism, as well as themes of ethnic and religious conflict (Hindi versus Muslim religion).

Narrative logic versus game logic

Slumdog Millionaire has an astute understanding of the current debate between the compatibility or incompatibility of narrative logic with game logic. As in the case of Lars von Trier (e.g., *The Five Obstructions*, and quite different from Hollywood blockbusters) Boyle and his scriptwriters have found a way of keeping the suspense and forward thrust of linear narrative, while modulating their story across the levels and stages familiar from interactive games. At the same time, the film knows that the television game show, which makes up the narrative core, is different from a generic interactive narrative. The police interrogation and the quiz-show Q & A format are cleverly exploited for their narrative potential (flashbacks and forward drive), suggesting a level at which narrative and game logic coalesce. On the other hand, regarding its narration and point of view structure, as well as focalization and temporal registers, the film is self-consciously cinematic, as if to reassert the cinematic over both its rivals: the television game show *and* the interactive video or computer game.

Gender and psychoanalysis: The Oedipal initiation

Slumdog Millionaire follows a long line of films that show the world as seen through a boy's eyes: from De Sica's *Bicycle Thieves* and Rossellini's *Germany Year Zero*, to Steven Spielberg's *Empire of the Sun* and *ET*, to Stephen Daldry's *Billy Elliot* and *The Reader*, Roberto Benigni's *La Vita e bella* and Fernando Mierelles' *City of God*. These male initiation stories are some of the most enduring narrative situations of all cinema (and socially significant prose, if one thinks of the bourgeois novel). As a coming of age story, *Slumdog Millionaire* is invariably Oedipal in how it both poses and eventually resolves the issue of male identity and the necessary entry into the social symbolic, usually referenced by marriage.

Such Oedipal coming-of-age can be symbolized by the two-brother motif, because Jamal's brother Salim's fate demonstrates the alternative path taken for becoming an adult male: part reworking of Cain and Abel motif, part submission to the rule of the enjoying superego, i.e. a lawless and violent patriarchal authority.[22] Salim has, as his father figure, the slumlord-turned-crime boss and as in *film noir*, it is the gangster boss as über-father, who "owns" the femme fatale, and who represents the dragon or monster that keeps the princess captive.

As in most (fairytale) narratives centered on boyhood, initiation and coming-of-age, there is no evidence of a biological father, and the quest is focused on a mother-substitute, i.e., Latika (in *Slumdog* made unusually explicit, as indeed is the dual identity of the mother-figure as virgin and whore). The gamut of challenges for the hero are the good father/bad father figures, with good fathers turning out to be bad fathers (the beggar-king) and bad fathers capable of good (the police sergeant), as well as ambiguous father figures (the quiz-master, on the hero's side, yet tempting him into giving the wrong answer).

Bio-politics, bio-power, control society

Finally, a further reason for the film attracting commentary well beyond cinephile circles is Boyle and Beaufoy's skill in touching on deep philosophical issues (and fears) in the West about the fraying of the social bond, and about zones of exclusion created by surveillance and new forms of social control that Michel Foucault summed up under the heading of bio-politics.[23] In *Slumdog Millionaire*, we encounter the commodification of life, the struggle for naked survival and conditions theorized by Giorgio Agamben as "bare life" and "homo sacer"[24] while, at the same time, allowing for the formation of the multitude: another powerful trope of contemporary theory. A further paradigm – this time associated with Gilles Deleuze – is present thanks to the transgressive word slumdog.[25] While the feral associations feed into the fascination with marginal groups in urban environments (reflected in other films with canine titles, such as *Amores Peros* and *Reservoir Dogs*), the notion of becoming animal has been in the forefront of redefining what is human: between intelligent machines and the bio-politics of human labor as raw resource under global capitalism. Against the generally dystopian and apocalyptic scenarios in the West, the film treats these conditions of abjection, exploitation and brute survivalism with an energy and vitality that suggests the triumph of hope and chance over evil and adversity. Other aspects of the so-called control societies are also evoked, perhaps most strikingly in the many parallels drawn between the police interrogation – including torture – and the quiz-show before a live audience and millions of TV viewers. It is as if the carceral and the ludic (to which one could add the call-center cubicles) were indeed the different faces of the same surveillance paradigm, comparable to the analogies drawn by avant-garde artists (such as Harun Farocki, inspired by Foucault) between prisons and shopping malls as totally monitored environments.[26]

Conclusion

If we now summarize our findings, we note several features. Each of our layers taps into rich and varied data which go beyond the usual connotations of response, since they have an existence prior to and beyond the film, and even film (festival) culture: the relation of the various East Asian and North American diasporas to India and its cinematic representation, and the post-colonial debates in the humanities and social sciences. The film inserts itself into life-worlds and discourses where its textual coherence might get dispersed, but its effervescence and energy also irrigate and refresh debates that might have become stale and predictable. Areas of overlap and direct correspondence between our chosen layers are surprisingly few, another indication that popular films can have a life that touches people in different aspects of their daily existence, affect their sense of selfhood and identity, and complement their professional as well as leisure activities.

Does every (festival) film elicit such a diverse response? Probably not, which raises the question of how representative a film we have chosen, and how much predictive power can be associated with our data-mining. Before trying to formulate a response to this by way of a conclusion, one last thought on the film itself and its internal construction: in line with an argument that Thomas Elsaesser has made elsewhere, in a discussion of James Cameron's *Avatar*,[27] Boyle's *Slumdog Millionaire* displays some of the features Elsaesser labeled "access for all," one of which is performative self-contradiction. Instead of aiming at coherence and unity at the different levels of meaning and reference, as in a classical narrative seeking closure, what seems to prevail in both Cameron's and Boyle's films is a deliberate attempt to generate contradictions. These either lead to passionate debates for and against (as was the case with both *Avatar* and *Slumdog*) or register as pleasurable intensifiers and energizers. The latter was clearly in evidence in *Slumdog Millionaire*, starting with the contradiction encapsulated in the title and reflected in the many judgments phrased as paradoxes: "a gripping narrative that's both heartbreaking and uplifting in equal measure"; "poor but pithy"; "criminal but energetic"; "realistic but fairy-tale"; "tragic and sad but suspenseful and full of hope."[28] Even the tag that sparked the most sustained debate – poverty porn – has all the hallmarks of the same semantic urge to produce paradox or cognitive dissonance. The film's most severe critics thus inadvertently contributed to a strategy that plays up the contrasts rather than mediate or resolve them: *Slumdog Millionaire* anticipated as well as inoculated itself against the criticism the makers knew they would encounter.

As a final point, we need to revisit our lifecycle metaphor, which compares the online reputation of films released at festivals throughout the globe with a living organism that goes through predictable stages of birth, maturity, decline and death. Does a film's online reputation in fact conform to this metaphor? Is the pattern of a film's online reception predictable? Traditional reception studies (such as Staiger's *Interpreting Films*) suggest that analyzing reception is a cumulative process, and that, given enough information, a predictable pattern of reception can be identified. However, our case study of *Slumdog Millionaire*, with its diverse (i.e. digital and print) sources of information, reaches the opposite conclusion – reception is inherently an unpredictable process and, as complexity theory teaches us, small fluctuations in this rich data stream (such as the introduction of the term poverty porn) can have enormous consequences in the reception of a film. Yet, this term disappeared as quickly as it appeared (see again Fig. 14.4). There was no slow decline, as the organic metaphor suggests. As this paper has tried to demonstrate, future studies not only of online reception of films require an epistemic shift: away from models based on the static, orderly accumulation of data, and towards models that are complex and emergent, if we are to understand the unpredictable, multiple and diverse lifecycles of contemporary cinema.

Notes

1 A longer version of the following outline of data mining and of Google's Insight for Search was first published in Warren Buckland, "Measuring Online Word-of-Mouth: The Initial Reception of *Inland Empire* on the Web," in *American Independent Cinema*, edited by Yannis Tzioumakis, Claire Molloy and Geoff King (London: Routledge, 2012).

2 Janet Staiger, *Interpreting Films: Studies in the Historical Reception of American Cinema* (Princeton: Princeton University Press, 1992), 8.

3 Daniel Soar, "It Knows." *London Review of Books*, 6 October 2011, 3.

4 Franco Moretti, *Graphs, Maps, Trees: Abstract Models for Literary History* (London: Verso, 2005).

5 Laura A. Granka, "Measuring Agenda Setting With Online Search Traffic: Influences of Online and Traditional Media." http://static.googleusercontent.com/external_content/untrusted_dlcp/research.google.com/en//pubs/archive/36915.pdf (accessed 16 September 2011).

6 Dina Iordanova, *Budding Channels of Peripheral Cinema: The Long Tail of Global Film Circulation* (St. Andrews: College Gate Press, 2008), 45.

7 Yair Shimshoni, Niv Efron and Yossi Matias, "On the Predictability of Search Trends." http://static.googleusercontent.com/external_content/untrusted_dlcp/research.google.com/en//archive/google_trends_predictability.pdf (accessed 16 September 2011).

8 Firstly, the search is represented as a graph. Secondly, it is represented in terms of geographical location. Thirdly, particular search terms are ranked in order of popularity. However, the searches are not given as raw figures – we do not know how many people actually entered search terms; instead we are given the relative frequency of search terms normalized to 100 (representing the highest volume of searches for a given term).

In terms of the graph at the top of Insight for Search, the highest volume of searches on a particular day is given the value of 100. All other searches on different days are then given a value relative to that highest volume. A day with the value of 50 means that the search term's volume is half that of the day on which the highest search rate was achieved. This ranking also applies to countries and to search terms. The country/search terms that generate the highest volume are given the value of 100. Furthermore, the data on search terms publicly available only stretches back to 2004. This process of measuring relative frequency of search terms can be carried out diachronically, a process which Shimshoni, Efron and Matias call a "time series of search trends," and which we are calling a film's lifecycle on the web.

9 The Julian calendar simply counts the number of days that have passed since 1 January 4713 BC, midday. 11 October 2011 is 2455845 on the Julian calendar system. Because a day is simply represented as a number, it is easy for computers to calculate the difference between two days, whereas a calendar consisting of days, months and years is more difficult. By entering a date range in the form of Julian calendar days (search term and then daterange [one word]), it is possible to narrow down a Google search to exact days. For example:

"Slumdog Millionaire" daterange: 2455844–2455845

will return Google pages dated between 10–11 October 2011 (33,000 pages out of the thirteen million devoted to the film – see note 10).

10 Anon., "India shooting," *Hindustan Times*, 23 March 2007 (a listing of four films shooting in India, including *Slumdog Millionaire*). Document HNTM000020070324e33n0003n from Factiva.com; Anon., "Oh, Danny Boy – so you love our Hinglish films?" *Hindustan Times*, 24 March 2007. Document HNTM000020070325e33o0005o from Factiva.com; "*Slumdog Millionaire*" – in quotation marks – generates over 13 million hits on Google, in comparison to the 34,000 hits on Factiva. This demonstrates that the 25,000 newspapers and newswires on Factiva.com simply represent the tip of the iceberg (in fact, a ratio of 1:382) when it comes to tracking the discussions around a film.

11 Christine Kearney, "Boyle film leads buzz at Telluride Film festival," *Reuters News*, 1 September 2008. Document LBA0000020080901e4910020k from Factiva.com (accessed 8 October 2011).

12 Todd McCarthy, "Telluride buzzing over 'Slumdog,'" *Daily Variety*, 1 September 2008. Document VARTY00020080904e491000ru from Factiva.com (accessed 8 October 2011).

13 Susan Wloszczyna. "Toronto: Star power, fewer prizes? Film festival lacks top picks," *USA Today*, 3 September 2008. Document USAT000020080903e4930000i from Factiva.com (accessed 8 October 2011).

14 Michael Phillips, "'Slumdog' artful, if extreme," *Chicago Tribune*, 8 September 2008. Document KRTTB00020080908e49800003 from Factiva.com (accessed 8 October 2011).

15 "Baz Bamigboye at the Toronto Film Festival," *Daily Mail*, 12 September 2008. Document DAIM000020080911e49c0002d from Factiva.com (accessed 8 October 2011).

16 Voynar claims that, "while Boyle immerses the viewer in the poverty and tragedy of life as an orphan in the slums of Mumbai, he deftly avoids delving into the murky realm of 'poverty porn,' which treats the lives of those caught in such circumstances gratuitously.

This is a character-intensive story, with the narrative lens focused firmly on Jamal, who, in spite of growing up amidst filth, abuse and the threat of starvation, emerges with his spirit, honesty and courage intact." "Telluride Review: Slumdog Millionaire," moviefone.com, 31 August 2008. Online: http://blog.moviefone.com/2008/08/31/telluride-review-slumdog-millionaire/ (accessed 8 October 2011).

17 Alice Miles, "Shocked by Slumdog's poverty porn; Danny Boyle's film is sweeping up awards, but it's wrong to revel in the misery of India's children," *Times*, 14 January 2009. Document T000000020090114e51e00043 from Factiva.com (accessed 8 October 2011).

18 Arifa Akbar and Guy Adams, "'Smear tactics' threaten to halt Slumdog's Oscar march," *Independent*, 31 January 2009. Document IND0000020090131e51v0002k from Factiva.com (accessed 8 October 2011).

19 "Les Fabulenses Aventures d'un Indien Malchanceux qui devint Millionaire," Le Portrait de Bollywood. Online: http://bollywood-sapna.over-blog.com/article-26769377.html (accessed 8 October 2011).

20 Quoted in "Slumdog Millionaire: critiques," Premiere. Online: http://www.premiere.fr/film/Slumdog-Millionaire-1358945/%28affichage%29/press (our translation, accessed 8 October 2011).

21 On *Slumdog* and subaltern studies, see A. J. Sebastian, "Voicing Slum-subaltern in Slumdog Millionaire," *Journal of Alternative Perspectives in the Social Sciences* 1.3 (2009): 897–920 and Ananya Roy, "Slumdog Cities: Rethinking Subaltern Urbanism," *International Journal of Urban and Regional Research* 35.2 (March 2011): 223–38.

22 The "enjoying superego" is a term coined by Slavoj Žižek. See "You May," *London Review of Books*, 18 May 1999. Online: http://www.lrb.co.uk/v21/n06/slavoj-zizek/you-may (accessed 8 October 2011).

23 See Ellen Dengel-Janic: "[w]hat the film negates and helps to mask in a pleasurable visual manner is a translocated fear of poverty and the abject [...]. The film's appeal reflects not only the West's exoticism of India, but also its repressed fear and paranoia of becoming abject and poor." Quoted in Shakuntala Banaji, "Seduced 'outsiders' versus sceptical 'insiders'? *Slumdog Millionaire* through its re/viewers," *Participations: Journal of Audience and Reception Studies*, 7.1 (2010): 3.

24 Giorgio Agamben, *Homo Sacer: Sovereign Power and Bare Life*, translated by Daniel Heller-Roazen (Stanford, CA: Stanford University Press, 1998).

25 See "Le corps, la viande et l'espirit, le devenir-animal," in Gilles Deleuze, *Francis Bacon* (Paris: Editions de la difference, 1981), 19–22.

26 See Harun Farocki, *I Thought I Was Seeing Convicts* (Germany, 2000).

27 Thomas Elsaesser, "James Cameron's *Avatar*: Access for All," *New Review of Film and Television Studies* 9.3 (2011): 247–63.

28 See, for instance, "Review: Slumdog Millionaire," *The Shiznit*, 7 January 2009. Online: http://www.theshiznit.co.uk/review/slumdog-millionaire.php and "Slumdog Millionaire," *Broad Street Review*, 2 March 2009. Online: http://www.broadstreetreview.com/index.php/main/article/slumdog_millionaire (accessed 8 October 2011).

Conclusion

JAI *WHO*?

Ajay Gehlawat

Riding on *Slumdog Millionaire*'s wave of success, the award winning Indian composer A. R. Rahman launched his "Jai Ho" world tour in 2010. This tour, whose Hindi title (meaning, "Let there be victory") stems from Rahman's Oscar-winning song featured during *Slumdog*'s end credits sequence, kicked off in June at the Nassau Coliseum in New York and went on to several cities in the US, the UK, Canada and South Africa, featuring twenty-three playback singers from India, along with multiple dancers and musicians. As was the case with *Slumdog*, this tour was a highly successful event, with many of the concert tickets selling out days in advance.[1] Though it traveled around the globe, one place the Jai Ho tour did not go was the Wagah border between India and Pakistan, near Amritsar. Nevertheless, "Jai Ho" plays at the ceremony that takes place every day, just before sunset, at this border. During this highly orchestrated event, featuring goose-stepping soldiers armed with bayonets, the large crowds (at least on the Indian side) seated in bleachers cheer and sing along to many of the songs broadcast through a loudspeaker system, while several Indians dance before the viewing stands and soldiers. The irony of a song composed by a Muslim being used to celebrate India's fractious border with Pakistan should not be overlooked. Indeed, one wonders what the film's Muslim protagonist, Jamal, whose mother is killed by rioting Hindu fundamentalists, would make of such a scene.

The use of "Jai Ho" at the Wagah border ceremony effectively demonstrates how this song and, by extension, *Slumdog*, continues to be appropriated by several competing forces around the world, each invoking the song's title lyrics to proclaim its own victory. Indeed, along with the cheering Indian crowds at the Wagah border (encouraged, one may surmise, by the Indian army), the Indian National Congress Party made "Jai Ho" its official campaign song during the 2009 election.[2] Thus, as with the previous "India Shining" slogan employed by the Hindu nationalist Bharatiya Janata Party (BJP) in the

2004 elections, or the current "Incredible India" phrase used by the Indian government to advertise tourism and tourist destinations in the country, "Jai Ho" becomes one in a long line of mantras used to promote a particular agenda, whether it be of (Hindu) nationalism, a Western-financed film or the latter's appeal to Indians.[3]

This question – of who takes ownership of *Slumdog* – becomes a fitting way of concluding a collection in which so many voices have laid claim to the competing ideological discourses on display in the film. From Warner Brothers originally planning to release the film straight to DVD (before Fox Searchlight began madly distributing it to various film festivals), to Amitabh Bachchan initially lambasting the film (only to ultimately be one of the first to praise Rahman after the soundtrack won so many awards in the West), one can chart the shifting identity of *Slumdog* via its fluctuating receptions around the globe. As with the disreputable figure of its title – personified most vividly in the shit-covered Jamal who emerges clutching a picture of Bachchan – no one seemed to want anything to do with this film until it became so successful, winning the laundry list of awards noted at the outset, at which point everyone began seeing it as their own.

The essays in this collection have attempted to come to terms with both the fraught relationships multiple audiences have had with *Slumdog*, as well as the film's equally fraught relations with the various components comprising its cinematic world. Like the format of the game show at the heart of the film, this book's four sections have laid out four possibilities, four possible ways of framing *Slumdog*: through its relations with the nation; with the slum; with Bollywood; and with numerous global audiences who went on to watch it and cheer or deride its subsequent victories. Yet, unlike the game show format, none of these four possibilities in and of itself provides the "correct" answer – the meaning of *Slumdog*, rather, is constituted through its competing and at times contradictory relations with all of these contexts. This is not to say that the question posed by this conclusion's title is a trick question, nor, for that matter, is it one that can definitively be answered. If anything, the ongoing spread of *Slumdog* through so many competing circuits signals the palimpsestic nature of this film, onto which everyone has projected his or her own vision(s). *Slumdog* is not an Indian film, yet (according to some) has been embraced by India as "its own" (at least, post-Oscar wins); *Slumdog* is not a Bollywood film, yet its success has helped bring more attention to this industry than any actual Bollywood film has; and, finally, "Jai Ho" is arguably not a "real" Bollywood song and dance but, thanks to its popularity, Bollywood dance has grown increasingly popular, "surfac[ing] in venues and programs previously reserved for non-Indian dance forms."[4]

In such a way, a triumphalist ("Jai Ho!") narrative becomes hard to avoid; indeed, as Priya Joshi has recently argued, "*Slumdog Millionaire*'s [...] landslide victory in just about every international film award competition seems to echo a lesson from the year's triumphant Obama playbook: yes, Jamal can; yes, India can; even maybe, yes, Bollywood can."[5] Yet, to return to a point made by several authors in this collection, such a complacent attitude overlooks a few points, chief among them being what, precisely, is "Jai Ho-ed" by *Slumdog*'s victories, and who ultimately benefits? While the essays in this collection have attempted to address these questions from multiple vantage points, they still remain unresolved. While Jamal and Latika's dance in Mumbai's Victoria Terminus station concludes with the duo walking off into the sunset, the song from this sequence continues playing every day, just before sunset, at the Wagah border.

Notes

1 "Rahman fans to shell 50K for concert," *Hindustan Times*, 4 June 2010. Online: http://www.hindustantimes.com/Lifestyle/CelebWatch/Rahman-fans-to-shell-50-k-for-concert/Article1-552191.aspx (accessed 1 July 2010). According to the *Times*, tickets for a special enclosure called the "*Jai Ho* Circle," cost $1,050.

2 It went on to win a majority of the seats in this election.

3 As *New York Times* columnist Somini Sengupta noted, while *Slumdog* was initially criticized by Indians for its negative portrayals of the less than shining aspects of the country, the day after the Oscars, "this movie-mad country went 'Jai Ho.'" Sengupta, "India Celebrates a Hollywood Victory," *New York Times*, 23 February 2009. Online: http://www.nytimes.com/2009/02/24/world/asia/24india.html (accessed 24 February 2009).

4 Sangita Shresthova, *Is It All About Hips? Around the World with Bollywood Dance* (New Delhi: Sage, 2011), 131. In a similar vein, a version of "Jai Ho" featuring English lyrics was subsequently released by the Pussycat Dolls, an American pop girl group and dance ensemble, rising to #2 on the European Hot 100 Singles chart and to #15 on the US Billboard Hot 100 chart. The video for this version references the original "Jai Ho" sequence, both in its setting and choreography, with the Pussycat Dolls taking the place of Jamal and Latika at the front of a group of dancers on a train platform. The after-life of *Slumdog*'s stars is also worth noting, with Dev Patel recently featured in *The Best Exotic Marigold Hotel* (2011) and in commercials promoting tourism to London in anticipation of the 2012 Olympic Games; Freida Pinto appearing in Woody Allen's *You Will Meet a Tall Dark Stranger* (2010) and as the title character in *Trishna* (2012), a British update of Thomas Hardy's *Tess of the d'Urbervilles* set in India; and Anil Kapoor appearing in numerous episodes of the American television series, *24* (2010), and in *Mission: Impossible – Ghost Protocol* (2011).

5 Priya Joshi, "Bollylite in America," *South Asian Popular Culture* 8.3 (2010): 245.

SELECT BIBLIOGRAPHY

Adiga, Aravind. *The White Tiger*. New York: Free Press, 2008.

Akbar, Arifa and Guy Adams, "'Smear tactics' threaten to halt Slumdog's Oscar March," *Independent*, 31 January 2009. Online: Document IND0000020090131e51v0002k from Factiva.com (accessed 8 October 2011).

Altman, Rick. "A Semantic/Syntactic Approach to Film Genre." *Cinema Journal* 23.3 (1 April 1984): 6–18.

Anjaria, Ulka and Jonathan Shapiro Anjaria. "Text, Genre, Society: Hindi youth films and postcolonial desire." *South Asian Popular Culture* 6.2 (2008): 125–140.

Appadurai, Arjun. *Modernity at Large: Cultural Dimensions of Globalization*. Minneapolis: University of Minnesota Press, 1996.

______. "The Capacity to Aspire." In *Culture and Public Action*, edited by Vijayendra Rao and Michael Walton. New Delhi: Permanent Black, 2004.

Arora, Poonam. "The Production of Third World Subjects for First World Consumption: *Salaam Bombay* and *Parama*." In *Multiple Voices in Feminist Film Criticism*, edited by Diane Carson, Linda Dittmar and Janice R. Welsch, 293–304. Minneapolis: University of Minnesota Press, 1994.

Banaji, Shakuntala. "Seduced 'Outsiders' Versus Sceptical 'Insiders'?: *Slumdog Millionaire* Through Its Re/Viewers." *Participations* 7.1 (2010): 1–30.

Bawa, Z. and Parth J. Shah, "Low-Income Housing in Indian Cities: Some Considerations for Policy," *Development Policy Review*, 28.3 (2010): 259–93.

Bazin, André. *What Is Cinema?*, 2 volumes, translated by Hugh Gray. Berkeley: University of California Press, 1967.

Beck, Bernard. "Angels With Dirty Faces: Who Invited *Slumdog Millionaire* and *The Visitor*?" *Multicultural Perspectives* 11.3 (2009): 146–9.

Blakely, Rhys. "Rubina Ali's Family Brawl after Father Denies Offering *Slumdog* Actress for Sale." *Sunday Times*, 20 April 2009. Online: http://www.timesonline.co.uk/tol/news/world/asia/article6126458.ece (accessed 20 April 2009).

Boo, Katherine. *Behind the Beautiful Forevers: Life, Death, and Hope in a Mumbai Undercity*. New York: Random House, 2012.

Bordwell, David. "Slumdogged by the Past," *Observations on Film Art*. Online: http://www.davidbordwell.net/blog/2009/02/01/slumdogged-by-the-past/ (accessed 28 February 2012).

Buckland, Warren. "Measuring Online Word-of-Mouth: The Initial Reception of *Inland Empire* on the Web." In *Reader in Independent American Cinema*, edited by Yannis Tzioumakis, Claire Molloy and Geoff King. London: Routledge, 2012.

Carr, David. "Oscar Night Is Starry Night for the Starless 'Slumdog Millionaire.'" *New York Times*. 23 February 2009, sec. Arts. Online: http://www.nytimes.com/2009/02/24/movies/awardsseason/24bagg.html (accessed 24 February 2009).

Chakrabarty, Dipesh. *Provincializing Europe: Postcolonial Thought and Historical Difference*. Princeton: Princeton University Press, 2000.

Chakravarty, Sumita S. *National Identity in Indian Popular Cinema, 1947–1948*. Austin: University of Texas Press, 1993.

Chan, Nadine. "*Slumdog Millionaire* and the Troubled Place of Cinema and Nation." *Post Identity* 30.2 (2010): 37–45.

Chatterjee, Partha. *The Politics of the Governed: Reflections on Popular Politics in most of the World*. New York: Columbia University Press, 2004.

_______. "Democracy and Economic Transformation in India." *Economic and Political Weekly* 43.16 (April 2008): 19–25.

Chion, Michel. *Audio-Vision*, translated by Claudia Gorbman. New York: Columbia University Press, 1994.

de Bruyn, Pippa, Keith Bain, David Allardice, and Shonar Joshi. *Frommer's India*. London: John Wiley and Sons, 2010.

Dabashi, Hamid. "Native Informers and the Making of the American Empire." *Al Ahram Weekly*, 1–7 June 2006. Online: http://weekly.ahram.org.eg/2006/797/special.htm (accessed 2 February 2009).

Deshpande, Shekhar. "A Million Slumdogs Now." *Little India*, 13 February 2009.

Dhaliwal, Nirpal. "Slumdog Millionaire could only have been made by a westerner." *Guardian*. 15 January 2009. Online: http://www.guardian.co.uk/film/filmblog/2009/jan/15/danny-boyle-shows (accessed 22 July 2009).

Dunham, Brent, ed. *Danny Boyle: Interviews*. Jackson: University Press of Mississippi, 2011.

Dwyer, Rachel. *All You Want Is Money, All You Need Is Love: Sex and Romance in Modern India*. London: Cassell, 2000.

Echanove, Matias and Rahul Srivastava. "Taking the Slum Out of 'Slumdog.'" *New York Times* 21 February 2009. Online: http://www.nytimes.com/2009/02/21/opinion/21srivastava.html (accessed 27 January 2012).

Elsaesser, Thomas. "James Cameron's *Avatar*: Access for All," *New Review of Film and Television Studies*, 9.3 (2011): 247–63.

Fanon, Frantz. *The Wretched of the Earth*, translated by Richard Philcox. New York: Grove Press, 2004 [1964].

Farred, Grant. "Wankerdom: *Trainspotting* as a rejection of the postcolonial?" *South Atlantic Quarterly* 103.1 (2004): 215–26.

Fernandes, Leela. *India's New Middle Class*. Minneapolis: University of Minnesota Press, 2006.

Friedman, Thomas. *The World is Flat: A Brief History of the Twenty-First Century*. New York: Farrar, Straus and Giroux, 2005.

Galt, Rosalind, and Karl Schoonover. "Introduction." In *Global Art Cinema: New Theories and Histories*, edited by Galt and Schoonover, 3–26. Oxford: Oxford University Press, 2010.

Gehlawat, Ajay. *Reframing Bollywood: Theories of Popular Hindi Cinema*. New Delhi: Sage, 2010.

Giridharadas, Anand. "Horatio Alger Relocates to a Mumbai Slum." *New York Times*, 17 January 2009. Online: http://www.nytimes.com/2009/01/18/weekinreview/18giridharadas.html (accessed 27 January 2012).

Gopal, Sangita. *Conjugations: Marriage and Form in New Bollywood Cinema*. Chicago: University of Chicago Press, 2011.

Gopalan, Lalitha. *Cinema of Interruptions: Action Genres in Contemporary Indian Cinema*. London: British Film Institute, 2002.

Gritten, David. "Slumdog Millionaire: The first film in the Obama era," *Telegraph*, 12 January 2009. Online: http://www.telegraph.co.uk/culture/film/4224827/Slumdog-Millionaire-the-first-film-of-the-Obama-era.html (accessed 20 January 2009).

Guha, Ramachandra. *India After Gandhi: The History of the World's Largest Democracy*. London: Macmillan, 2007.

Hansen, Thomas Blom. *Wages of Violence: Naming and Identity in Postcolonial Bombay*. Princeton: Princeton University Press, 2001.

Hardikar, Ashwini and Laurel Mei Turbin. "*Slumdog Millionaire* for popular educators: Globalization, feminism, and media." *South Asian Popular Culture* 9.2 (2011): 205–14.

Hardt, Michael and Antonio Negri. *Empire*. Cambridge, MA: Harvard University Press, 2000.

Harvey, David. *Social Justice and the City*. Oxford: Blackwell Publishers, 1973.

Spaces of Hope. Berkeley: University of California Press, 2000.

The New Imperialism. Oxford: Oxford University Press, 2003.

Hetsroni, Amir. "The Millionaire Project: A Cross-Cultural Analysis of Quiz Shows From the United States, Russia, Poland, Norway, Finland, Israel, and Saudi Arabia." *Mass Communication and Society* 7.2 (2004) 133–56.

Iordanova, Dina. *Budding Channels of Peripheral Cinema: The Long Tail of Global Film Circulation*. St. Andrews: College Gate Press, 2008.

Jackson, Stephanie Lou. "Beyond Kitsch: A. R. Rahman and the Global Routes of Indian Popular Music." Unpublished master's thesis, Bowling Green State University, 2010. Online: http://etd.ohiolink.edu/view.cgi?acc_num=bgsu1276889390 (accessed 15 August 2012).

Joshi, Priya. "Bollylite in America." *South Asian Popular Culture* 8.3 (2010): 245–59.

Kazmi, Fareeduddin. "How Angry is the Angry Young Man? 'Rebellion' in Conventional Hindi Films." In *The Secret Politics of Our Desires: Innocence, Culpability and Indian Popular Cinema*, edited by Ashis Nandy, 134–56. London: Zed Books, 1998.

Khilnani, Sunil. *The Idea of India*. New York: Farrar, Straus and Giroux, 1998.

Kumar, Amitava. "Slumdog Millionaire's Bollywood Ancestors." *Vanity Fair*, 23 December 2008. Online: http://www.vanityfair.com/online/oscars/2008/12/slumdog-millionaires-bollywood-ancestors.html (accessed 25 December 2008).

Lim, Dennis. "What, Exactly, Is *Slumdog Millionaire*?" *Slate*, 26 January 2009. Online: http://www.slate.com/id/2209783/pagenum/all/#p2 (accessed 7 May 2010).

Magnier, Mark. "Indians Don't Feel Good About *Slumdog Millionaire*." *Los Angeles Times*, 24 January 2009. Online: http://www.latimes.com/entertainment/news/la-fg-india-slumdog24-2009jan24,0,1162547.story (accessed 25 January 2009).

Martin-Jones, David. *Deleuze, Cinema, and National Identity*. Edinburgh: Edinburgh University Press, 2006.

Mazumdar, Ranjani. *Bombay Cinema: An Archive of the City*. Minneapolis: University of Minnesota Press, 2007.

_______. "Terrorism, Conspiracy, and Surveillance in Bombay's Urban Cinema." *Social Research* 78.1 (2011): 143–72.

McDonald, Mark. "A Diplomat's Unlikely Rise to 'Slumdog' Acclaim." *New York Times*, 1 April 2008. Online: http://www.nytimes.com/2009/04/02/arts/02iht-zslumdog.html?pagewanted=all (accessed 13 September 2011).

McFarlane, Colin. *Learning the City: Knowledge and Translocal Assemblage.* Oxford: Wiley-Blackwell, 2011.

Mehta, Suketu. *Maximum City: Bombay Lost and Found.* New York: Vintage, 2004.

Metz, Christian, and Georgia Gurrieri. "Aural Objects." *Yale French Studies* 60 (1980): 24–32.

Miles, Alice. "Shocked by Slumdog's poverty porn; Danny Boyle's film is sweeping up awards, but it's wrong to revel in the misery of India's children," *Times.* 14 January 2009. Online: Document T000000020090114e51e00043 from Factiva.com (accessed 8 October 2011).

Mishra, Pankaj. "Fighting for Scraps." *New York Times Book Review*, 12 February 2012.

Moretti, Franco. *Graphs, Maps, Trees: Abstract Models for Literary History.* London: Verso, 2005.

Nabar, Vrinda. "Slumdog Millionaire Bizarrely Plausible?" *DNA*, 10 January 2009. Online: http://www.dnaindia.com/opinion/main-article_slumdog-millionaire-bizarrely-plausible_1220495 (accessed 7 May 2010).

Nandy, Ashis. "Introduction: Indian Popular Cinema as a Slum's Eye View of Politics." In *The Secret Politics of Our Desires: Innocence, Culpability, and Indian Popular Cinema*, edited by Nandy. New Delhi: Oxford University Press, 1998.

Nandy, Ashis and Vinay Lal. "Introduction: Popular Cinema and the Culture of Indian Politics." In *Fingerprinting Popular Culture: The Mythic and the Iconic in Indian Cinema*, edited by Nandy and Lal. New Delhi: Oxford University Press, 2006.

Nilekani, Nandan. *India Imagined: the Idea of a Renewed Nation.* New York: Penguin, 2009.

Patel, S. and J. Maselos, eds. *Bombay and Mumbai.* New Delhi: Oxford University Press, 2003.

Pendakur, Manjunath. *Indian Popular Cinema: Industry, Ideology, and Consciousness.* New York: Hampton Press, 2003.

Rai, Amit. *Untimely Bollywood: Globalization and India's New Media Assemblage.* Durham, NC: Duke University Press, 2009.

Roy, Ananya. "Slumdog Cities: Rethinking Subaltern Urbanism," *International Journal of Urban and Regional Research*, 35.2 (March 2011), 223–38.

Roy, Sandip. "The New Bollywood." *San Francisco Chronicle,* 22 February 2009: 16.

Said, Edward. *Orientalism.* New York: Random House, 1978.

Sebastian, A. J. "Voicing Slum-subaltern in Slumdog Millionaire," *Journal of Alternative Perspectives in the Social Sciences* 1.3 (2009): 897–920.

Sengupta, Somini. "Extreme Mumbai, Without Bollywood's Filtered Lens." *New York Times*, 11 November 2008. Online: http://www.nytimes.com/2008/11/16/movies/16seng.html?pagewanted=1&adxnnl=1&adxnnlx=1299819049-QBVV2M8pb389Fkbhcsdfog (accessed 3 January 2009).

"Indians Embrace the Triumph of 'Slumdog' as a Victory for Their Country." *New York Times*, 24 February 2009. Online: http://query.nytimes.com/gst/fullpage.html?res=9401E3DA1331F937A15751C0A96F9C8B63 (accessed 25 February 2009).

Shresthova, Sangita. *Is It All About Hips? Around the World with Bollywood Dance.* New Delhi: Sage, 2011.

Spivak, Gayatri Chakravorty. *A Critique of Postcolonial Reason: Toward a History of the Vanishing Present.* Cambridge, MA: Harvard University Press, 1999.

Staiger, Janet. *Interpreting Films: Studies in the Historical Reception of American Cinema.* Princeton: Princeton University Press, 1992.

Swarup, Vikas. *Q & A.* New York: Scribner, 2005.

Thomas, Rosie. "Indian Cinema: Pleasures and Popularity." *Screen* 26 (1985).

Tieber, Claus. "Kino im Ausnahmezustand: Amitabh Bachchan als nationaler Held in Krisenzeiten." In *Fokus Bollywood: Das indische Kino in wissenschaftlichen Diskursen*, edited by Tieber, 84–98. Berlin: Lit Verlag, 2009.

Tyree, J. M. "Against the Clock: *Slumdog Millionaire* and the *Curious Case of Benjamin Button*." *Film Quarterly* 62.4 (2009): 34–8.

Varma, Pavan. *The Great Indian Middle Class*. London: Penguin, 1998.

Varma, Rashmi. *The Postcolonial City and its Subjects: London, Nairobi, Bombay*. New York: Routledge, 2012.

Vieira, João Luiz. "The Transnational Other: Street Kids in Contemporary Brazilian Cinema." In *World Cinemas, Transnational Perspectives*, edited by Nataša Ďurovičová and Kathleen Newman, 226–43. New York: Routledge, 2009.

Windsor, D. A. "Nargis, Ray, Rushdie and the real." *South Asia* 21.1 (1998).

Zakaria, Fareed. *The Post-American World*. New York: W. W. Norton, 2008.

______. "Slum Voyeurism?" *Newsweek* (International Edition), 30 January 2009. Online: http://www.newsweek.com/id/182341 (accessed 1 February 2009).

FILMS CITED

3 Idiots (Rajkumar Hirani, 2009, India)
Avatar (James Cameron, 2009, US)
Best Exotic Marigold Hotel, The (John Madden, 2011, UK)
Bicycle Thieves (Vittorio De Sica, 1948, Italy)
Bombay (Mani Ratnam, 1995, India)
Born into Brothels: Calcutta's Red Light Kids (Zana Briski and Ross Kauffman, 2004, US)
Calcutta (Louis Malle, 1969, France)
Citizen Kane (Orson Welles, 1941, US)
City of God (Fernando Meirelles and Katia Lund, 2002, Brazil)
City of Joy (Roland Joffe, 1992, US)
Coolie (Manmohan Desai, 1983, India)
Darjeeling Limited, The (Wes Anderson, 2007, US)
Deewaar (Yash Chopra, 1975, India)
Dil Se (Mani Ratnam, 1998, India)
Dilwale Dulhania le Jayenge (DDLJ) (Aditya Chopra, 1995, India)
Don (Chandra Barot, 1978, India)
Gandhi (Richard Attenborough, 1982, UK)
Guru (Mani Ratnam, 2007, India)
Jodhaa Akbar (Ashutosh Gowariker, 2008, India)
Kadhalan/ Humse Hai Muqabala (S. Shankar, 1994, India)
Krantiveer (Mehul Kumar, 1994, India)
Lagaan: Once Upon a Time in India (Ashutosh Gowariker, 2001, India)
Lamhe (Yash Chopra, 1991, India)
Mission: Impossible – Ghost Protocol (Brad Bird, 2011, US)
Mother India (Mehboob Khan, 1957, India)
Moulin Rouge (Baz Luhrmann, 2001, US)
Namesake, The (Mira Nair, 2006, US)
Oliver Twist (David Lean, 1948, UK)
Pather Panchali (Satyajit Ray, 1955, India)
Phantom India (Louis Malle, 1969, France)
Pineapple Express (David Gordon Green, 2008, US)
Ram Balram (Vijay Anand, 1980, India)
Rang De Basanti (Rakeysh Omprakash Mehra, 2006, India)
Rangeela (Ram Gopal Varma, 1995, India)
Roja (Mani Ratnam, 1992, India)
Saathiya (Shaad Ali, 2002, India)
Salaam Bombay! (Mira Nair, 1988, US)

Shoeshine (Vittorio De Sica, 1946, Italy)
Slumdog Millionaire (Danny Boyle and Loveleen Tandan, 2008, UK)
Smile Pinki (Megan Mylan, 2008, US)
Swades (Ashutosh Gowariker, 2004, India)
Taal (Subhash Ghai, 1999, India)
Trainspotting (Danny Boyle, 1996, UK)
Trishna (Michael Winterbottom, 2011, UK)
Trishul (Yash Chopra, 1978, India)
You Will Meet a Tall Dark Stranger (Woody Allen, 2010, US)
Zanjeer (Prakash Mehra, 1973, India)

INDEX

3 Idiots 118
24 (TV series) 203n4

Academy Awards: and Amitabh Bachchan 116; India's reactions to *Slumdog Millionaire*'s 82, 169–70, 202; and A. R. Rahman 134; *Slumdog Millionaire*'s nominations for and total xxiin1, 53, 69, 128, 166; and 2009 ceremony xxi, 72, 143, 146–7, 149–51, 153, 164, 187–8
Adiga, Aravind xvii, 10, 14, 57
Ahmad, Aijaz xvii, 3–4, 6
Akhtar, Javed 116
Alger, Horatio 168
Ali, Rubina 39, 48, 122, 151–2, 157
Amritsar: *see* Wagah border
"angry young man" xx, 33, 113–15, 131; *see also* Bachchan, Amitabh
Anjaria, Jonathan Shapiro xix, 53
Anjaria, Ulka xix, 53
Appadurai, Arjun 76–7, 81, 150, 165
Arab Spring 104
assemblage, media xviii–xix, 39–41, 47–9
audiences: *see Slumdog Millionaire*
Avatar 196

Bachchan, Amitabh: as Bollywood superstar xx, 160; filmic personae of 111–15, 117, 131, 168; and Nargis 5; and role in *Slumdog Millionaire* 27n23, 45, 60; and views on *Slumdog Millionaire* 3, 32–3, 54, 111, 116, 152, 165, 202
Bazin, André xx, 123–6, 130, 134–5
Beaufoy, Simon: and Bollywood 11, 17, 20; and Danny Boyle 158, 195; as British screenwriter 3, 15, 156, 167, 192
Bend It Like Beckham 144
Best Exotic Marigold Hotel, The 203n4
Bhagidari system 80
Bharatiya Janata Party (BJP) 102, 201
Bicycle Thieves 124–5, 130, 194
Bollywood: actors of 32, 91, 95, 116, 170; aesthetic of 166–7; and globalization 144, 153; Hindu domination in 113–14; and Hollywood 15, 26n16; and "impersonation" 168–9; popularity of 194; and A. R. Rahman 130–32, 187; and *Slumdog Millionaire* xv, xvii, xx–xxi, xxiiin19, 10–13, 17, 19–20, 23–4, 35, 40, 45, 47–8, 118, 122–3, 129, 133, 135–6, 155, 157–60, 172–3, 188–91, 193, 202–3; depiction of slums in 150–51, 168; as thriving film industry 171; western misconceptions of 110, 164–6
Bombay/Mumbai (city): and Amitabh Bachchan 111; and beautification projects 81; and Bollywood 35, 122; inhabitants of 33, 151–2, 172, 193; and name change xxiin3, 44; and 1992–93 riots 114; real estate prices of 80; and *Salaam Bombay!* 32, 66n2; and Shiv Sena 76; and

Slumdog Millionaire 9, 14–17, 21, 41, 44, 46, 54–7, 61, 69, 72–4, 78, 82, 85, 129–30, 135, 146, 157; and slums xv–xvi, 30, 48, 62–3, 75, 126–8, 136, 145, 165; and terrorist attacks 159; *see also* Dharavi
Bombay (film) 114, 131
Boo, Katherine xvi
Born into Brothels 66, 165
Boyle, Danny: and Bollywood 17, 20, 155, 160; and Bombay xvi; brand of 192; as British director 3, 40, 69, 186–7; and Deepak Chopra 25n8; and Christian Colson 110; and Dickensian sensibility 159; ethnic and class composition of 15; filmic vision of 57–8, 61, 73, 77–8, 156, 189; and game show format 65, 194; and experience in India xxi; intentions of 165, 172–3; and Anthony Dod Mantle 193; global perceptions of 188–90; and A. R. Rahman 130, 166; and India's schizophrenia 152–3; and studio bosses 32; and Vikas Swarup 63, 94; and Loveleen Tandan xxiiin17, 151; as fly-by-night tourist 161; and urban life 54; and Fareed Zakaria 164
Buckland, Warren xxi, 179–80
Bush, George W. 170

Calcutta (city) 44, 83, 165
Calcutta (film) 32, 165
call centers: in India 35, 160, 171, 189; in *Slumdog Millionaire* 14, 20–21, 33, 44, 46, 55, 159, 195
Celador Films 35, 48, 149, 152
Chakrabarty, Dipesh xviii, 10–11, 14, 22, 25n9
Chakravarty, Sumita 168–9
Chandra, Nandini xviii, 29
Chatterjee, Partha xviii, 33–4, 77
child actors: *see Slumdog Millionaire*
China 10, 13, 190
Chion, Michel 123, 126
Chopra, Anupama 168
City of God 121–2, 132, 194
City of Joy xix, 54, 70, 74, 83–4, 165
colonialism 25n8, 84, 159; *see also* neocolonialism
Colson, Christian 110, 172
compradors: *see Slumdog Millionaire*
Coolie 111, 113

Dabashi, Hamid 163–4
Darjeeling Limited, The 128
De Sica, Vittorio 121, 124, 194
Deewar 111–14, 116–17; *see also* "angry young man"
Deleuze, Gilles xviii, 39–40, 46, 72, 195
Denby, David 166
Dharavi: and child actors 72; and Dharavi Redevelopment Project (DRP) 79–81; and Madonna 34; reality of xvi, 62, 75–7; as setting of *Slumdog Millionaire* 31, 78, 113, 149–50; and Vikas Swarup 27n19, 62–3, 98–9, 101; and tourists 153; *see also* Bombay; India; slums
Dickens, Charles: and Horatio Alger 168; and Indian landscape 145; and melodrama 32, 116; and picaresque tales 159; and *Q & A* (Swarup) 16; and *Slumdog Millionaire* xvii, 155–6, 189, 194
Dilwale Dulhania Le Jayenge (*DDLJ*) 117

Elsaesser, Thomas xxi, 179–80, 188, 196

Fanon, Frantz 19
favelas 121, 136n2
Fernandes, Leela 80
Forster, E. M. 166
Fox Searchlight Pictures xvii, 48, 149, 158, 170, 202

game show: *see Kaun Banega Crorepati?*; *Slumdog Millionaire*; *Who Wants to Be a Millionaire?*
Gandhi (film) 71, 163, 170, 173
Gandhi, Indira 114
Gandhi, Mahatma 17, 21, 171–2
Gehlawat, Ajay xv, 53, 163
General Agreement on Tariffs and Trade (GATT) 30
Global War on Terror (GWOT) 170
globalization: and Bollywood 122, 153; and global economic crises 145; and India 11, 18–20, 22, 24, 43, 82; and "Paper Planes" 48; and *Slumdog Millionaire* 14, 56–7, 65, 160–61; and urban navigation xix, 54
Google 16, 27n19, 101–2, 180–83, 186
Gopalan, Lalitha 47

Hardt, Michael 11
Harvey, David 70, 79, 81
Hindi cinema: *see* Bollywood
Hindu–Muslim conflicts: *see Slumdog Millionaire*
Hollywood: and André Bazin 124–6; and Bollywood 15, 110, 118, 122, 189–90; and coming-of-age story 194; dominance of 128; as geographically indeterminate term 26n15; lens of 13; and Muslim lead 32; and Oscars xxi, 69; typical protagonist of 112, 117; and SFX 135; silent movies of 116; and *Slumdog Millionaire* 40, 71, 129, 147, 149, 171, 173, 179
India: and Bollywood 110, 114, 116; emerging centrality of 9–10, 22; definition of 26n14; and education problem 118; and Emergency 114–15; and Hindi 23–4; political and economic history of 112; and its many languages 161; middle class of xviii, 100, 102, 118; and global modernity 14, 20, 156; movie theatres in 48; national emblem of 64; reception of *Slumdog Millionaire* in 70, 82–3, 110, 166, 169, 190, 202; representations of 3, 5–6, 53–4, 109–11; "rise" of xvi–xvii; *Slumdog Millionaire*'s depiction of 11, 13, 17–19, 21, 35, 41, 155, 164, 173; and social welfare net 103; upward class mobility in xx, 98; and ties to US 170–71; and Wagah border 201; as WTO/GATT signatory 30; *see also* Bombay; slums
Indian Administrative Service (IAS) 29
Indian National Congress Party 82, 201
Inland Empire 180
International Monetary Fund (IMF) 79
Iraq War 174n9

Jai Ho (song): and Bollywood 202; and end credits sequence in *Slumdog Millionaire* 47, 126, 134, 136, 167–8, 175n25; and Hindu concept of destiny 33; and Indian Congress Party 82, 201; and Pussycat Dolls 203n4; translation of 176n39; and Wagah border ceremony 201; *see also* Rahman, A. R.
Jaikumar, Priya xxi, 149
Jameson, Fredric xvii, 3–6, 68n22
Joffe, Roland 54, 70, 74, 83
Joshi, Priya 202

Kapoor, Anil: and Bollywood 32, 116, 170; as game show host 46, 128, 145, 156, 159; and roles after *Slumdog Millionaire* 203n4

Kaun Banega Crorepati? (*KBC*) 29, 31–2, 93, 115, 160; *see also* *Who Wants to Be a Millionaire?*
Kavoori, Anandam xx, 13, 143
Kazmi, Fareed 111
Khan, Irrfan 128, 156
Khan, Shah Rukh 110, 113, 115, 117, 152
Khilnani, Sunil xvi
Kidman, Nicole 152
Koehler, Robert xxi, 155
Krantiveer 115

Lane, Anthony 175n25
Larkin, Brian xvii–xviii, 3
Lawrence of Arabia 83
liberalism 92, 97, 103–4; *see also* neoliberalism
Lim, Dennis 164, 173, 175n25

Madonna 34
Malle, Louis 32, 165
Martin-Jones, David 46
Mazumdar, Ranjani 60
Metz, Christian 123, 125
M. I. A.: and "Paper Planes" 42, 48, 126; and A. R. Rahman 130, 132, 187, 189
Miles, Alice 166, 187–8
Mishra, Pankaj xvi–xvii
Mission: Impossible – Ghost Protocol 203n4
Moretti, Franco 181
Mother India 5, 112–13, 117
Moulin Rouge 110
MTV 192–3
Mukherjee, Sharmila xviii, 9
Mumbai: *see* Bombay
Muqaddar ka Sikandar 113

Nair, Mira: and Bollywood, 193; and *The Namesake* 128; and *Salaam Bombay!* 32, 54, 71, 74, 118, 165
Nandy, Ashis 115, 165–6, 172–3
Nargis 5, 109, 111, 118
Negri, Antonio 11
neocolonialism 187
neoliberalism: and neoliberal audience xviii, 34; and capitalist development 94; and neoliberal economy 14, 18, 33–4, 37; and promise of egalitarianism 149; and globalization 56, 65; and hegemony 53; and Jamal and Latika 84; and liberalism 103–4; and the nation's redundancy 31; and optimism 34, 55; rise of 81; and *Slumdog Millionaire*'s culturalization of poverty 70; and social capital 96; and the West's neoliberal present 82
neorealism 31, 123–5, 130, 135, 194; *see also* realism
9/11 85, 163–4; *see also* Iraq War

Obama, Barack: and Cinderella effect 31; and narrative of hope xvii; as self-described "mutt" 40; and "Obama effect" 146; and *Slumdog Millionaire* as "Obama-like" xxiiin, 13, 149, 170, 202
Occupy movements 104, 146
Oliver Twist 121, 156, 189
Olympic Games, 2012 203n4
Orientalism: and *City of Joy* 70, 83; and the lens of Hollywood 13; and inequality 69; and Orientalist intervention 19; and the mapping of real India and real America 27n24; and Orientalist motifs xviii; and Orientalist stereotypes 85; and translated title of *Slumdog Millionaire* 190–91; and the Orientalist trap 192
Oscars: *see* Academy Awards

Padmanabhan, Lakshmi xviii–xix, 39
Pakistan 13, 76, 85, 100–101, 185, 201

Patel, Dev: as British 15, 84, 172; as Dickensian protagonist 156; hybridity of 26n17, 144; as Jamal 42, 159
Pather Panchali xviii, 5–6, 109
Phantom India 165
Pineapple Express 48
Pinto, Freida 84, 144, 156, 203n4
postcolonialism: and Britain 15; and postcolonial debates 196; and "global cities" xvi; and literature 6; and politics 21; and the state 19; and postcolonial studies 27n20, 180, 193; and postmodernism 192
"poverty porn": *see Slumdog Millionaire*
Puar, Jasbir 39, 48
Pussycat Dolls 203n4

Q & A (Swarup): as anti-cinematic novel 94–6; and Dickens's picaresque novels 156; info-dumping in 98–9; and descriptions of the slum 62–3; and *Slumdog Millionaire* xix, 3, 15–17, 30, 71, 91, 103
quiz show: *see* game show

Rahman, A. R.: and Academy Awards 134, 149; and Amitabh Bachchan 116, 202; career of 131–2, 187; as composer 128, 138n31; and *Slumdog Millionaire*'s end credits sequence 85; and "Jai Ho" world tour 201; and *Slumdog Millionaire*'s score xx, 122, 126, 130–31, 143, 158, 166, 173, 189; *see also Jai Ho*
Rai, Amit xviii, 39–41
Ray, Satyajit xviii, 5–6, 109–11, 118
realism: and André Bazin xx; and Bollywood 35, 110; and interpretation of the city 65–6; and fantasy 68n22; films' claims to 71; and Indian films 118; and magic realism 194; and melodrama 54, 109; and *Slumdog Millionaire* 77, 122–3, 130–32, 135, 151; and Vikas Swarup 94, 101–3

Said, Edward 73
Salaam Bombay!: *see* Nair, Mira
Sengupta, Mitu xix, 67n19, 69
Sengupta, Somini 169, 174n7
Shantaram 34
Shingavi, Snehal xix–xx, 91
Shoeshine 121
Singh, Manmohan 170
Slumdog Millionaire: and film festival audiences 157, 185–6; and Indian audiences xix, 45–6, 130, 134; and international audiences 96–7, 194, 202; and middle class audiences 92–3, 104; and neoliberal audience 34; and "new middlebrow" audience 155, 160–61; and Turkish audiences 189; and Western audiences 13–14, 19, 23, 70–73, 78, 82, 85, 110, 143–6, 165–7, 172–3, 187; child actors of 39, 48, 72, 86n12, 126, 128, 149–51, 187; and comprador critics xxi, 163–4, 167, 169, 172–3; as crossover text 144, 147; and game show format 47, 63–6, 71, 122, 126, 152, 158–9, 167–8, 194, 202; Hindu/Muslim conflicts in 21, 55, 62, 91, 114, 157, 194, 201; and "poverty porn" 3, 44, 166, 187–9, 196–7
slums, Indian: children of 23, 41, 92, 122; during Emergency 114–15; and luxury high-rises 20, 85; journalistic accounts of 123; as melodramatic settings 116; rise of xv–xvi, 79; *Slumdog Millionaire*'s portrayal of xix, 54, 69, 74, 128,

135, 153; screening of *Slumdog Millionaire* in 190; *see also* Bombay; Dharavi

Smile Pinki 66

soundtrack: *see* M. I. A.; Rahman, A. R.

Spivak, Gayatri 25n6, 27n20

Staiger, Janet 180, 197

Sunya, Samhita xx, 121

Swarup, Vikas: as "accidental" writer 27n21; on *Slumdog Millionaire* adaptation 91–4; as possible auteur of *Slumdog Millionaire* 192; and Dharavi 27n19, 99, 101–2; on *Q & A* 16–17; and *Quiz Time* 31; *see also Q & A*

Tandan, Loveleen: and child actors 41; as co-director of *Slumdog Millionaire* 3, 122, 151, 169, 192; as cover-up officer for cultural gaffes 32; precise status of xxiiin17

Tea Party movement 146

Third World: authenticity of the 124; and Third World city 55, 66n2, 79; and First World xvi, 71, 82, 84, 121, 136, 170, 173; India as 3, 10, 152; *Slumdog Millionaire*'s setting as 61, 126, 129, 135; texts of the xvii, 3–5, 147

Three Cups of Tea (Mortenson) 85

Tieber, Claus xx, 109

Trainspotting 17, 57–61, 153, 156, 190, 193

Trishna 203n4

Trishul 168

United States: and Bollywood 166; and the Gilded Age xvii; and India 170–71; and internet traffic 180–81; and response to 9/11 164; and Pakistan 85; and *Slumdog Millionaire* 145–6

Varma, Rashmi xv–xvi

Victoria Terminus 32, 203

Wagah border 201, 203

Warner Brothers 149, 171, 179, 190, 202

White Tiger, The (Adiga) xvii, 10, 15, 57

Who Wants to Be a Millionaire?: and Amitabh Bachchan xx, 115; and Celador Films 35, 152; as ultimate text of consumption 147; and Charles Ingram 16; and Jamal xvii, 55, 63, 71, 156; and *Kaun Banega Crorepati?* 29; and Prem Kumar 44, 159; and *Slumdog Millionaire*'s narrative structure 111; and opening sequence of *Slumdog Millionaire* 46; and values of merit and neutrality 82; and Western audiences 167; *see also Kaun Banega Crorepati?*

World Bank 79

World Trade Organization (WTO) 30, 79

You Will Meet a Tall Dark Stranger 203n4

Zanjeer 111